Foundation Chemistry

John Raffan and Brian Ratcliff

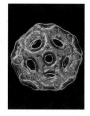

Series editor
Fred Webber

Consultant editors
John Raffan
Michael Reiss

CAMBRIDGE
UNIVERSITY PRESS

Published by the Press Syndicate of the University of Cambridge
The Pitt Building, Trumpington Street, Cambridge CB2 1RP
40 West 20th Street, New York, NY 10011-4211, USA
10 Stamford Road, Oakleigh, Melbourne 3166, Australia

First published 1995

Printed in Great Britain at the University Press, Cambridge

A catalogue record for this book is available from the British Library

ISBN 0 521 42198 5 paperback

Designed and produced by Gecko Ltd, Bicester, Oxon

This book is one of a series produced to support
individual modules within the Cambridge Modular
Sciences scheme. Teachers should note that written
examinations will be set on the content of each module as
defined in the syllabus. This book is the authors'
interpretation of the module.

Front cover photograph: Simulation of electron distribution in a
molecule of buckminsterfullerene (C_{60}); J. Bernholc *et al.*, North
Carolina State University/Science Photo Library

Contents

Acknowledgements

1cr, Malcolm Fielding, Johnson Matthey/Science Photo Library; 1 (all others), 43t, 50br, 65b, 68b, Tick Ahearn; 3t, 6l, University of Cambridge Cavendish Laboratory, Madingley Road, Cambridge; 4b, Manchester University/Science & Society Picture Library; 17, 30cr (fluorite: Blue John), 39b, 42l, Dr B. Booth/GeoScience Features Picture Library; 18, Heine Schneebeli/Science Photo Library; 21tl, 22, courtesy of AgrEvo Agrochemicals Ltd; 21tr, courtesy of Bruker-Franzen Analytik GmbH; 21b, Gray Mortimore/Allsport; 25, 81, 86bl, 92, 93t, Andrew Lambert; 29, Photo Library International; 30tl (calcite), 30tr (pyrite) A. Fisher/GeoScience Features Picture Library; 30cl (galena), 39l, r, 42r, 45t, 70tl (sulphur), cr (bromine), cbl (iodine), cbr (gold), GeoScience Features Picture Library; 30bl, courtesy of ICI; 30br, NASA/ Science Picture Library; 32l, The Natural History Museum, London; 33t, 33l, 43b, 45b, 50t, 70tr (chlorine), 82, 91, 110, Peter Gould; 35, courtesy of Argonne National Laboratory; 40, 67, Ancient Art & Architecture Collection; 44, Britstock–IFA/TPL; 46t, courtesy of Dr Jonathan Goodman, Department of Chemistry, Cambridge University, using the program Eadfrith (©J.M. Goodman, Cambridge University, 1994)/photo by Cambridge University Chemistry Department Photographic Unit; 46b, Dr Arthur Lesk, Laboratory of Molecular Biology/Science Photo Library; 49, 70tc (zinc), Astrid & Hanns-Frieder Michler/Science Photo Library; 50c, 57, 60r, Ann Ronan at Image Select; 50bl, courtesy of Buxton Lime Industries/photo: S.J. Hambleton; 59, Paolo Koch/Robert Harding Picture Library; 60l, source: DTI; 61, Kieran Murray/ Ecoscene; 62t, 63bl, Schaffer/Ecoscene; 62c, Pascal Rondeau/Allsport; 62b, Prof. David Hall/Science Photo Library; 63tl, US Department of Energy/Science Photo Library; 63tr, John Mead/Science Photo Library; 63br, Wilkinson/Ecoscene; 64tl, r, Simon Fraser/Science Photo Library; 64bl, Helene Rogers/TRIP; 65t, FPG International/Robert Harding Picture Library; 68t, Adam Hart-Davis/Science Photo Library; 70ctl (plutonium), ctr (button of uranium), US Department of Energy/Science Photo Library; 70bl (drops of mercury), Vaughan Fleming/Science Photo Library; 70br (drops of liquid lead), Erich Schrempp/Science Photo Library; 71, courtesy of the Library & Information Centre of the Royal Society of Chemistry; 72r, courtesy of Gordon Woods, Malvern School; 86tl, John Raffan; 86r, James Green/Robert Harding Picture Library; 93l, Paul Silverman/Fundamental Photos/Science Photo Library; 93b, Richard Megna/Fundamental Photos/Science Photo Library; 94, Robert Harding Picture Library; 101t, courtesy of Allyn and Bacon publishers, USA; 101b, 102, Shell Photo Service; 111t, Tim Benton; 118b, James Holmes/Zedcor/Science Photo Library

Atomic structure

By the end of this chapter you should be able to:

1 appreciate some of the evidence for the internal structure of atoms in terms of protons, neutrons and electrons, and describe their relative charges and relative masses;

2 describe the distributions of mass and charge within an atom and deduce the numbers of protons, neutrons and electrons present in both atoms and ions, from given proton numbers and nucleon numbers;

3 understand that isotopes of an element are distinguished on the basis of different numbers of neutrons present in their nuclei;

4 explain and use the term *first ionisation energy* of an element;

5 realise that ionisation energy data give evidence for the distribution of electrons in atoms;

6 predict the simple electronic configurations of elements, and their positions in the Periodic Table, from the sequence of their successive ionisation energies;

7 describe the number and relative energies of the s, p and d orbitals for the shells (energy levels) of principal quantum numbers 1, 2 and 3 and also the 4s orbital;

8 describe the shapes of s and p orbitals;

9 state the electronic configurations of atoms and ions in terms of shells and s, p and d orbitals, given their proton numbers and charges.

● **Figure 1.1** All of these useful chemicals, and many more, have been created by applying chemistry to natural materials. Chemists must also find answers to problems caused when people misuse chemicals.

Chemistry is a science of change. Over the centuries people have heated rocks, distilled juices and probed solids, liquids and gases with electricity. From all this activity we have gained a great wealth of new materials – metals, medicines, plastics, dyes, ceramics, fertilisers, fuels and many more (*figure 1.1*). But this creation of new materials is only part of the science and technology of chemistry. Chemists also want to *understand* the changes, to find patterns of behaviour and to discover the innermost nature of the materials.

Our 'explanations' of the chemical behaviour of matter come from reasoning and model-building based on the limited evidence available from experiments. The work of chemists and physicists has shown us the following:

■ All known materials, however complicated and varied they appear, can be broken down into the fundamental substances we call **elements**. These elements cannot be broken down further into simpler substances. So far, about 109 elements are recognised. Most exist in combinations with other elements in **compounds** but some, such as gold, nitrogen, oxygen and sulphur, are also found in an uncombined state. Some elements would not exist on Earth without the artificial use of nuclear reactions. Chemists have given each element a symbol. This symbol is usually the first one or two letters of the name of the element; some are derived from their names in Latin. Some examples are:

Element	Symbol
carbon	C
lithium	Li
iron	Fe (from the Latin *ferrum*)
lead	Pb (from the Latin *plumbum*)

■ Groups of elements show patterns of behaviour related to their atomic masses. A Russian chemist, Dmitri Mendeleev, summarised these patterns by arranging the elements into a 'Periodic Table'. Modern versions of the Periodic Table are widely used in chemistry. (A Periodic Table is shown in the appendix on page 115 and explained, much more fully, in chapter 5.)

■ All matter is composed of extremely small particles (atoms). About 100 years ago, the accepted model for atoms included the assumptions that (i) atoms were tiny particles, which could not be divided further nor destroyed, and (ii) all atoms of the same element were identical. The model had to give way to other models, as science and technology produced new evidence. This evidence could only be interpreted as atoms having other particles inside them – they have an internal structure.

Scientists now believe that there are two basic types of particles – 'quarks' and 'leptons'. These are the building-blocks from which everything is made, from microbes to galaxies. For many explanations or predictions, however, scientists find it helpful to use a model of atomic structure that includes three basic particles in any atom, the **electron**, the **proton** and the **neutron**. Protons and neutrons are made from quarks, and the electron is a member of the family of leptons.

Discovering the electron

Effect of electric current in solutions (electrolysis)

When electricity flows in an aqueous solution of silver nitrate, for example, silver metal appears at the negative electrode (cathode). This is an example of **electrolysis** and the best explanation is that:

■ the silver exists in the solution as positively charged particles known as **ions** (Ag^+);
■ one silver ion plus one unit of electricity gives one silver atom.

The name 'electron' was given to this unit of electricity by the Irish scientist George Johnstone Stoney in 1891.

Study of cathode rays

At normal pressures gases are usually very poor conductors of electricity, but at low pressures they conduct quite well. Scientists, such as William Crookes, who first studied the effects of passing electricity through gases at low pressures, saw that the glass of the containing vessel opposite the **cathode** (negative electrode) glowed when the applied potential difference was sufficiently high. A solid object, placed between the cathode and the glow, cast a shadow (*figure 1.2*). They proposed that the glow was caused by rays coming from the cathode and called these **cathode rays**.

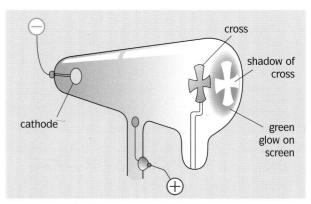

● *Figure 1.2* Cathode rays cause a glow on the screen opposite the cathode, and the 'Maltese Cross' casts a shadow. The shadow will move if a magnet is brought near to the screen. This shows that the cathode rays are deflected in a magnetic field. The term 'cathode ray' is still familiar today, as in 'cathode-ray oscilloscopes'.

For a while there was some argument about whether cathode rays are waves, similar to visible light rays, or particles. The most important evidence is that they are strongly deflected in a magnetic field. This is best explained by assuming that they are streams of electrically charged particles. The direction of the deflection shows that the particles in cathode rays are negatively charged.

J. J. Thomson's e/m experiment

The great leap in understanding came in 1897, at the Cavendish Laboratory in Cambridge (*figures 1.3 and 1.4*). J. J. Thomson measured the deflection of a narrow beam of cathode rays in both magnetic and electric fields. His results allowed him to calculate the charge/mass (*e/m*) ratio and the velocity of the particles. Their charge/mass ratio was found to be exactly the same, whatever gas or type of electrodes were used in the experiment. The cathode-ray particles had a tiny mass, only approximately 1/2000 of the mass of a hydrogen atom. Thomson then decided to call them **electrons** – the name suggested earlier by Stoney for the 'units of electricity'.

Millikan's 'oil-drop' experiment

The electron charge was first measured accurately in 1909 by the American physicist Robert Millikan using his famous 'oil-drop' experiment (*figure 1.5*). He found the charge to be 1.602×10^{-19} C (coulombs). The mass of an electron was calculated to be 9.109×10^{-31} kg, which is 1/1837 of the mass of a hydrogen atom.

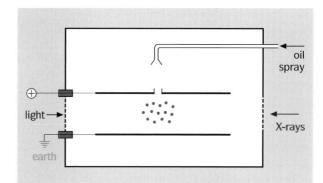

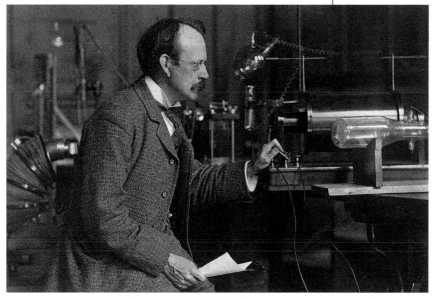

● **Figure 1.3** Joseph (J. J.) Thomson (1856–1940) using his cathode-ray tube.

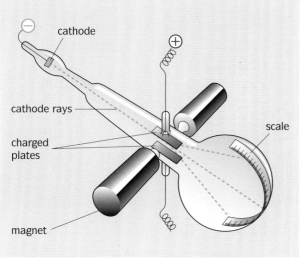

● **Figure 1.4** A drawing of Thomson's apparatus. The electrons move from the hot cathode (negative) through slits in the anode (positive).

● **Figure 1.5** Robert Millikan's 'oil-drop' experiment. Millikan gave the oil drops negative charge by spraying them into air ionised by X-ray bombardment. He adjusted the charge on the plates so that the upward force of attraction equalled the downward force due to gravity, and a drop could remain stationary. Calculations on the forces allowed him to find the charges on the drops. These were multiples of the charge on an electron.

Discovering protons and neutrons

New atomic models: 'plum-pudding' or 'nuclear' atom

The discoveries about electrons demanded new models for atoms. If there are negatively charged electrons in all electrically neutral atoms, there must also be a positively charged part. For some time the most favoured atomic model was J. J. Thomson's 'plum-pudding', in which electrons (the plums) were embedded in a 'pudding' of positive charge (*figure 1.6*).

Then, in 1909, came one of the experiments that changed everything. Two members of Ernest Rutherford's research team in Manchester University, Hans Geiger and Ernest Marsden, were investigating how α-particles (α is the Greek letter alpha) from a radioactive source were scattered when fired at very thin sheets of gold and other metals (*figure 1.7*). They detected the α-particles by the small flashes of light (called 'scintillations') that they caused on impact with a fluorescent screen. Since (in atomic terms) α-particles are heavy and energetic, Geiger and Marsden were not surprised that most particles passed through the metal with only slight deflections in their paths. These deflections could be explained, by the 'plum-pudding' model of the atom, as small scattering effects caused while the positive α-particles moved through the diffuse mixture of positive charge and electrons.

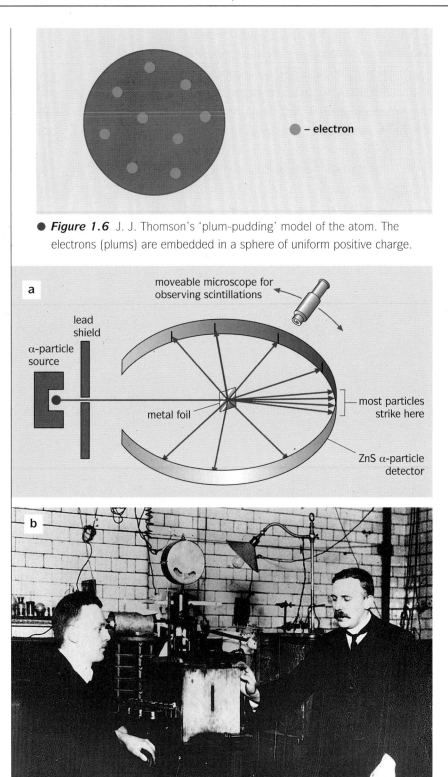

● *Figure 1.6* J. J. Thomson's 'plum-pudding' model of the atom. The electrons (plums) are embedded in a sphere of uniform positive charge.

● *Figure 1.7* Geiger and Marsden's experiment, which investigated how α-particles are deflected by thin metal foils.
a A drawing showing the arrangement of the apparatus.
b Ernest Rutherford (right) and Hans Geiger using their apparatus for detecting α-particle deflections. Interpretation of the results led Rutherford to propose the nuclear model for atoms.

However, Geiger and Marsden also noticed some large deflections. A few (about one in 20 000) were so large that scintillations were seen on a screen placed on the same side of the gold sheet as the source of α-particles. This was most unexpected. Rutherford said: 'it was almost as incredible as if you had fired a 15-inch shell at a piece of tissue paper and it came back and hit you!'

The plum-pudding model, with its diffuse positive charge, could not explain the surprising Geiger–Marsden observations. Rutherford, however, soon proposed his convincing **nuclear model** of the atom. He suggested that atoms consist largely of empty space and that the mass is concentrated into a very small, positively charged, central core called the **nucleus**. The nucleus is about 10 000 times smaller than the atom itself – rather like a marble placed at the centre of an athletics stadium.

Most α-particles will pass through the empty space in an atom with very little deflection. When an α-particle approaches on a path close to a nucleus, however, the positive charges strongly repel each other and the α-particle is deflected through a large angle (*figure 1.8*).

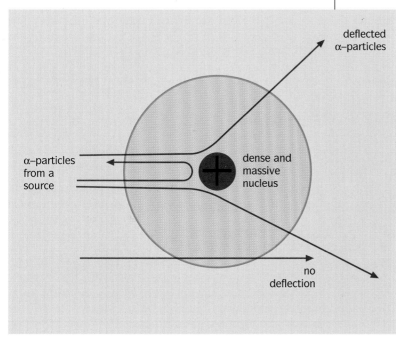

● *Figure 1.8* Ernest Rutherford's interpretation of the Geiger–Marsden observations. The α-particles are deflected by the tiny, dense, positively charged nucleus. Most of the atom is empty space.

Nuclear charge and 'atomic' number

In 1913, Henry Moseley, a member of Rutherford's research team in Manchester, found a way of comparing the positive charges of the nuclei of elements. The charge increases by one unit from element to element in the Periodic Table. Moseley showed that the sequence of elements in the Table is related to the nuclear charges of their atoms, rather than to their relative atomic masses (see page 73). The size of the nuclear charge was then called the **atomic number** of the element. Atomic number also defined the position of the element in the Periodic Table.

Particles in the nucleus

The proton

After the discovery of the nuclear atom, Rutherford proposed that there must be particles in the nucleus that are responsible for the positive nuclear charge. He and Marsden fired α-particles through hydrogen, nitrogen and other materials. They detected new particles with positive charge and the approximate mass of a hydrogen atom. Rutherford eventually called these particles **protons**. A proton carries a positive charge of 1.602×10^{-19} C, equal in size but opposite in sign to the charge on an electron. It has a mass of 1.673×10^{-27} kg, about 2000 times as heavy as an electron.

Each electrically neutral atom has the same number of electrons outside the nucleus as there are protons within the nucleus.

The neutron

The mass of an atom, which is concentrated in its nucleus, cannot depend only on protons; usually the protons provide around half of the atomic mass. Rutherford proposed that there is a particle in the nucleus with a mass equal to that of a proton but with zero electrical charge. He thought of this particle as a proton and an electron bound together.

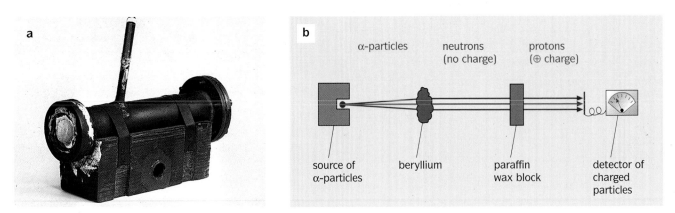

● *Figure 1.9*

a Using this apparatus, James Chadwick discovered the neutron.

b Drawing of the inside of the apparatus. Chadwick bombarded a block of beryllium with α-particles ($^4_2$He). No charged particles were detected on the other side of the block. However, when a block of paraffin wax (a compound containing only carbon and hydrogen) was placed near the beryllium, charged particles were detected and identified as protons (H^+). Alpha-particles had knocked neutrons out of the beryllium, and in turn these had knocked protons out of the wax.

Without any charge to make it 'perform' in electrical fields, detection of this particle was very difficult. It was not until 12 years after Rutherford's suggestion that, in 1932, one of his co-workers, James Chadwick, produced sufficient evidence for the existence of a nuclear particle with a mass similar to that of the proton but with no electrical charge (*figure 1.9*). The particle was named the **neutron**.

Proton and nucleon numbers

Proton (atomic) number (Z)

The most important difference between atoms of different elements is in the number of protons in the nucleus of each atom. The number of protons in an atom determines the element to which the atom belongs. This is why the atomic number of an element is now known as the **proton number**. The proton number of an element thus shows:

■ the number of protons in the nucleus of an atom of that element;

■ the number of electrons in a neutral atom of that element;

■ the position of the element in the Periodic Table.

Nucleon (mass) number (A)

It is useful to have a measure for the total number of particles in the nucleus of an atom. This is called the **nucleon number**, where *nucleon* means any nuclear particle (an older name is *mass number*). For any atom:

nucleon number = number of protons + number of neutrons

Summary table

Particle name	Nucleon number	Relative charge	Charge/C
electron	0	−1	-1.6×10^{-19}
proton	1	+1	$+1.6 \times 10^{-19}$
neutron	1	0	0

Isotopes

In Rutherford's model of the atom, the nucleus consists of protons and neutrons, each with a mass of one atomic unit. The relative atomic masses of elements should then be whole numbers. It was thus a puzzle why chlorine has a relative atomic mass of 35.5.

The answer is that atoms of the same element are not all identical. In 1913, Frederick Soddy proposed that atoms of the same element could have different atomic masses. He named such atoms **isotopes**. The word means 'equal place', i.e. occupying the same place in the Periodic Table and having the same proton number.

The discovery of protons and neutrons explained the existence of isotopes of an element. In isotopes of one element, the number of protons must be the same, but the number of neutrons may be different.

Remember:

proton number (Z) = number of protons
nucleon number (A) = number of protons + number of neutrons

Isotopes are atoms with the same proton number, but different nucleon numbers. The symbol for isotopes is shown as

$$_{\text{proton number}}^{\text{nucleon number}} X \quad \text{or} \quad _{Z}^{A}X$$

■ For example, hydrogen has three isotopes:

	Protium, $_{1}^{1}H$	*Deuterium*, $_{1}^{2}H$	*Tritium*, $_{1}^{3}H$
protons	1	1	1
neutrons	0	1	2

■ An α-particle is now known to be like the nucleus of a helium atom. It consists of two protons and two neutrons, and is shown as $_{2}^{4}He$.

It is also common practice to identify isotopes by name or symbol plus nucleon number only. For example, uranium, the heaviest naturally occurring element ($Z = 92$), has two particularly important isotopes of nucleon numbers 235 and 238. They are often shown as uranium-235 and uranium-238, as U-235 and U-238 or as ^{235}U and ^{238}U.

Numbers of protons, neutrons and electrons

It is easy to calculate the composition of a particular atom or ion:

$$\text{number of protons} = Z$$
$$\text{number of neutrons} = A - Z$$
number of electrons in neutral atom $= Z$
number of electrons in positive ion $= Z -$ charge on ion
number of electrons in negative ion $= Z +$ charge on ion

For example, magnesium is element 12; it can form doubly charged ions. The ionised isotope magnesium-25 thus has the full symbol $_{12}^{25}Mg^{2+}$, and

number of protons = 12
number of neutrons = 13
number of electrons = 10

SAQ 1.1

a What is the composition (numbers of electrons, protons and neutrons) of neutral atoms of the two main uranium isotopes, U-235 and U-238?

b What is the composition of the ions of potassium-40 (K^+) and chlorine-37 (Cl^-)?

(Use the Periodic Table, page 115, for the proton numbers.)

Electrons in atoms

Electrons hold the key to almost the whole of chemistry. Protons and neutrons give atoms their mass, but electrons are the outer part of the atom and only electrons are involved in the changes that happen during chemical reactions. If we knew everything about the arrangements of electrons in atoms and molecules, we could predict most of the ways that chemicals behave, purely from mathematics. So far this has proved very difficult, even with the most advanced computers – but it may yet happen.

SAQ 1.2

Suggest why the isotopes of an element have the same chemical properties, though they have different relative atomic masses.

What evidence do we have about how electrons are arranged around the nucleus? The first simple idea – that they just orbit randomly around the nucleus – was soon rejected. Calculations showed that any moving, electrically charged particles, like electrons, would lose energy and fall into the nucleus.

The best evidence for the arrangements of electrons in atoms has come from two sets of experiments: observations on emission spectra and measurements of ionisation energies.

Arrangements of electrons: energy levels and 'shells'

There was a great advance in atomic theory when, in 1913, the Danish physicist Niels Bohr proposed his ideas about arrangements of electrons in atoms.

Earlier the German physicist Max Planck had proposed, in his 'Quantum Theory' of 1901, that energy, like matter, is 'atomic'. It can only be transferred in packets of energy he called **quanta**; a single packet of energy is a **quantum**. Bohr applied this idea to the energy of electrons. He suggested that, as electrons could only possess energy in quanta, they would not exist in a stable way, anywhere outside the nucleus, but only in fixed or 'quantised' energy levels. If an electron gained or lost energy, it could move to higher or lower energy levels, but not somewhere in between. It is a bit like climbing a ladder; you can only stay in a stable state on one of the rungs. You will find that, as you read more widely, there are several names given to these energy levels. The most common name is **shells**.

A hydrogen atom has one electron. The electron usually exists in the lowest energy level (the 'ground state') but may be excited by an input of energy to a higher energy level. On returning to a lower level, it loses the excess energy by emission of radiation (visible or ultraviolet light). The emitted radiation has a precise energy value, as it is the difference between two fixed energy levels.

The energy levels (shells) are given numbers, called the **principal quantum numbers**, with the lowest energy at level $n = 1$, then $n = 2$, ...

Ionisation energy

When an atom loses an electron it becomes a positive ion. We say that it has been **ionised**. Energy is needed to remove electrons and this is generally called **ionisation energy**. More precisely, the **first ionisation energy** of an element is the amount of energy needed to remove one electron from each atom in a mole of atoms of an element in the gaseous state.

The general symbol for ionisation energy is ΔH_i and for a first ionisation energy it is ΔH_{i1}. The

process may be shown by the example of calcium as:

$$Ca(g) \rightarrow Ca^+(g) + e^-; \quad \Delta H_{i1} = +590\,kJ\,mol^{-1}$$

(If the symbols seem unfamiliar at this stage, see page 51.)

The energy needed to remove a second electron from each ion in a mole of ions is the **second ionisation energy**. This process for calcium is:

$$Ca^+(g) \rightarrow Ca^{2+}(g) + e^-;$$
$$\Delta H_{i2} = +1150\,kJ\,mol^{-1}$$

Note that the second ionisation energy is much larger than the first. The reasons for this are discussed on page 10.

Ionisation energies of elements are measured mainly by two techniques:

■ calculating the energy of the radiation causing particular lines in the spectrum of the element;
■ using electron bombardment of gaseous elements in discharge tubes.

We now know the ionisation energies of all of the elements.

Ionisation energies and electronic configurations

An interesting graph may be plotted with ionisation energies on the y axis and proton numbers on the x axis *(figure 1.10)*. We shall consider here only the first 36 elements of the Periodic Table.

Look at the first three elements. The atomic structures of their main isotopes are:

	H	He	Li
protons	1	2	3
neutrons	0	2	4
electrons	1	2	3

Helium has a higher first ionisation energy than hydrogen. This is easily explained, as more energy is needed to remove one electron away from the attraction of the two protons in helium compared with only one proton in hydrogen. But lithium has a much lower first ionisation energy. Why is it easier to remove one electron away from *three* protons in lithium?

The explanation is that lithium's three electrons are not all in the same energy level (shell). The

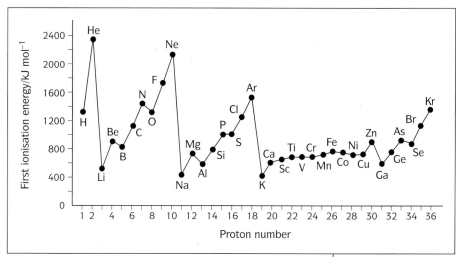

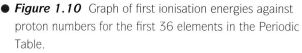

● **Figure 1.10** Graph of first ionisation energies against proton numbers for the first 36 elements in the Periodic Table.

shell with quantum number $n = 1$ must be filled with two electrons and the third electron is in shell $n = 2$. This outer electron is both further away from the positive charge of the protons in the nucleus, and screened (shielded) by the negative charge of shell $n = 1$ electrons. It is more easily removed than electrons in shell $n = 1$.

From lithium to neon the general trend of first ionisation energies is an increase. Electrons are filling up shell $n = 2$ and are attracted more strongly by an increasing nuclear charge. Shell $n = 2$ must be full in neon, however, because the next ionisation energy (for sodium) shows a sharp decrease. Sodium must have one electron in shell

$n = 3$. This type of pattern is repeated between sodium and potassium.

This explanation, based on evidence from ionisation energies and from the Rutherford–Bohr model of the atom, gives us a simple pattern for the arrangements of electrons in atoms of elements in the early part of the Periodic Table. The arrangement is usually called the **electronic configuration** of the atom *(table 1.1)*.

When writing out one of these simple electronic configurations, we use the form, for example, fluorine F (2,7) and sodium Na (2,8,1). We may also represent these in a simple diagrammatic way, as in *figure 1.11*.

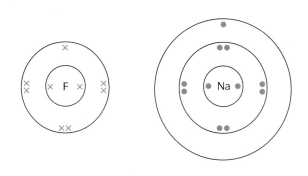

fluorine (2,7)   sodium (2,8,1)

● **Figure 1.11** Simple diagram of electronic configurations of fluorine and sodium atoms.

SAQ 1.3

a What are the likely, simple electronic configurations for atoms of elements 12 (magnesium) to 18 (argon)?

b What patterns do you notice in the electronic configurations of similar elements, such as lithium and sodium, or carbon and silicon, or fluorine and chlorine?

Successive ionisation energies

Further evidence for the general pattern of electronic configurations is provided by using the *successive* ionisation energies of elements. These are the first, second, third, fourth, etc. ionisation

		Electron in shells		
	Proton number	$n=1$	$n=2$	$n=3$
H	1	1		
He	2	2		
Li	3	2	1	
Be	4	2	2	
B	5	2	3	
C	6	2	4	
N	7	2	5	
O	8	2	6	
F	9	2	7	
Ne	10	2	8	
Na	11	2	8	1

● **Table 1.1** Electronic configurations of the first 11 elements in the Periodic Table

	Electrons removed										
	1	2	3	4	5	6	7	8	9	10	11
1 H	1310										
2 He	2370	5250									
3 Li	520	7300	11800								
4 Be	900	1760	14800	21000							
5 B	800	2420	3660	25000	32800						
6 C	1090	2350	4610	6220	37800	47300					
7 N	1400	2860	4590	7480	9400	53300	64300				
8 O	1310	3390	5320	7450	11000	13300	71300	84100			
9 F	1680	3370	6040	8410	11000	15200	17900	92000	106000		
10 Ne	2080	3950	6150	9300	12200	15200	–	–	–	131200	
11 Na	490	4560	6940	9540	13400	16600	20100	25500	28900	141000	158700

● *Table 1.2* Ionisation energies for the first 11 elements in the Periodic Table (to nearest $10\,kJ\,mol^{-1}$)

energies. They cannot all be measured with great precision, but even the approximations are helpful. *Table 1.2* shows the successive ionisation energies for the first 11 elements of the Periodic Table (hydrogen to sodium). The values are rounded to the nearest $10\,kJ\,mol^{-1}$.

We see that the following hold for any one element:

■ The ionisation energies increase. As each electron is removed from an atom, the remaining ion becomes more positively charged. Removing the next electron away from the increased positive charge is more difficult and the next ionisation energy is even larger.

■ There are one or more particularly large rises within the set of ionisation energies of each element (except hydrogen and helium).

These data may be interpreted in terms of the proton numbers of elements and their simple electronic configurations.

Consider the example of the successive ionisation energies of lithium. We see a low first ionisation energy, followed by much larger second and third ionisation energies. This confirms that lithium has one electron in its outer shell $n = 2$, which is easier to remove than either of the two electrons in the inner shell $n = 1$. The large increase in ionisation energy indicates where there is a change from shell $n = 2$ to shell $n = 1$.

The pattern is seen even more clearly if we plot a graph of ionisation energies (*y* axis) against number of electrons removed (*x* axis). As the ionisation energies are so large, we must use logarithm to base 10 (log_{10}) to make the numbers fit on a reasonable scale. The graph for sodium is shown in *figure 1.12*.

SAQ 1.4

a In *figure 1.12* why are there large increases between the first and second ionisation energies and again between the ninth and tenth ionisation energies?

b How does this graph confirm the suggested simple electronic configuration for sodium of (2,8,1)?

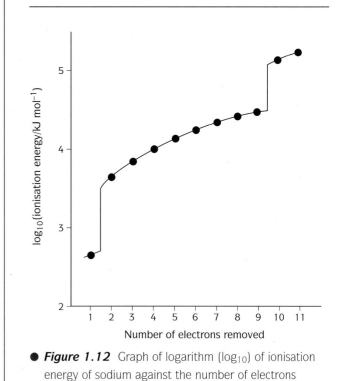

● *Figure 1.12* Graph of logarithm (log_{10}) of ionisation energy of sodium against the number of electrons removed.

Successive ionisation energies are thus helpful for predicting or confirming the simple electronic configurations of elements. In particular, they confirm the number of electrons in the outer shell. This leads also to confirmation of the position of the element in the Periodic Table. As you will read in more detail in chapter 5, elements with one electron in their outer shell are in Group I, elements with two electrons in their outer shell are in Group II, and so on.

SAQ 1.5

The first four ionisation energies of an element are, in kJ mol^{-1}: 590, 1150, 4940 and 6480. Suggest the Group in the Periodic Table to which this element belongs.

Need for a more complex model

Electronic configurations are not quite so simple as the pattern shown in *table 1.1*. You will see from the graph of first ionisation energies *(figure 1.10)* that there are variations from the general trends. For example:

- the first ionisation energies, from elements 3 (lithium) to 10 (neon) and from 11 (sodium) to 18 (argon), do not increase evenly;
- after element 20 (calcium) the pattern is distinctly different for a series of elements from 21 (scandium) to 30 (zinc), before resuming something like the previous trend. (The series of elements from scandium to zinc is discussed in more detail in chapter 5.)

These variations from the general trends of first ionisation energies show the need for a more complex model of electronic configurations. A brief account of a developed model is given in the next section.

In chapter 5 there is a more detailed look at ionisation energies and the factors that influence their values. There is also more detail about electronic configurations and their relationships with the position of the element in the Periodic Table. Chapter 5 also deals with relationships between ionisation energies and reactivities of elements.

More recent models of electrons in atoms

Bohr's model of electronic configurations was found to be too simple. The newer models are much more complex. They depend upon an understanding of the mathematics of **quantum mechanics** and, in particular, the **Schrödinger equation** and **Heisenberg's uncertainty principle**. Explanations of these will not be attempted in this book, but an outline of some implications for the chemist's view of atoms is given.

It is now thought that the following hold:

- The energy levels (shells), of principal quantum numbers $n = 1, 2, 3, 4$, etc., do not have precise energy values. Instead, they each consist of a set of subshells, which contain **orbitals** with different energy values.
- The subshells are of different types labelled **s**, **p**, **d** and **f**. An s subshell contains one orbital; a p subshell contains three orbitals; a d subshell contains five orbitals; and an f subshell contains seven orbitals.
- Orbitals represent the mathematical probabilities of finding an electron at any point within certain spatial distributions around the nucleus.
- Each orbital has its own approximate, three-dimensional shape. It is not possible to draw the shape of orbitals precisely. They do not have exact boundaries but are fuzzy, like clouds; indeed, they are often called 'charge-clouds'.

Approximate representations of orbitals are shown in *figure 1.13*. Some regions, where there is a greater probability of finding an electron, are shown as more dense than others. To make drawing easier, however, we usually show orbitals as if they have a boundary; this encloses over 90% of the probability of finding an electron. Note that there is only one type of s orbital but three different p orbitals (p_x, p_y, p_z). There are five different d orbitals.

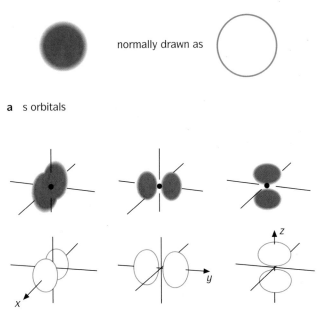

a s orbitals

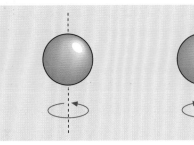

● *Figure 1.14* Representation of opposite spins of electrons.

b p orbitals

● *Figure 1.13* Representations of orbitals:
a s orbitals with spherical symmetry;
b p orbitals, p_x, p_y and p_z, with 'lobes' along x, y and z axes.

Orbitals: Pauli exclusion principle and spin-pairing

The shell $n = 1$ consists of a single s orbital called 1s; $n = 2$ consists of s and p orbitals in subshells called 2s and 2p; $n = 3$ consists of s, p and d orbitals in subshells called 3s, 3p and 3d.

There is an important principle concerning orbitals that affects all electronic configurations. This is the theory that any individual orbital can hold *one* or *two* electrons but not more. The principle was proposed by the Austro-Swiss physicist Wolfgang Pauli in 1921 and is called the **Pauli exclusion principle.**

You may wonder how an orbital can hold two electrons with negative charges that repel each other strongly. It is explained by the idea of **spin-pairing.** Two electrons can exist as a pair in an orbital through each having opposite spin *(figure 1.14)*; this reduces the effect of repulsion (see also later in this chapter).

From the ionisation energy and spectroscopic evidence, and using the Pauli exclusion principle, scientists have decided that: shell $n = 1$ contains up to two electrons in an s orbital; shell $n = 2$ contains up to eight electrons, two in an s orbital and six in the p subshell, with two in each of the p_x, p_y, p_z orbitals; shell $n = 3$ contains up to 18 electrons, two in an s orbital, six in the p subshell and ten in the d subshell, with two in each of the five orbitals.

Order of filling shells and orbitals

The order of filling the shells and orbitals is the order of their relative energy. The electronic configuration of each atom is the one that gives as low an energy state as possible to the atom as a whole. This means that the lowest-energy orbitals are filled first. The order of filling is:

first 1s, then 2s, 2p, 3s, 3p, 4s, 3d, 4p, ...

As you see, the order (shown diagrammatically in *figure 1.15*) is not quite what we might have predicted! An expected order is followed up to the 3p subshell, but then there is a variation, as the 4s is filled before the 3d. This variation and other variations further along in the order are caused by the increasingly complex influences of nuclear attractions and electron repulsions upon individual electrons.

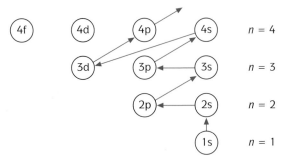

● *Figure 1.15* Diagram to show the order in which orbitals are filled up to shell $n = 4$.

Electronic configurations

Representing electronic configurations

The most common way of representing the electronic configurations of atoms is shown below. For example, hydrogen has one electron in an s orbital in the shell with principal quantum number $n = 1$. We show this as

Helium has two electrons, both in the 1s orbital, and is shown as $1s^2$.

The electronic configurations for the first 18 elements (H to Ar) are shown in *table 1.3*.

For the set of elements 19 (potassium) to 36 (krypton), it is more convenient to represent part of the configuration as a 'noble-gas core'. In this case the core is the configuration of argon. For convenience we sometimes represent $1s^2\ 2s^2\ 2p^6\ 3s^2\ 3p^6$ as [Ar] rather than write it out each time. Some examples are shown in *table 1.4*.

The following points should be noted:

- When the 4s orbital is filled, the next electron goes into a 3d orbital (see scandium). This begins a pattern of filling up the 3d subshell, which finishes at zinc. The elements that add electrons to the d subshells are called the **d-block elements**; a subset of these is called **transition elements** (see chapter 5).
- There are variations in the pattern of filling the d subshell at elements 24 (chromium) and 29 (copper). These elements have only one electron in their 4s orbital. Chromium has five d electrons, rather than the expected four; copper has ten d electrons rather than nine. This is the outcome of the complex interactions of attractions and repulsions in their atoms.
- From element 31 (gallium) to 36 (krypton) the electrons add to the 4p subshell. This is similar to the pattern of filling the 3p subshell from elements 13 (aluminium) to 18 (argon) in Period 3.

1	H	$1s^1$
2	He	$1s^2$
3	Li	$1s^2\ 2s^1$
4	Be	$1s^2\ 2s^2$
5	B	$1s^2\ 2s^2\ 2p^1$
6	C	$1s^2\ 2s^2\ 2p^2$
7	N	$1s^2\ 2s^2\ 2p^3$
8	O	$1s^2\ 2s^2\ 2p^4$
9	F	$1s^2\ 2s^2\ 2p^5$
10	Ne	$1s^2\ 2s^2\ 2p^6$
11	Na	$1s^2\ 2s^2\ 2p^6\ 3s^1$
12	Mg	$1s^2\ 2s^2\ 2p^6\ 3s^2$
13	Al	$1s^2\ 2s^2\ 2p^6\ 3s^2\ 3p^1$
14	Si	$1s^2\ 2s^2\ 2p^6\ 3s^2\ 3p^2$
15	P	$1s^2\ 2s^2\ 2p^6\ 3s^2\ 3p^3$
16	S	$1s^2\ 2s^2\ 2p^6\ 3s^2\ 3p^4$
17	Cl	$1s^2\ 2s^2\ 2p^6\ 3s^2\ 3p^5$
18	Ar	$1s^2\ 2s^2\ 2p^6\ 3s^2\ 3p^6$

● **Table 1.3** Electronic configurations for the first 18 elements in the Periodic Table

19	Potassium (K)	$[Ar]\ 4s^1$
20	Calcium (Ca)	$[Ar]\ 4s^2$
21	Scandium (Sc)	$[Ar]\ 3d^1\ 4s^2$
24	Chromium (Cr)	$[Ar]\ 3d^5\ 4s^1$
25	Manganese (Mn)	$[Ar]\ 3d^5\ 4s^2$
29	Copper (Cu)	$[Ar]\ 3d^{10}\ 4s^1$
30	Zinc (Zn)	$[Ar]\ 3d^{10}\ 4s^2$
31	Gallium (Ga)	$[Ar]\ 3d^{10}\ 4s^2\ 4p^1$
35	Bromine (Br)	$[Ar]\ 3d^{10}\ 4s^2\ 4p^5$
36	Krypton (Kr)	$[Ar]\ 3d^{10}\ 4s^2\ 4p^6$

● **Table 1.4** Electronic configurations for some of the elements 19 to 36

Filling of orbitals

Whenever possible, electrons will occupy orbitals singly. This is due to the repulsion of electron charges. Electrons remain unpaired until the available orbitals of equal energy have one electron each. When there are more electrons than the orbitals can hold as singles, they pair up by spin-pairing. This means that, if there are three electrons available for a p subshell, one each will go to the p_x, p_y and p_z orbitals, rather than two in p_x, one in p_y and none in p_z. When there are four electrons available, two will spin-pair in one orbital, leaving single electrons in the other orbitals. Similarly, five electrons in a d subshell will remain unpaired in the five orbitals. (See *figure 1.16*.)

As an example, we can show how orbitals are occupied in atoms of carbon, nitrogen and oxygen as:

carbon (six electrons)
$1s^2 \; 2s^2 \; 2p_x^{\;1} \; 2p_y^{\;1} \; 2p_z^{\;0}$
nitrogen (seven electrons)
$1s^2 \; 2s^2 \; 2p_x^{\;1} \; 2p_y^{\;1} \; 2p_z^{\;1}$
oxygen (eight electrons)
$1s^2 \; 2s^2 \; 2p_x^{\;2} \; 2p_y^{\;1} \; 2p_z^{\;1}$

(Normally electronic configurations are shown in less detail – as on page 13.)

Electronic configurations of ions

The number of electrons in an ion is found from the proton number of the element and the charge of the ion. Some examples are:

	Sodium atom	Sodium ion	Fluorine atom	Fluoride ion
symbol	Na	Na$^+$	F	F$^-$
proton number	11	11	9	9
electrons	11	10	9	10
configuration	$1s^2\,2s^2\,3p^6\,3s^1$	$1s^2\,2s^2\,2p^6$	$1s^2\,2s^2\,2p^5$	$1s^2\,2s^2\,2p^6$

Note that both the sodium ion Na$^+$ and the fluoride ion F$^-$ have the same electronic configuration as the noble gas neon. This has implications for the formation of, and bonding in, the compound sodium fluoride (see chapter 3, page 29 for a discussion of ionic bonding).

Electronic configurations in boxes

Another useful way of representing electronic configurations is in box form. We can show the electrons as arrows with their spin as up ↑ or down ↓.

Some elements, on this representation, will have the configurations shown in *figure 1.16*.

SAQ 1.6

Draw box-form electronic configurations for: boron, oxygen, argon, nickel and bromine.

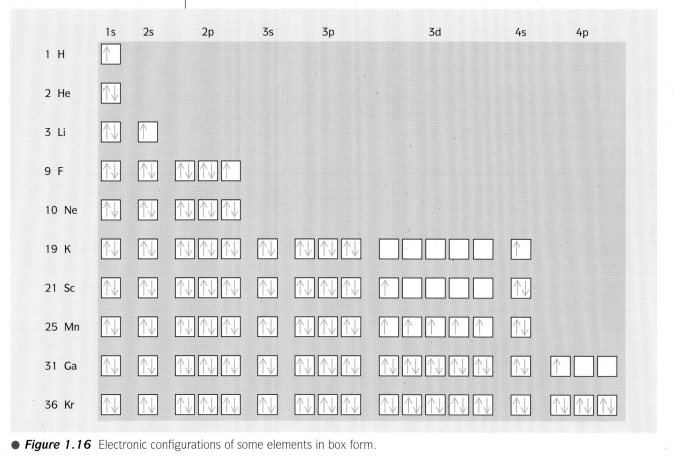

● *Figure 1.16* Electronic configurations of some elements in box form.

SUMMARY

- Any atom has an internal structure with almost all of the mass in the nucleus, which has a diameter about 10^{-4} that of the diameter of the atom.

- The nucleus contains protons (+ charge) and neutrons (0 charge). Electrons (− charge) exist outside the nucleus.

- All atoms of the same element have the same proton number (Z); that is, they have equal numbers of protons in their nuclei.

- The nucleon number (A) of an atom is the total number of protons and neutrons. Thus the number of neutrons = $A-Z$.

- The isotopes of an element are atoms with the same proton number but different nucleon numbers. If neutral, they have the same number of protons and electrons but different numbers of neutrons.

- Electrons can exist only at certain energy levels and gain or lose 'quanta' of energy when they move between the levels.

- The main energy levels or 'shells' are given principal quantum numbers $n = 1$, 2, 3, etc. Shell $n = 1$ is the closest to the nucleus.

- The shells consist of subshells known as s, p, d or f and each subshell consists of orbitals. Subshells s, p, d and f have one, three, five and seven orbitals respectively. Orbitals s, p, d, and f have different, distinctive shapes; we have looked at the shapes of s and p orbitals.

- Each orbital holds a maximum of two electrons, so that full subshells of s, p, d and f orbitals, contain two, six, ten and fourteen electrons respectively. The two electrons in any single orbital are spin-paired.

- Electrons remain unpaired among orbitals of equal energy until numbers require them to spin-pair.

- The first ionisation energy of an element is the energy required to remove one electron from each atom in a mole of atoms of the element in the gaseous state. This is often called the **molar ionisation energy**. The second ionisation energy is the energy required to remove a second electron, and so on.

- Large changes in the values of successive ionisation energies of an element indicate that the electrons are being removed from different shells. This gives evidence for the electronic configuration of atoms of the element and helps to confirm the position of the element in the Periodic Table.

Questions

1 An element X has a proton number between 10 and 20. It has the following values for 11 of its successive molar ionisation energies/kJ mol^{-1}: 790, 1600, 3200, 4400, 16 100, 19 800, 23 800, 29 200, 33 900, 38 700 and 45 900.
   a What is meant by the terms **proton number** and **molar ionisation energy**?
   b Explain the pattern of successive increases in the ionisation energies of the element X.
   c Suggest the likely electronic configuration of element X.
   d Suggest the Group in the Periodic Table to which element X belongs.

2 A relative of yours did not do much science at school. He says he thinks of atoms as extremely small and hard, like tiny marbles. How would you explain why we now accept a nuclear model of the atom with electrons, protons and neutrons?

3 Suggest an explanation for the fact that samples of pure lead, extracted from ores from different parts of the world, have slightly different relative atomic masses.

4 What are the electronic configurations of the following atoms or ions: Li^+, K^+, Ca^{2+}, N^{3-}, O^{2-}, S^{2-}, Cl and Cl^-?

Chapter two

Atoms, molecules and the mole

By the end of this chapter you should be able to:

1   recall the definitions of the terms *relative atomic mass, isotopic mass, molecular mass* and *formula mass* based on the carbon-12 scale;

2   recall the definition of the term *mole* in terms of Avogadro's constant;

3   interpret mass spectra in terms of isotopic abundances and molecular fragmentation;

4   calculate the relative atomic mass of an element given the relative abundance of its isotopes, or its mass spectrum;

5   define the terms *empirical formula* and *molecular formula*;

6   calculate empirical and molecular formulae, using composition by mass;

7   perform calculations, including use of the mole concept, involving **a** reacting masses (from formulae and equations), **b** volumes of gases (e.g. in the burning of hydrocarbons) and **c** volumes and concentrations of solutions (e.g. using titrations involving acids and bases of different strengths);

8   deduce stoichiometric relationships from calculations such as those in 7.

Counting atoms and molecules

If you have ever had to sort and count coins, you will know that it is a very time-consuming business! Banks do not need to count sorted coins, as they can quickly check the amount by weighing. For example, as a 2p coin has twice the mass of a 1p coin, a bag containing £2.00 could contain one hundred 2p coins or two hundred 1p coins. Chemists are also able to count atoms and molecules by weighing them. This is possible because atoms of different elements also have different masses.

We rely on tables of relative atomic masses for this purpose. The **relative atomic mass**, A_r, of an element is the average mass of the naturally occurring isotopes of the element relative to the mass of an atom of carbon-12; one atom of this isotope (see chapter 1, page 6) is given a relative isotopic mass of exactly 12. The relative atomic masses, A_r, of the other elements are then found by comparing the average mass of their atoms with that of the carbon-12 isotope. Notice that we use the average mass of their atoms. This is because we take into account the abundance of their naturally occurring isotopes. Thus the relative atomic mass of hydrogen is 1.0079, whilst that of chlorine is 35.49. (Relative atomic masses are shown on the Periodic Table in the appendix on page 115.)

We use the term **relative isotopic mass** for the mass of an isotope of an element relative to carbon-12. For example, the relative isotopic mass of carbon-13 is 13.003. If the natural abundance of each isotope is known, together with their relative isotopic masses, we can calculate the relative atomic mass of the element as follows.

Chlorine, for example, occurs naturally as chlorine-35 and chlorine-37 with percentage natural abundances 75.53% and 24.47% respectively. So

$$\text{relative atomic mass} = \frac{(75.53 \times 35 + 24.47 \times 37)}{100}$$

$$= 35.49$$

SAQ 2.1

Carbon has a relative atomic mass of 12.011. Naturally occurring carbon is 98.89% carbon-12 and 1.11% carbon-13. Use these figures, together with the relative isotopic masses given above, to show that they indeed correspond to a relative atomic mass of 12.011.

The masses of different molecules are compared in a similar fashion. The **relative molecular mass**, M_r, of a compound is the mass of a molecule of the compound relative to the mass of an atom of carbon-12, which is given a mass of exactly 12.

To find the relative molecular mass of a molecule, we add up the relative atomic masses of all the atoms present in the molecule. For example, the relative molecular mass of methane, CH_4, is $12 + 4 \times 1 = 16$.

Where compounds contain ions, we use the term **relative formula mass**. Relative molecular mass refers to compounds containing molecules.

SAQ 2.2

Use the Periodic Table in the appendix (page 115) to calculate the relative formula mass of the following:

a magnesium chloride, $MgCl_2$;

b copper sulphate, $CuSO_4$;

c sodium carbonate, $Na_2CO_3.10H_2O$ ($10H_2O$ means ten water molecules).

In the next section we shall see how these relative atomic and molecular masses help us to count atoms by mass.

Counting chemical substances in bulk

The mole and Avogadro's constant

When chemists write a formula for a compound, it tells us how many atoms of each element are present in the compound. For example, the formula of water is H_2O, and this tells us that two atoms of hydrogen are combined with one atom of oxygen. As the A_r of hydrogen is 1 and the A_r of oxygen is 16, the M_r is $2 + 16 = 18$ and the hydrogen and oxygen are combined in a mass ratio of 2:16. Although atoms are too small to be weighed individually, any mass of water will have hydrogen and oxygen in this ratio.

For example, consider 18 g of water ($2 + 16 = 18$). This will actually contain 2 g of hydrogen and 16 g of oxygen. In 2 g of hydrogen there will be twice as many hydrogen atoms as there are oxygen atoms in 16 g of oxygen. We can use any unit of mass as long as we keep to the same mass ratio. In 18 tonnes of water there will be 2 tonnes of hydrogen and 16 tonnes of oxygen. The actual number of atoms present will be very large indeed!

When we take the relative molecular mass or relative atomic mass of a substance in grams, we say that we have one mole of the substance. The mole is the chemist's unit of amount. A **mole** of substance is the amount of substance that has the same number of particles as there are atoms in exactly 12 g of carbon-12. The particles may be atoms, molecules, ions or even electrons.

The number of atoms or molecules in one mole is a constant known as Avogadro's constant. Avogadro's constant, L, is approximately $6 \times 10^{23} \, mol^{-1}$.

Units used by chemists:

Mass is measured in g (kg in SI units)
Volume is measured in cm^3 or dm^3
  ($1 \, dm^3 = 1000 \, cm^3 = 1 \, litre$).
Amount of substance is measured in moles
  (abbreviation is mol).

You need to remember that *amount* has a specific meaning, as do *mass* and *volume*. Each has its own unit. SI is an abbreviation for the Système International d'Unités. In this internationally recognised system, kilogram, metre and mole are three of the seven base units from which all supplementary units are derived.

We often refer to the mass of one mole of a substance as the molar mass, M. The units of molar mass are $g \, mol^{-1}$.

In *figure 2.1* a mole of some elements may be compared.

Moles are particularly helpful when we need to measure out reactants or calculate the mass of

● *Figure 2.1* From left to right, one mole of each of copper, bromine, carbon, mercury and lead.

product from a reaction. Such information is very important when manufacturing chemicals. For example, if the manufacture of a drug requires a particularly expensive reagent, it is important to mix it with the correct amounts of the other reagents to ensure that it all reacts and none is wasted. You will need to be able to write formulae in order to calculate amounts in moles. (See page 23 for some help with writing formulae.)

To find the amount of substance present in a given mass, we must divide that mass by the molar mass, M, of the substance. For example, for NaCl, $M = 23 + 35.5 = 58.5\,g$; so in $585\,g$ of sodium chloride (NaCl) there are $585/58.5\,mol$ of NaCl, i.e. $10\,mol$ NaCl.

SAQ 2.3

What amount of substance is there in:

a $35.5\,g$ of chlorine *atoms*?

b $71\,g$ of chlorine *molecules*, Cl_2?

SAQ 2.4

Use Avogadro's constant to calculate the total number of atoms of chlorine in:

a $35.5\,g$ of chlorine atoms.

b $71\,g$ of chlorine molecules.

To find the mass of a given amount of substance, we multiply the number of moles of the substance by the molar mass.

SAQ 2.5

Calculate the mass of the following:

a $0.1\,mol$ of carbon dioxide.

b $10\,mol$ of calcium carbonate, $CaCO_3$.

If we are given the mass of a reactant, we can find out the mass of product formed in a chemical reaction. To do this, a balanced equation is used. (See page 24 for revision on balancing equations.)

Consider the formation of water from hydrogen and oxygen:

	$2H_2$	$+ O_2$	$\rightarrow 2H_2O$
this reads	2 molecules hydrogen	+ 1 molecule oxygen	$\rightarrow$ 2 molecules water
or	2 moles hydrogen	+ 1 mole oxygen	$\rightarrow$ 2 moles water
masses/g	$2 \times 2 = 4$	$+ 32$	$\rightarrow 2 \times 18 = 36$

If we mix $4\,g$ of hydrogen with $32\,g$ of oxygen we should produce $36\,g$ of water on exploding the mixture.

Suppose we wish to calculate the mass of iron that can be obtained from a given mass of iron oxide, Fe_2O_3. When iron ore is reduced by carbon monoxide in a blast furnace *(figure 2.2)*, the equation for the reaction is:

$$Fe_2O_3 + 3CO \rightarrow 2Fe + 3CO_2$$

The molar mass of Fe_2O_3 is $2 \times 56 + 3 \times 16 = 160\,g\,mol^{-1}$. One mole of Fe_2O_3 produces two moles of iron. Hence $160\,g$ of Fe_2O_3 will produce $2 \times 56 = 112\,g$ iron; or

$$1000\,g \text{ of } Fe_2O_3 \text{ will produce } 112 \times \frac{1000\,g}{160} = 700\,g \text{ iron.}$$

SAQ 2.6

Hydrogen burns in chlorine to produce hydrogen chloride:

$$H_2 + Cl_2 \rightarrow 2HCl$$

a   Calculate the ratio of the masses of reactants.

b   What mass (in g) of hydrogen is needed to produce $36.5\,g$ of hydrogen chloride?

● **Figure 2.2** Workers taking the slag from the top of the molten iron in an open-hearth blast furnace.

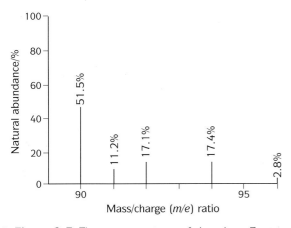

● *Figure 2.3* The mass spectrum of zirconium, Zr.

In a mass spectrometer, atoms are converted to positive ions; these may then be sorted by electric and magnetic fields before being detected. For an element, the detector enables the mass of each isotope to be found as well as its relative abundance.

The mass spectrum of the element zirconium is shown in *figure 2.3*. Notice that the natural abundance is on the vertical axis. The horizontal axis displays the mass/charge (*m/e*) ratio. Remember, the mass spectrometer sorts and detects positive ions. The ions almost always carry a single positive charge. Hence you often see this axis simply labelled mass as, numerically, mass/charge = mass.

SAQ 2.7

Calculate the mass of iron produced from 1000 tonnes of Fe_2O_3. How many tonnes of Fe_2O_3 would be needed to produce 1 tonne of iron? If the iron ore contains 12% of Fe_2O_3, how many tonnes of ore are needed to produce 1 tonne of iron? (Note: 1 tonne = 1000 kg)

SAQ 2.8

a List the isotopes present in zirconium.

b Use the percentage abundance of each isotope to calculate the relative atomic mass of zirconium.

Determination of A_r and M_r from mass spectra

You may have wondered how tables of relative atomic masses have been obtained. An instrument called a mass spectrometer is used for this purpose; such instruments are too expensive to be found in schools or colleges. Academic or industrial chemical laboratories will have one or two, depending on their needs and resources. Mass spectrometers have even been sent into space (e.g. to study the surface of Mars).

Molecular masses

A mass spectrometer can also be used to find molecular masses. When a molecular compound is placed in a mass spectrometer, it also is ionised. The molecule will lose one electron and the positive ion will be detected. This ion, which has a mass equal to the M_r of the compound, is called the molecular ion. Many other ions will also be detected. These are formed by the fragmentation of the molecular ion in the mass spectrometer. Identification of these fragments can be very helpful in determining the structure of an organic compound.

The mass spectrum of dodecane, $C_{12}H_{26}$, is shown in *figure 2.4*. The molecular ion is the peak with the highest mass/charge (*m/e*) ratio. Dodecane has a relative molecular mass of 170 and the spectrum shows the molecular ion, $C_{12}H_{26}^+$, peak at *m/e* 170. As a molecule breaks down in the spectrometer, it forms fragments, which appear as ions of lower mass/charge ratio. Dodecane produces peaks at *m/e* ratios 29, 43, 57, 71 and 85. These correspond to the fragment ions $C_2H_5^+$,

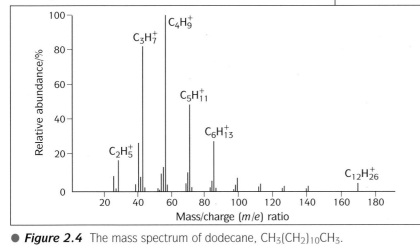

● *Figure 2.4* The mass spectrum of dodecane, $CH_3(CH_2)_{10}CH_3$.

$C_3H_7^+$, $C_4H_9^+$, $C_5H_{11}^+$ and $C_6H_{13}^+$. The relative heights of these peaks partly depend on the individual stability of the fragments. The peak with the highest abundance is called the base peak. This may be a fragment ion but it can be the molecular ion. Notice that the base peak has, by convention, a relative abundance of 100. The base peak for dodecane corresponds to $C_4H_9^+$.

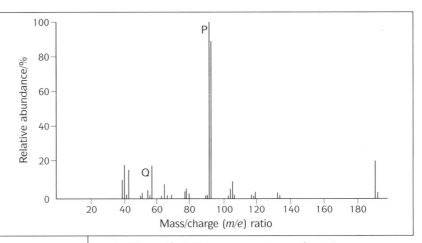

● **Figure 2.5** The mass spectrum of octylbenzene.

SAQ 2.9

Look at the mass spectrum of octylbenzene in *figure 2.5*.

a Find the relative molecular mass of the compound.

b The mass/charge ratios of the peaks labelled P and Q are 91 and 57 respectively; suggest formulae for the fragment ions P and Q.

Examination of the fragmentation pattern can lead to suggestions regarding the structure of a compound where only the molecular formula is known. The molecular formula shows the total number of atoms of each element. The structural formula shows the way in which these atoms are joined together in the molecule. You will find more information on these different types of formulae in chapter 6.

When isotopes of an element are present in a compound, a group of peaks will appear close to the molecular-ion peak. Each of these peaks will correspond to the molecular ion with a different isotope. For example, chloromethane, CH_3Cl, will show peaks with mass/charge ratios of 50 and 52 (*figure 2.6*). The first of these corresponds to the molecular ion with a chlorine-35 isotope, i.e. $[CH_3{}^{35}Cl]^+$; the second to the molecular ion with a chlorine-37 isotope present, i.e. $[CH_3{}^{37}Cl]^+$. The ratio of the heights of these two peaks will be in the same ratio as the natural abundance of these two isotopes.

A study of peaks arising from the presence of carbon-13 in organic molecules can help to establish the number of carbon atoms in the molecule. The probability of finding one or more carbon-13

atoms in a molecule increases with the total number of carbon atoms.

SAQ 2.10

The mass spectrum of dichloromethane shows molecular-ion peaks at mass/charge ratios of 84, 86 and 88. Explain how the three peaks arise and deduce their relative abundances assuming that chlorine-35 has a natural abundance of 75% and chlorine-37 has a natural abundance of 25%. (Consider how these natural abundances affect the probabilities of finding each molecular ion.)

Some modern mass spectrometers can be set up to determine isotopic masses to four or five decimal places. *Figure 2.7* shows a photograph of such a spectrometer.

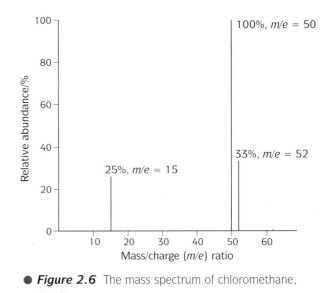

● **Figure 2.6** The mass spectrum of chloromethane, CH_3Cl.

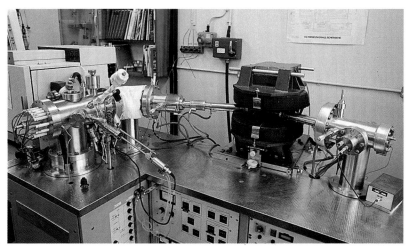

● *Figure 2.7* A high-resolution mass spectrometer. The magnet and the flight tube for the ions are clearly visible.

The relative molecular masses of compounds can be determined to a similar accuracy. This technique can actually be used to identify a compound. Books and computer databases exist listing the accurate molecular masses of a huge number of possible molecular formulae.

SAQ 2.11

Nitrogen (N_2), ethane (C_2H_4) and carbon monoxide (CO) all have molecular masses close to 28. The accurate atomic masses are: carbon 12.0111; nitrogen 14.0067; oxygen 15.9994; hydrogen 1.0079.

a Calculate the *accurate* molecular masses of N_2, C_2H_4 and CO.

b Which compound is present if the mass spectrometer trace shows a molecular ion at 28.0105?

Analytical applications of the mass spectrometer

Water analysis

The very tiny amounts of industrial and agricultural organic chemicals that find their way into our water supplies can be monitored by means of a mass spectrometer. *Figure 2.8* shows a modern portable mass spectrometer that has been developed for this purpose. It is comforting to know that these instruments are capable of detecting such pollutants at levels well below the point where the pollutants might harm us. A recent example comes from British Rail. SAC Scientific have developed analytical methods for determining the concentration of triazine herbicides, which have been found in ground-water. British Rail has used these herbicides to control weeds on railway lines, but it is now trying less persistent herbicides such as

● *Figure 2.8* A mobile mass spectrometer used for environmental chemical analysis.

glyphosate (Tumbleweed), which rapidly breaks down in soil into harmless products.

Drug analysis

In most sports competitions, a careful watch is kept for athletes who may have taken drugs to enhance their performance (*figure 2.9*). As in water analysis, mass spectrometry is linked with gas–liquid chromatography to provide a rapid method of detecting tiny quantities of a drug in a sample of blood or urine.

● *Figure 2.9* Drug analysis is needed to detect the use of performance-enhancing drugs by athletes.

Calculation of empirical and molecular formulae

The **empirical formula** of a compound shows the simplest whole-number ratio of the elements present. For many simple compounds it is the same as the molecular formula. The **molecular formula** shows the total number of atoms of each element present in a molecule of the compound. Some examples are shown below:

Compound	Empirical formula	Molecular formula
water	H_2O	H_2O
methane	CH_4	CH_4
butane	C_2H_5	C_4H_{10}
benzene	CH	C_6H_6

SAQ 2.12

Write down the empirical formulae of the following:
a hexane, C_6H_{14}; **b** hydrogen peroxide, H_2O_2.

The molecular formula is far more useful. It enables us to write balanced chemical equations and to calculate masses of compounds involved in the reaction. However, the empirical formula can be found from the percentage composition by mass of a compound. To find this, experimental methods that determine the mass of each element present in a compound are needed.

If magnesium is burned in oxygen, magnesium oxide is formed. Suppose that a piece of magnesium of known mass is burned completely and the

● **Figure 2.10** Modern microanalytical equipment used for routine determination of percentage of carbon and hydrogen in a compound.

magnesium oxide produced is weighed. The weighings enable us to calculate the empirical formula of magnesium oxide.

In such an experiment, 0.240 g of magnesium ribbon produced 0.400 g of magnesium oxide:

	Mg	O
Mass /g	0.240	0.400 − 0.240
		= 0.160

$$\text{Amount/mol} = \frac{\text{mass}}{A_r} \qquad = \frac{\text{mass}}{A_r}$$
$$= \frac{0.240}{24} \qquad = \frac{0.160}{16}$$
$$= 0.0100 \qquad = 0.0100$$

Divide by the smallest amount to give whole numbers:

Atoms /mol	1	1

Hence the empirical formula of magnesium oxide is MgO. Notice that we convert the mass of each element to the amount in moles, as we need the ratio of the number of atoms of each element present.

SAQ 2.13

An oxide of copper has the following composition by mass: Cu, 0.635 g; O, 0.080 g. Calculate the empirical formula of the oxide.

Combustion analysis

The composition by mass of organic compounds can be found by combustion analysis. This involves the complete combustion in oxygen of a weighed sample. In combustion analysis, all the carbon is converted to carbon dioxide and all the hydrogen to water. The carbon dioxide and water produced are carefully collected by absorption and weighed. The apparatus is shown in *figure 2.10*. Calculation then gives the mass of carbon and hydrogen present. If oxygen is also present, its mass is found by subtraction (see example below). Other elements require further analytical determinations.

Let us consider an example. Suppose that 0.500 g of an organic compound X (containing only carbon, hydrogen and oxygen) produces 0.733 g of carbon dioxide and 0.300 g of water on complete combustion. The mass spectrum of the compound shows a molecular-ion peak at a mass/charge ratio of 60. Determine the molecular formula of the compound.

The calculation goes as follows. As 12 g of carbon are present in 1 mol (= 44 g) CO_2,

$$\text{mass of carbon in} \atop 0.733\,\text{g of } CO_2 = \frac{12}{44} \times 0.733\,\text{g}$$

$$= 0.200\,\text{g}$$

$$= \text{mass of carbon in X}$$

As 2 g of hydrogen are present in 1 mol (= 18 g) H_2O,

$$\text{mass of hydrogen in} \atop 0.300\,\text{g of } H_2O = \frac{2}{18} \times 0.300\,\text{g}$$

$$= 0.033\,\text{g}$$

$$= \text{mass of hydrogen in X}$$

Hence

$$\text{mass of oxygen in X} = 0.500 - 0.199 - 0.033$$
$$= 0.268\,\text{g}$$

	C	H	O
Mass/g	0.200	0.033	0.268
Amount/mol	0.200/12	0.033/1	0.268/16
	= 0.0167	= 0.033	= 0.0168

Divide by the smallest amount to give whole numbers:

Atoms /mol	1	2	1

Hence the empirical formula is CH_2O. This has $M_r = 12 + 2 + 16 = 30$. As M_r of X is 60, the molecular formula of the compound is $C_2H_4O_2$.

SAQ 2.14

On complete combustion of 0.400 g of a hydrocarbon, 1.257 g of carbon dioxide and 0.514 g of water were produced.

a Calculate the empirical formula of the hydrocarbon.

b If the relative molecular mass of the hydrocarbon is 84, what is its molecular formula?

Writing chemical formulae

By this point in your study of chemistry you will already know the formulae of some simple compounds. For advanced chemistry you will need to learn the formulae of a wide range of compounds. These formulae are determined by the electronic configurations of the elements involved

and the ways in which they combine with other elements to form compounds. The chemical bonding of elements in compounds is studied in chapter 3. It will help if you learn some generalisations about the names and formulae of compounds.

To write the formula of a compound, it is important to use all the oxidation numbers (see chapter 5, page 83) of each element. In the case of ionic compounds, this means that the total number of positive charges in the compound must exactly equal the total number of negative charges. For magnesium oxide, magnesium (in Group II) forms Mg^{2+} ions. Oxygen (in Group VI) forms O^{2-} ions. Magnesium oxide is thus MgO ($+2 - 2 = 0$). Aluminium forms 3+ ions. Two Al^{3+} ions and three O^{2-} ions are needed in aluminium oxide ($2\times(+3) + 3\times(-2) = 0$). The formula is Al_2O_3. Note how the number of ions of each element in the formula is written as a small number following and below the element symbol.

Some compounds do not contain ions; in such compounds the sum of the oxidation numbers of each element must be the same. Carbon (in Group IV) has an oxidation number of -4, hydrogen (in Group I) has an oxidation number of $+1$. This means that one carbon will combine with four hydrogen atoms to form CH_4 (methane). In chapter 3, you will see that each hydrogen forms one bond to carbon whilst the carbon forms four bonds to the four hydrogen atoms.

Table 2.1 summarises the oxidation numbers and charges on some of the common ions that you need to learn. The position of the elements in the Periodic Table is helpful. In many instances, the Group in which an element lies indicates the oxidation number of the element. Many non-metals show oxidation numbers lower than the number of their Group. One common oxidation number corresponds to their Group number subtracted from eight. (Remember that filling all the s and p orbitals in a Period requires eight electrons – see chapter 1.) Note that metals form positive ions, whilst non-metals form negative ions.

Metals do not usually change their names in compounds. However, non-metals change their

Charge	Oxidation number	Examples
1+	+1	H^+ and Group I, the alkali-metal ions, e.g. Li^+, Na^+, K^+
2+	+2	Group II, the alkaline-earth-metal ions, e.g. Mg^{2+}, Ca^{2+}
3+	+3	Al^{3+}
1−	−1	Group VII, the halogens, e.g. F^-, Cl^-, Br^-, I^-
	+5	Nitrogen in NO_3^- (nitrate)
2−	−2	Group VI, O^{2-} and S^{2-}
	+4	Carbon in CO_3^{2-} (carbonate) and sulphur in SO_3^{2-} (sulphite)
	+6	Sulphur in SO_4^{2-} (sulphate)
3−	+5	Phosphorus in PO_4^{3-} (phosphate)

● **Table 2.1** Charges on and oxidation numbers of some common ions

name by becoming -ides. For example, chlorine becomes chloride in sodium chloride. Sodium has not changed its name, although its properties are now dramatically different! Many non-metals (and some metals) combine with other non-metals such as oxygen to form negative ions. These negative ions start with the name of the element and end in -ate (or sometimes -ite), e.g. sulphate (sulphite). Some of these ions are also included in *table 2.1*.

SAQ 2.15

Write the formula for each of the following compounds:

a magnesium bromide   **d** sodium sulphate

b hydrogen iodide   **e** potassium nitrate

c calcium sulphide   **f** nitrogen dioxide

SAQ 2.16

Name each of the following compounds:

a K_2CO_3 **d** $Ca_3(PO_4)_2$

b Al_2S_3 **e** SiO_2

c $LiNO_3$ **f** NO

Calculations involving concentrations and gas volumes

Before we look at calculations involving these, some revision on how to balance chemical equations may be helpful.

■ Write down the formulae of all the reactants and all the products. It may help you to write these in words first.

■ Now inspect the equation and count the atoms of each element on each side. As the elements present cannot be created or lost in the chemical reaction, we must balance the number of each formula.

■ Decide what numbers must be placed in front of each formula to ensure that the same number of each atom is present on each side of the equation.

It is most important that the formulae of the reactants and products are not altered; only the total number of each may be changed.

We shall now do an example. When iron(III) oxide is reduced to metallic iron by carbon monoxide, the carbon monoxide is oxidised to carbon dioxide (the III in iron(III) oxide indicates that the iron has an oxidation number of +3).

> Iron(III) oxide + carbon monoxide
> → iron + carbon dioxide

The formulae are:

$$Fe_2O_3 + CO \rightarrow Fe + CO_2$$

On inspection we note that there are two iron atoms in the oxide on the left-hand side but only one on the right-hand side. We thus write

$$Fe_2O_3 + CO \rightarrow 2Fe + CO_2$$

There is one carbon atom on each side of the equation, so we next count the oxygen atoms: three in the oxide plus one in carbon monoxide, on the left-hand side. As there are only two on the right-hand side in carbon dioxide, we double the number of CO_2 molecules:

$$Fe_2O_3 + CO \rightarrow 2Fe + 2CO_2$$

On checking we see we have solved one problem but created a new one. There are now two carbon atoms on the right but only one on the left. Doubling the number of CO molecules still does not balance the equation. If we examine the equation again, we see that Fe_2O_3 needs to lose three oxygen atoms. One CO molecule requires only one oxygen atom to form CO_2. Thus three CO molecules are required to combine with the three oxygen atoms lost from Fe_2O_3. Three CO_2 molecules will be formed:

$$Fe_2O_3 + 3CO \rightarrow 2Fe + 3CO_2$$

The equation is now balanced.

We often need to specify the physical states of chemicals in an equation. This can be important when, for example, calculating enthalpy changes (see chapter 4). The symbols used are: (s) for solid; (l) for liquid; (g) for gas. A solution in water is described as aqueous, so (aq) is used. Addition of the physical states to the equation for the reaction of iron(III) oxide with carbon monoxide produces:

$$Fe_2O_3(s) + 3CO(g) \rightarrow 2Fe(s) + 3CO_2(g)$$

SAQ 2.17

Balance the equations for the following reactions.

a The thermite reaction (used for chemical welding of lengths of rail):

$$Al + Fe_2O_3 \rightarrow Al_2O_3 + Fe$$

b Petrol contains octane, C_8H_{18}. Complete combustion in oxygen produces only carbon dioxide and water.

c Lead nitrate decomposes on heating to produce PbO, NO_2 and O_2.

Concentrations of solutions

When one mole of a compound is dissolved in a solvent to make one cubic decimetre ($1\,dm^3$) of solution, the concentration is $1\,mol\,dm^{-3}$. Usually the solvent is water and an aqueous solution is formed.

Traditionally, concentrations in $mol\,dm^{-3}$ have been expressed as molarities. For example, $2\,mol\,dm^{-3}$ aqueous sodium hydroxide is 2M aqueous sodium hydroxide, where M is the molarity of the solution. Although this is still a convenient method for labelling bottles, etc., it is better to use

the units of $mol\,dm^{-3}$ in your calculations. Although you may have used mol/dm^3 or mol/litre in the past, advanced chemistry requires you to use $mol\,dm^{-3}$.

In titrations *(figure 2.11)* there are five things you need to know:

- the balanced equation for the reaction showing the moles of the two reactants;
- the volume of the solution of the first reagent;
- the concentration of the solution of the first reagent;
- the volume of the solution of the second reagent;
- the concentration of the solution of the second reagent.

If we know four of these, we can calculate the fifth. Remember that concentrations may be in $mol\,dm^{-3}$ or $g\,dm^{-3}$.

● *Figure 2.11* Titrations form part of Royal Society of Chemistry competitions for first-year advanced chemistry students. A titration enables the reacting volumes of two solutions to be accurately determined. One solution is measured with a graduated pipette into a conical flask, the other is added slowly from a burette. The point where complete reaction just occurs is usually shown using an indicator, which changes colour at this point (called the end-point).

Many titration calculations start by finding the amount of a reagent (in moles) from a given concentration and volume. For example, what amount of sodium hydroxide is present in $24.0\,cm^3$ of an aqueous $0.010\,mol\,dm^{-3}$ solution?

Convert the volume to dm^3:

$$1\,dm^3 = 10 \times 10 \times 10\,cm^3 = 1000\,cm^3$$

$$24.0\,cm^3 = \frac{24.0}{1000}\,dm^3$$

$$\text{amount of NaOH} = \frac{24.0}{1000} \times 0.010\,mol$$

$$= 2.4 \times 10^{-4}\,mol \text{ in } 24\,cm^3$$

Notice how the units multiply and cancel: $dm^3 \times mol\,dm^{-3} = mol$. Use this as a check. Another check is to ask yourself: should the numerical value of your answer be greater than or less than that of the concentration?

We also often need to find the concentration of a solution from the amount in a given volume. For example, what is the concentration of an aqueous solution containing $2 \times 10^{-4}\,mol$ of sulphuric acid in $10\,cm^3$?

As before, convert the volume to dm^3:

$$10\,cm^3 = \frac{10}{1000}\,dm^3 = 1 \times 10^{-2}\,dm^3$$

$$\begin{aligned}\text{concentration of} \\ \text{sulphuric acid}\end{aligned} = \frac{2 \times 10^{-4}}{1 \times 10^{-2}}\,mol\,dm^{-3}$$

$$= 2 \times 10^{-2}\,mol\,dm^{-3}$$

Again check by looking at the units:

$$\frac{mol}{dm^3} = mol\,dm^{-3}.$$

SAQ 2.18

a Calculate the amount in moles of nitric acid in $25.0\,cm^3$ of a $0.1\,mol\,dm^{-3}$ aqueous solution.

b Calculate the concentration in $mol\,dm^{-3}$ of a solution comprising $0.125\,mol$ of nitric acid in $50\,cm^3$ of water.

Changing concentrations expressed in $mol\,dm^{-3}$ to $g\,dm^{-3}$ and vice versa is straightforward. We multiply by the molar mass M to convert $mol\,dm^{-3}$ to $g\,dm^{-3}$. To convert $g\,dm^{-3}$ to $mol\,dm^{-3}$ we divide by M.

SAQ 2.19

a What is the concentration in $g\,dm^{-3}$ of $0.50\,mol\,dm^{-3}$ aqueous ethanoic acid (CH_3CO_2H)?

b What is the concentration in $mol\,dm^{-3}$ of an aqueous solution containing $4.00\,g\,dm^{-3}$ of sodium hydroxide?

A worked example follows of how such calculations are combined with a balanced chemical equation to interpret the result of a titration. Try to identify the 'five things to know' in this calculation. In the titration $20.0\,cm^3$ of $0.200\,mol\,dm^{-3}$ aqueous sodium hydroxide exactly neutralises a $25.0\,cm^3$ sample of sulphuric acid. What is the concentration of the sulphuric acid in **a** $mol\,dm^{-3}$, **b** $g\,dm^{-3}$?

The working goes as follows:

$$20.0\,cm^3 = \frac{20}{1000}\,dm^3 = 2.00 \times 10^{-2}\,dm^3$$

amount of sodium hydroxide

$$= 2 \times 10^{-2} \times 0.200\,mol$$
$$= 4.00 \times 10^{-3}\,mol$$

The balanced equation for the reaction is:

$$2NaOH(aq) + H_2SO_4(aq)$$
$$\rightarrow Na_2SO_4(aq) + 2H_2O(l)$$

Exact neutralisation requires $2\,mol$ of NaOH to $1\,mol$ of H_2SO_4. So

amount of H_2SO_4 neutralised in the titration

$$= \tfrac{1}{2} \times \text{amount of NaOH}$$
$$= \tfrac{1}{2} \times 4 \times 10^{-3}\,mol$$
$$= 2 \times 10^{-3}\,mol$$

Volume of $H_2SO_4 = 25.0\,cm^3 = 25.0/1000\,dm^3$
$$= 2.5 \times 10^{-2}\,dm^3.$$

a Concentration of H_2SO_4
$$= \frac{2 \times 10^{-3}}{2.5 \times 10^{-2}}\,mol\,dm^{-3}$$
$$= 0.080\,mol\,dm^{-3}$$

b As $M(H_2SO_4) = 2 + 32 + 4 \times 16 = 98\,g$
concentration of $H_2SO_4 = 98 \times 0.080\,g\,dm^{-3}$
$$= 7.84\,g\,dm^{-3}$$

SAQ 2.20

$20.0\,cm^3$ of $0.100\,mol\,dm^{-3}$ potassium hydroxide exactly neutralises a $25.0\,cm^3$ sample of hydrochloric acid. What is the concentration of the hydrochloric acid in **a** $mol\,dm^{-3}$, **b** $g\,dm^{-3}$?

It is possible to use a titration result to arrive at the reacting mole ratio (called the **stoichiometric ratio**) and balanced equation for a reaction.

The example that follows illustrates how this is done. A $25.0\,cm^3$ sample of $0.0400\,mol\,dm^{-3}$ aqueous metal hydroxide is titrated against $0.100\,mol\,dm^{-3}$ hydrochloric acid. $20.0\,cm^3$ of the acid were required for exact neutralisation.

The working is as follows:

$$\text{amount of metal hydroxide} = \frac{25.0}{1000} \times 0.0400\,mol$$
$$= 1.00 \times 10^{-3}\,mol$$
$$\text{amount of hydrochloric acid} = \frac{20.0}{1000} \times 0.100\,mol$$
$$= 2.00 \times 10^{-3}\,mol$$

Hence the reacting (i.e. stoichiometric) mole ratio of metal hydroxide : hydrochloric acid is

$$1.00 \times 10^{-3} : 2.00 \times 10^{-3}$$
or $\qquad 1 : 2$

i.e. exactly one mole of the metal hydroxide neutralises exactly two moles of hydrochloric acid. One mole of HCl will neutralise one mole of hydroxide ions, so the metal hydroxide must contain two hydroxide ions in its formula. The balanced equation for the reaction is

$$M(OH)_2(aq) + 2HCl(aq)$$
$$\rightarrow MCl_2(aq) + 2H_2O(l)$$

where M is the metal.

SAQ 2.21

Determine the stoichiometric ratio, and hence the balanced equation, for the reaction of an insoluble iron hydroxide with dilute nitric acid, HNO_3. $4.00 \times 10^{-4}\,mol$ of the iron hydroxide is exactly neutralised by $24.0\,cm^3$ of $0.05\,mol\,dm^{-3}$ nitric acid.

Gas volumes

It was Avogadro who, in 1811, first suggested that equal volumes of all gases contain the same number of molecules. (Note that the volumes must be measured under the same conditions of temperature and pressure.) This provides an easy way of calculating the amount of gas present in a given volume. At room temperature and pressure, one mole of any gas occupies approximately $24.0\,dm^3$.

SAQ 2.22

a Calculate the amount of helium present in a balloon with a volume of $2.4\,dm^3$. Assume that the pressure inside the balloon is the same as atmospheric pressure and that the balloon is at room temperature.

b Calculate the volume occupied by a mixture of $0.5\,mol$ of propane and $1.5\,mol$ of butane gases at room temperature and pressure.

SUMMARY

■ Definitions of atomic, isotopic and molecular masses are relative to carbon-12, which has a mass of exactly 12.

■ One mole of a substance is the amount of substance that has the same number (called Avogadro's constant) of particles as there are atoms in exactly 12 g of carbon-12.

■ Mass spectra of elements enable isotopic abundances and relative atomic masses to be found. Mass spectra of compounds enable molecular masses and molecular formulae to be found from molecular ions. The structures of compounds may be found by using a 'jigsaw puzzle' approach with the fragment ions.

■ Empirical formulae show the simplest whole-number ratio of atoms in a compound whilst molecular formulae show the total number of atoms for each element present. Empirical formulae may be determined from the composition by mass of a compound. The molecular formula may then be found if the molecular mass is known.

■ Molar masses enable calculations to be made using moles and balanced chemical equations involving reacting masses, volumes and concentrations of solutions and volumes of gases.

Questions

1 Oxygen, O_2, was discovered by Joseph Priestley in 1774. He heated mercury(II) oxide, HgO, which readily decomposed into its elements.

   a Write a balanced equation for the thermal decomposition of mercury(II) oxide.

   b Priestley's experiment was repeated in the laboratory by heating 4.34 g of mercury(II) oxide.

   (i) How many moles of mercury(II) oxide were heated? [A_r: Hg, 201; O, 16]

   (ii) How many moles of oxygen were formed?

   (iii) What volume of oxygen was obtained at room temperature and pressure? [One mole of gas occupies 24.0 dm^3 at room temperature and pressure.]

   c Priestley also isolated several other gases including ammonia. Ammonia is dissolved in water to form a solution of concentration 2.0 mol dm^{-3}.

   (i) Explain what is meant by the term **concentration of 2.0 mol dm^{-3}**.

   (ii) What mass of ammonia must be dissolved to prepare 250 cm^3 of a 2.0 mol dm^{-3} solution? [M_r: NH$_3$, 17]

   (iii) Outline an experiment to determine the concentration of an unknown solution of ammonia.

2 a What is meant by the terms
   (i) isotopic abundance;
   (ii) relative atomic mass?

   Naturally occurring gallium, Ga, is a mixture of two isotopes, gallium-69 and gallium-71. The relative atomic mass of gallium is 69.735. Use this information to calculate the percentage abundance of each isotope.

   b What is meant by the terms:
   (i) mass/charge (m/e) ratio;
   (ii) molecular ion;
   (iii) fragmentation pattern?

   Illustrate your answer with a fully labelled diagram of the mass spectrum of a simple molecule.

   c The mass spectrum of chlorine, Cl$_2$(g), consists of peaks at m/e ratios of 70, 72 and 74.

   (i) Explain these observations as fully as you can.

   (ii) Give the m/e ratios of any other peaks that will appear.

What holds atoms, ions and molecules together?

1 describe ionic (electrovalent) bonding, as in sodium chloride and magnesium oxide, including the use of 'dot-and-cross' diagrams;

2 describe, including the use of 'dot-and-cross' diagrams, **a** covalent bonding, as in hydrogen, oxygen, chlorine, hydrogen chloride, carbon dioxide, methane and ethene, and **b** coordinate (dative covalent) bonding, as in $BF_3 \cdot NH_3$;

3 explain the shapes of, and bond angles in, molecules by using the qualitative model of electron-pair repulsion (including lone-pairs), using simple examples, e.g. BF_3 (trigonal), CO_2 (linear), CH_4 (tetrahedral), NH_3 (pyramidal), H_2O (non-linear) and SF_6 (octahedral), and predict the shapes of, and bond angles in, other similar molecules;

4 describe covalent bonding in terms of orbital overlap, giving σ and π bonds;

5 explain the terms *bond energy*, *bond length* and *bond polarity*, and use them to compare the reactivities of covalent bonds;

6 describe hydrogen bonding, using ammonia and water as simple examples of molecules containing –NH and –OH groups;

7 describe intermolecular forces (van der Waals' forces), based on permanent and induced dipoles, as in $CHCl_3(l)$, $Br_2(l)$ and the liquid noble gases;

8 describe, using a kinetic-molecular model, the liquid state, melting, vaporisation and vapour pressure;

9 describe metallic bonding in terms of a lattice of positive ions surrounded by mobile electrons;

10 describe, in simple terms, the lattice structure of a crystalline solid that is **a** ionic, as in sodium chloride and magnesium oxide, **b** simple molecular, as in iodine, **c** giant molecular, as in graphite, diamond and silicon(IV) oxide, **d** hydrogen-bonded, as in ice, and **e** metallic, as in copper;

11 describe, interpret and/or predict the effect of the different types of bonding (ionic bonding, covalent bonding, hydrogen bonding, other inter-molecular interactions, metallic bonding) on the physical properties of substances;

12 deduce the type of bonding present from information provided.

Ionic bonding

Many familiar substances are ionic compounds. An example is common salt (sodium chloride). Sodium chloride and many other ionic compounds are present in sea-water. Crystals of salt are readily obtained by the partial evaporation of sea-water (*figure 3.1*).

We need to understand the bonding in compounds in order to understand their properties. In sodium chloride, the ions are arranged in a crystal lattice, which determines the shape of the crystals grown from sea-water. Most other minerals are also found as well-formed crystals. The shapes of these crystals arise from the way in which the ions are packed together in the lattice. Some crystals are shown in *figure 3.2*.

● *Figure 3.1* A salt mountain with a salt pan in the foreground, Sardinia.

● *Figure 3.2* A selection of minerals.

Another important characteristic of ionic compounds is their ability to conduct electricity, with decomposition, when in aqueous solution or when they are molten. This process is called **electrolysis**. Electrolysis is used to produce chlorine from brine (concentrated aqueous sodium chloride) *(figure 3.3)* and aluminium from molten aluminium oxide.

Ions are free to move through the aqueous solution or molten compound and are attracted to the oppositely charged electrode. Positive ions (cations) are attracted to the negative electrode (cathode) and negative ions (anions) to the positive electrode (anode). At the electrode, the ions discharge; e.g. chloride ions to chlorine or aluminium ions to aluminium metal. On being discharged, an ion will either gain or lose electrons. Electrons will be gained by **cations** (positively charged ions) and lost by **anions** (negatively charged ions). The number of electrons gained or lost will depend on the magnitude of the charge on the ion. A chloride ion will lose one electron; an aluminium ion will gain three electrons. These changes may be represented as follows:

at the positive electrode (anode): $Cl^- \rightarrow \frac{1}{2}Cl_2 + e^-$
at the negative electrode (cathode):

$$Al^{3+} + 3e^- \rightarrow Al$$

SAQ 3.1

Write similar equations, including electrons, for the discharge of copper and bromide ions during the electrolysis of copper bromide, $CuBr_2$, using carbon electrodes. Indicate the electrode at which each reaction will occur.

Use is often made of the very high melting points of ionic compounds, e.g. aluminium oxide (melting point 2345 K, where K refers to the Kelvin scale for temperature, $0°C = 273 K$). A fibrous form of aluminium oxide is used in tiles on the Space Shuttle for protection from the high temperatures experienced on re-entry into the atmosphere *(figure 3.4)* and in the lining of the portable gas forges of a modern 'high-tech' farrier.

Formation of ions from elements

Positive ions are formed when electrons are removed from atoms. This happens most easily with metallic elements. Atoms of non-metallic elements tend to gain electrons to form negative ions. Hence when metals combine with non-metals, electrons are transferred from the metal atoms to the non-metal atoms. Usually a metal atom will lose all of its outer-shell electrons and a non-metal atom will accept electrons to fill its

● *Figure 3.3* Industrial electrolysis: chlorine cell.

● *Figure 3.4* The space shuttle *Columbia,* seen during the fitting of the thermal insulation tiles.

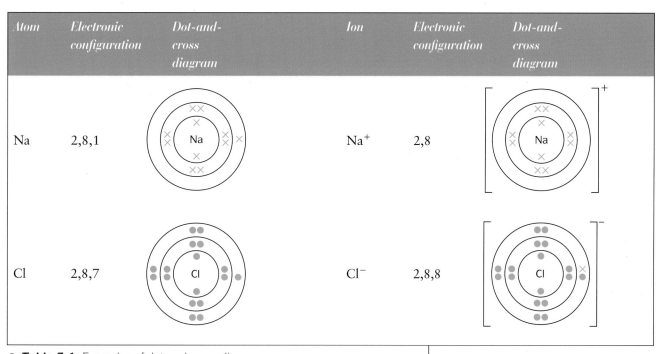

Atom	Electronic configuration	Dot-and-cross diagram	Ion	Electronic configuration	Dot-and-cross diagram
Na	2,8,1		Na^+	2,8	
Cl	2,8,7		Cl^-	2,8,8	

● **Table 3.1** Examples of dot-and-cross diagrams

outer shell. The net result of electron transfer from a metal atom to a non-metal atom is to produce filled outer shells similar to the noble-gas electronic configurations for both elements. The ionic bonding results from the electrostatic attraction between the oppositely charged ions.

Dot-and-cross diagrams are used to show the electronic configurations of elements and ions. The electrons of one element in the compound are shown by dots, those of the second element by crosses. *Table 3.1* shows some examples.

Usually when we draw a dot-and-cross diagram, the filled inner electron shells are omitted. A circle is drawn round the outer-shell electrons. In the case of a sodium ion Na^+, this shell no longer contains any electrons. The nucleus of the element is shown by the symbol for the element. The dot-and-cross diagram for an ion is placed in square brackets with the charge outside the brackets. Electrons are placed in pairs for clarity.

Often only the outer shell dot-and-cross diagram for the compound is needed. For sodium chloride this is:

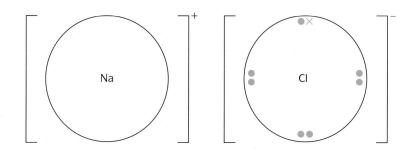

SAQ 3.2

Draw dot-and-cross diagrams for the following: **a** KF, **b** Na_2O, **c** MgO, and **d** $CaCl_2$.

The typical properties of ionic compounds may be explained by the presence of ions, which are arranged in a giant ionic lattice. In the ionic lattice, positive and negative ions alternate in a three-dimensional arrangement. The ions pack together in several basic ways, which depend on their relative sizes. Sodium chloride has a cubic ionic lattice, which is shown in *figure 3.5*.

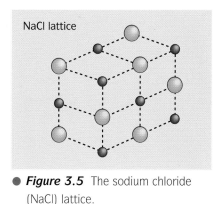

NaCl lattice

● **Figure 3.5** The sodium chloride (NaCl) lattice.

Magnesium oxide has the same cubic structure with magnesium ions in place of sodium ions and oxide ions in place of chloride ions. In the lattice, the attraction between oppositely charged ions binds them together. These attractions greatly outweigh repulsions between similarly charged ions, as the oppositely charged ions approach each other more closely. Hence the melting points of ionic compounds are very high. The melting point usually increases as the charges on the ions increase. Sodium chloride with its singly charged ions has a melting point of 1074 K, and magnesium oxide with its doubly charged ions has a melting point of 3125 K.

Ionic compounds are hard and brittle. The cleavage of gemstones and other ionic crystals occurs between planes of ions in the ionic lattice. If an ionic crystal is tapped sharply in the direction of one of the crystal planes with a sharp-edged knife, it will split cleanly. As a plane of ions is displaced, ions of similar charge come together and the repulsions between them cause the crystal to split apart. The natural shape of ionic crystals is the same as the arrangement of the ions in the lattice. This is because the crystal grows as ions are placed in the lattice and this basic shape continues to the edge of the crystal. Hence sodium chloride crystals are cubic. The smallest repeating unit in the lattice is known as the **unit cell**.

Gemstones and other semi-precious stones, such as emeralds, sapphires and rubies *(figure 3.6)*, are ionic compounds valued for their colour and hardness. Gemstones are crystalline and are cut so that they sparkle in the light. They are cut by exploiting the cleavage planes between layers of ions in the crystal structure.

Ionic compounds may dissolve in water. As a general rule all metal nitrates and most metal chlorides are soluble, as are almost all of the salts of the Group I metals. Ionic compounds that carry higher charges on the ions tend to be less soluble or insoluble. For example, whilst Group I hydroxides are soluble, Group II and III hydroxides are sparingly soluble or insoluble in water (a **sparingly soluble** compound has only a very low solubility, e.g. calcium hydroxide as lime water). When ionic compounds dissolve, energy must be provided to overcome the strong attractive forces between the ions in the lattice. This energy is provided by the similarly strong attractive forces that occur in the hydrated ions. In the case of a cation, the oxygen atoms of the water molecules are attracted by the positive charge on the ion. Negative ions are attracted to the hydrogen end of the water molecule. This is possible as water molecules are polar (see page 43). The diagram below shows a hydrated sodium ion (grey) and a hydrated chloride ion (green). The water molecules are shown with oxygen = red and hydrogen = white.

● *Figure 3.6* Sapphires, both rough crystals and cut gemstones.

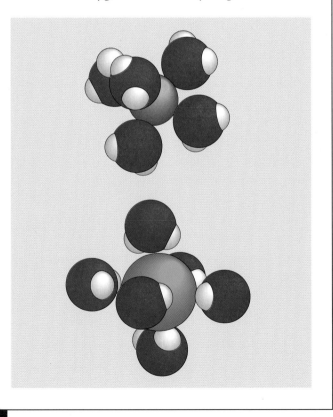

You will learn how to calculate the energy change when an ionic compound dissolves if you study the *How Far, How Fast?* module in this series.

Electrolysis of ionic compounds can only occur when the ions are free to move. In the lattice the ions are in fixed positions, and ionic solids will thus not conduct electricity. On melting, or dissolving in water, the ions are no longer in fixed positions so they are free to move towards electrodes (*figure 3.7*).

Covalent bonding

Many familiar compounds are liquids or gases or solids with low melting points e.g. water, ammonia, methane, ethanol, sucrose and poly(ethene). Such compounds have very different properties to ionic compounds. They all contain molecules in which groups of atoms are held together by covalent bonds. They are non-conductors of electricity and are usually insoluble in water. They may dissolve in organic solvents.

Some crystalline compounds are very hard, have high melting points and are more difficult to cleave than ionic compounds. Such compounds also contain covalent bonds, which extend throughout the crystal in a giant lattice structure, e.g. quartz crystals (*figure 3.8*).

In covalent compounds, electrons are shared in pairs. The negative charge of the electron-pair will attract the positively charged nuclei of the elements, and this holds the atoms together in a molecule. The

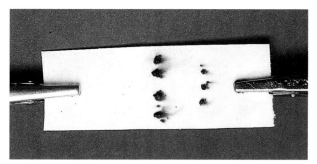

● **Figure 3.7** A sample of an ionic mixture has been spread along the centre of a porous card. The electrodes connected to each end cause ions to move from left to right, or from right to left, at different speeds, depending on the sign and size of the ionic charge.

● **Figure 3.8**
a Quartz crystals.
b Model of quartz lattice.

○ O
○ Si

electron-pair must lie between the nuclei for the attraction to outweigh the repulsion between the nuclei. Under such circumstances two atoms will be bound together by a covalent bond. In a molecule, atoms will share electrons, and, as a general rule, the number shared gives each atom filled outer shells similar to the electronic configuration of a noble gas. Covalent bonds are usually formed between pairs of non-metallic elements.

In a molecule the bonding electrons are now in molecular orbitals rather than atomic orbitals. The molecular orbitals may be considered to arise from overlap of atomic orbitals. Molecular orbitals are given labels using Greek letters: σ, π, δ, etc. (pronounced sigma, pi, delta, respectively). These parallel the labels for atomic orbitals: s, p, d, etc. A single covalent bond consists of a σ orbital and is often called a σ bond. The σ bond in a hydrogen molecule is shown in *figure 3.9*. The π orbitals are found as π bonds. A double covalent bond consists of a σ bond and a π bond. You will find more on σ and π bonds on page 106.

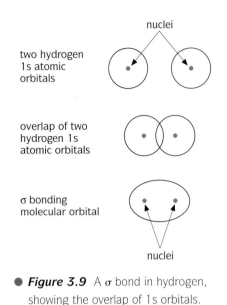

● **Figure 3.9** A σ bond in hydrogen, showing the overlap of 1s orbitals.

Dot-and-cross diagrams for some examples of covalent compounds are shown in *figure 3.10*. Diagrams of molecules often show the covalent bonds as lines. A double line is used for a double bond. Such diagrams are called displayed formulae. Examples are shown with the dot-and-cross diagrams in *figure 3.10*. Remember that each covalent bond is a shared pair of electrons.

SAQ 3.3

a Draw dot-and-cross diagrams together with displayed formulae for each of the following: (i) H_2, (ii) HCl, (iii) O_2, (iv) PCl_3, (v) BF_3 and (vi) SF_6.

b How many electrons are present in the outer shell of boron in BF_3 and of sulphur in SF_6?

SF_6 is now being used as a less hazardous alternative to poly-chlorinated biphenyls, commonly known as PCBs, in large electrical transformers. BF_3 is an example of a molecule in which an atom does not achieve a noble-gas

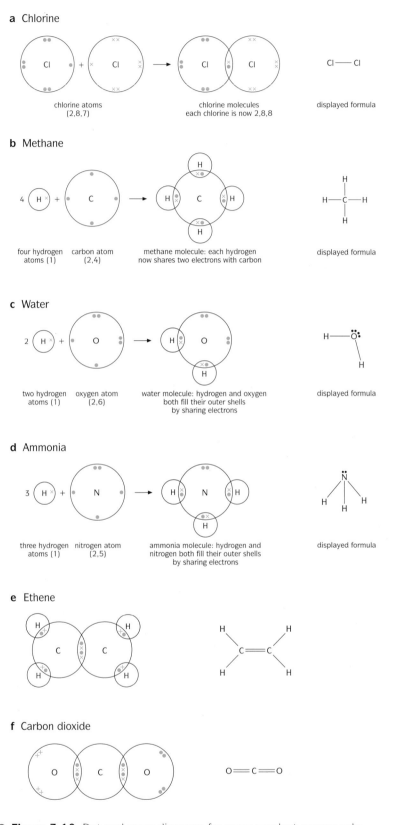

● **Figure 3.10** Dot-and-cross diagrams for some covalent compounds: **a** chlorine (Cl_2), **b** methane (CH_4), **c** water (H_2O), **d** ammonia (NH_3), **e** ethene (C_2H_4) and **f** carbon dioxide (CO_2), also showing the displayed formulae.

configuration in its outer shell. The sulphur atom in SF_6 has more electrons in its outermost shell than the next noble gas, argon. When chemists realised that it was possible for atoms to expand their outer shells in this way, it was suggested that noble gases, hitherto thought to be unreactive, might form compounds in the same way *(figure 3.11)*.

Lone-pairs

Atoms in molecules frequently have pairs of electrons in their outer shells that are not involved in covalent bonds. These non-bonding electron-pairs are called **lone-pairs**. In ammonia, nitrogen has one lone-pair, and in water, oxygen has two lone-pairs. Sometimes these lone-pairs are used to form a covalent bond to an atom that can accommodate two further electrons in its outer shell. An example is when ammonia and the hydrogen ion combine to form the ammonium ion, NH_4^+ (shown below):

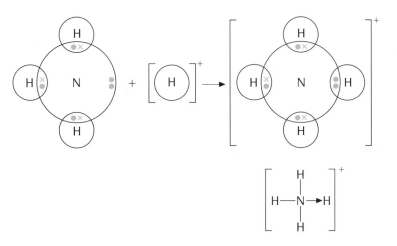

The covalent bond from the nitrogen atom to the H^+ ion is formed by sharing the nitrogen lone-pair. As both electrons come from the nitrogen atom, this is called a **dative covalent bond**. The word 'dative' derives from the Latin for 'give'. Dative covalent bonds are represented by arrows in displayed formulae of molecules. Dative covalent bonds are also called **coordinate bonds** in metal complexes (see chapter 5, page 92).

SAQ 3.4

a   Water molecules will hydrate the aqueous hydrogen ion to form the oxonium ion, H_3O^+. Draw a dot-and-cross diagram and the displayed formula of the oxonium ion.

b BF_3 forms a white solid when it reacts with gaseous ammonia. A bond forms between boron and nitrogen. The formula of the solid is F_3BNH_3. Draw a dot-and-cross diagram and the displayed formula of this product.

c   Draw a dot-and-cross diagram and the displayed formula for carbon monoxide.

● *Figure 3.11* In noble-gas compounds, the outer electron shell expands beyond eight electrons. XeF_4 contains 12 outer-shell electrons. The photograph shows crystals of XeF_4.

Bonds of intermediate character

There are compounds that might be expected to be ionic which have properties more typical of covalent compounds. For example, some salts sublime (i.e. change from a solid to a gas without melting) at quite low temperatures, e.g. aluminium chloride or iron(III) chloride.

Similarly there are covalent compounds that dissolve readily in water to produce ionic solutions, e.g. hydrogen chloride gas or ammonia.

Compounds that are purely ionic or covalent are best regarded as extremes. Between the two extremes a gradual transition from one to the other takes place. We shall start by examining an ionic compound.

Polarisation of ions

Ionic compounds that show some properties more characteristic of covalent compounds contain anions that have become **polarised**. This means that the cation distorts the electron charge-cloud on the anion. Polarisation brings more electron charge between the ionic nuclei, and thus produces a significant degree of covalent bonding between the ions.

Anions with a greater charge or a larger radius are more easily polarised than those with a smaller charge or smaller radius. Cations with a smaller radius or a greater charge will have a greater charge density. Such cations will exert a greater degree of polarisation on an anion than will cations with a larger radius or lower charge.

Figure 3.12 shows the increasing polarisation of an anion by a cation. The effect of this polarisation is to place some of the electron charge-cloud from the larger ion between the two ions. If the process is continued, a covalent bond is created between the two nuclei. When this occurs, the molecule still has some separation of positive and negative charge. The molecule has an electric dipole; it is described as a **polar molecule**.

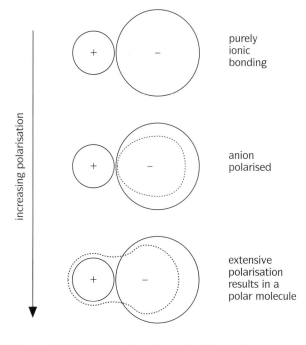

● *Figure 3.12* Polarisation of an anion by a cation.

Polar molecules

Covalent bonds in molecules are polar if there is a difference in electronegativity between the elements. **Electronegativity** is the ability of an atom to attract electron charge.

The electronegativity of the elements increases from Group I to Group VII across the Periodic Table. Electronegativity also increases up a Group of elements as the proton number decreases. Several attempts have been made to put numerical values on electronegativity. For our purposes, it is sufficient to recognise that electronegativities increase **a** moving from left to right across a Period in the Periodic Table and **b** vertically up Groups. The electronegativity of hydrogen is lower than that of most non-metallic elements. In the few cases where it is not lower, it is of a very similar magnitude to that of the non-metal.

increasing electronegativity
$$Cl < N < O < F$$

These electronegativity differences between atoms introduce a degree of polarity in covalent bonds between different atoms. A bigger difference in electronegativity will cause a greater degree of bond polarity. This accounts for the polarity of many simple diatomic molecules such as hydrogen chloride, HCl.

The situation is more complicated in polyatomic molecules, where the shape of the molecule must be taken into account. A symmetrical distribution of polar covalent bonds produces a non-polar molecule. The dipoles of the bonds exert equal and opposite effects on each other. An example is tetra-chloromethane, CCl_4. This tetrahedral molecule has four polar C–Cl bonds. The four dipoles point towards the corners of the tetrahedral molecule, cancelling each other out. In the closely related trichloromethane, $CHCl_3$, the three C–Cl dipoles point in a similar direction. Their combined effect is not cancelled out by the C–H bond. (The C–H bond has a weak dipole, pointing towards the carbon atom.) Hence trichloromethane is a very polar molecule.

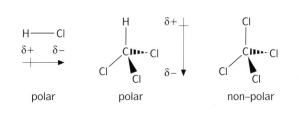

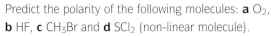

| polar | polar | non–polar |

SAQ 3.5

Predict the polarity of the following molecules: **a** O_2, **b** HF, **c** CH_3Br and **d** SCl_2 (non-linear molecule).

Bond polarity can be a helpful indication of the reactivity of a molecule. This is clearly illustrated by a comparison of nitrogen and carbon monoxide. Both molecules contain triple bonds, which require a similar amount of energy to break them. (The CO bond actually requires more energy than the N_2 bond!) However, carbon monoxide is a very reactive molecule, whereas nitrogen is very unreactive. Non-polar nitrogen will only undergo reactions at high temperatures or in the presence of a catalyst. Carbon monoxide may be burned in air and it combines more strongly with the iron in haemoglobin than does oxygen (see page 94). Many chemical reactions are started by a reagent attacking one of the electrically charged ends of a polar bond. Non-polar molecules are consequently much less reactive towards ionic or polar reagents.

Other important polar molecules include water and ammonia. As a knowledge of molecular shape is needed to predict the polarity of a polyatomic molecule, the next section shows how you can predict the shapes of simple molecules.

Shapes of simple molecules

Molecules vary in shape, as shown by the six examples in *figure 3.13*.

Electron-pair repulsion theory

As electrons are negatively charged, they exert a repulsion on each other. In chapter 1 (page 12), you saw that electrons may pair up with opposite spins in orbitals. This is also true in molecules. An electron-pair in the bonding (outermost) shell of the central atom in a simple molecule will exert a

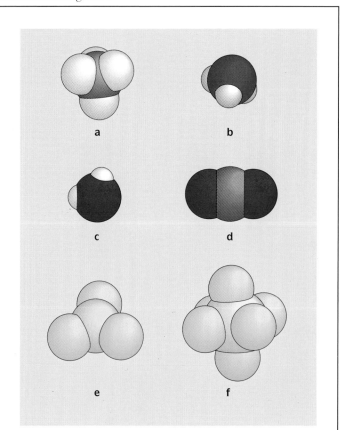

● *Figure 3.13* Shapes of molecules. These space-filling models show the molecular shapes of **a** methane (CH_4), **b** ammonia (NH_3), **c** water (H_2O), **d** carbon dioxide (CO_2), **e** boron trifluoride (BF_3) and **f** sulphur hexafluoride (SF_6).

repulsion on the other electron-pairs. Each pair will repel each of the other pairs. The effect of these repulsions will cause the electron-pairs to move as far apart as possible within the confines of the bonds between the atoms in the molecule. This will determine the three-dimensional shape of the molecule.

The concept of electron-pair repulsion is a powerful theory, as it successfully predicts shapes, which are confirmed by modern experimental techniques.

In order to predict the shape of a molecule, the number of pairs of outer-shell electrons on the central atom is needed. It is best to start with a dot-and-cross diagram and then to count the electron-pairs, as shown in the following examples.

■ *Methane*

As there are four bonding pairs of electrons, these repel each other towards the corners of a regular tetrahedron. The molecule thus has a tetrahedral shape. A tetrahedron has four faces.

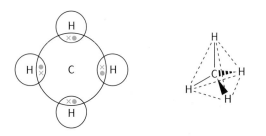

■ *Ammonia*

This has three bonding pairs and one lone-pair on the central atom, nitrogen. The four electron-pairs repel each other and occupy the corners of a tetrahedron as in methane. However, the nitrogen and three hydrogen atoms form a triangular pyramidal molecule.

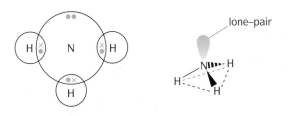

■ *Water*

There are two bonding pairs and two lone-pairs. Again, these repel each other towards the corners of a tetrahedron, leaving the oxygen and two hydrogen atoms as a non-linear (or bent) molecule.

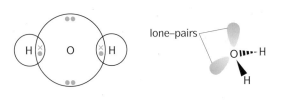

■ *Carbon dioxide*

This has two carbon–oxygen double bonds. Multiple bonds are best considered in the same way as single electron-pairs. If the two double bond pairs repel each other as far as possible, the molecule is predicted to be linear (i.e. the OCO angle is 180°):

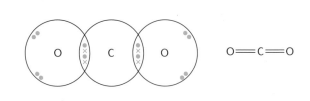

■ *Boron trifluoride*

This is an interesting molecule, as it only has six electrons in the bonding shell on boron, distributed between three bonding pairs. The three bonding pairs repel each other equally, forming a trigonal planar molecule with bond angles of 120°. Boron trifluoride is very reactive and will accept a non-bonding (lone) pair of electrons. For example, with ammonia $H_3N{\rightarrow}BF_3$ is formed (note the dative covalent bond).

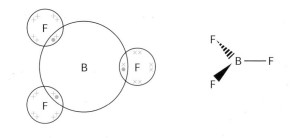

■ *Sulphur hexafluoride*

There are six bonding pairs and no lone-pairs. Repulsion between six electron-pairs produces the structure shown. All angles are 90°. The shape produced is an octahedron (i.e. eight faces).

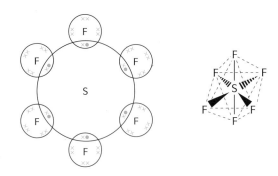

Lone-pairs, bonding pairs and bond angles

Lone-pairs of electrons are attracted by only one nucleus, unlike bonding pairs, which are shared between two nuclei. As a result, lone-pairs occupy a molecular orbital that is pulled closer to the nucleus than bonding pairs. The electron charge-cloud in a lone-pair has a greater width than a bonding pair. The diagram below shows the repulsions between lone-pairs (pink) and bonding pairs (white) in a water molecule.

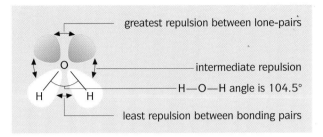

The repulsion between lone-pairs is thus greater than that between a lone-pair and a bonding pair. The repulsion between a lone-pair (LP) and a bonding pair (BP) is greater than that between two bonding pairs. To summarise:

LP–LP repulsion > LP–BP repulsion > BP–BP repulsion

This variation in repulsion produces small but measurable effects on the bond angles in molecules. In methane, all the HCH angles are the same at 109.5°. In ammonia, the slightly greater repulsion of the lone-pair pushes the bonding pairs slightly closer together and the angle reduces to 107°. In water, two lone-pairs reduce the HOH angle to 104.5°.

Bond	Bond energy/kJ mol^{-1}	Bond length/nm
C–C	347	0.154
C=C	612	0.134
C–O	358	0.143
C=O	805	0.116

● *Table 3.2* Examples of bond energies and bond lengths

	Density /g cm^{-3}	Tensile strength /10^{10} Pa	Thermal conductivity /W m^{-1} K^{-1}	Electrical conductivity /10^8 S m^{-1}
Aluminium	2.70	7.0	238	0.38
Iron	7.86	21.1	82	0.10
Copper	8.92	13.0	400	0.59
Sulphur	2.07		0.029	1×10^{-23}

● *Table 3.3* Properties of three metals and sulphur

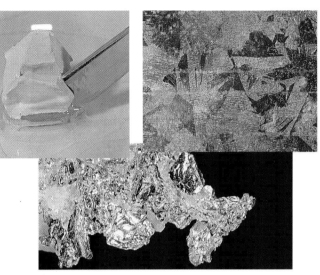

● *Figure 3.14* Metals. From left to right: sodium, gold and zinc.

Bond energy and bond length

In general, double bonds are shorter than single bonds. The energy required to break a double bond is also greater than that needed to break a single bond. The **bond energy** is the energy required to break one mole of the given bond in the gaseous molecule (see also chapter 4, page 53). *Table 3.2* shows some examples of bond energies and bond lengths.

Metallic bonding

Metals have very different properties to both ionic and covalent compounds. In appearance they are usually shiny (*figure 3.14*). They are good conductors of both heat and electricity (the latter in the solid state and without decomposition, unlike ionic compounds). They are easily worked and may be drawn into wires or hammered into a different shape, i.e. they are ductile and malleable. They often possess high tensile strengths and they are usually hard. *Table 3.3* provides information on some of the properties of aluminium, iron and copper, with the non-metal sulphur for comparison.

It is this range of properties that has led humans to use

● *Figure 3.15* Bronze age statue.

them to make tools, weapons and jewellery. Two major periods in our history are named after the metals in use at the time (*figure 3.15*). The change from bronze (an alloy of tin and copper) to iron reflected the discovery of methods for extracting different metals.

Bonding

A simplified model is adequate for our purposes. In a metallic lattice, the atoms lose their outer-shell electrons to become positive ions. The outer-shell electrons occupy new energy levels, which extend throughout the metal lattice. The bonding is often described as a 'sea' of mobile electrons surrounding a lattice of positive ions. This is shown in *figure 3.16*. The lattice is held together by the

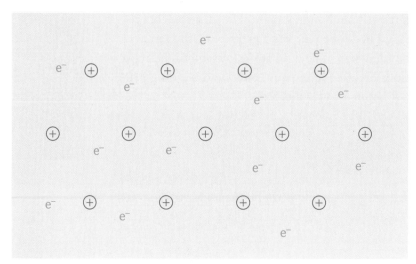

● *Figure 3.16* Metallic bonding.

strong attractive forces between the mobile electrons and the positive ions.

The properties of metals can be explained in terms of this model of the bonding. Electrical conduction can take place in any direction, as electrons are free to move throughout the lattice. Conduction of heat occurs by vibration of the positive ions as well as via the mobile electrons.

Metals are both ductile and malleable because the bonding in the metallic lattice is not broken when they are physically deformed. As a metal is hammered or drawn into a wire, the metal ions slide over each other to new lattice positions. The mobile electrons continue to hold the lattice together. Some metals will even flow under their own weight. Lead has a problem in this respect. It is often used on roofs where, over the years, it suffers from 'creep'. This is not only from thieves but also because the metal slowly flows under the influence of gravity.

The transition elements (see chapter 5, page 88) are metals that possess both hardness and high tensile strength. Hardness and high tensile strength are also due to the strong attractive forces between the metal ions and the mobile electrons in the lattice.

SAQ 3.6

Use *table 3.3* to answer the following questions and give full explanations in terms of metallic bonding. (Assume steel and stainless steel have similar properties to iron.)

a Why do some stainless steel saucepans have a copper base?

b Aluminium with a steel core is used for overhead power cables in preference to copper. Why is aluminium preferred? What is the function of the steel core?

c Apart from overhead power cables, copper is chosen for almost all other electrical uses. Suggest reasons for the choice of copper.

Intermolecular forces

Before we discuss the attractive forces that exist between molecules, it may be helpful to review the **kinetic theory of matter**. Matter exists in solid, liquid and gaseous states. In the solid state, the particles are packed together in a regularly ordered way. This order breaks down when a substance melts. In the liquid state, there may be small groups of particles with some degree of order. Overall in the liquid, particles are free to move past each other. In order to do this, many of the forces that bind the particles together must be overcome on melting. In the gaseous state, the particles are widely separated. They are free to move independently, and all the forces that bind the particles together in the solid or liquid have been overcome on vaporisation. In the gaseous state, the particles move randomly in any direction. As they do so, they exert a pressure (vapour pressure) on the walls of their container.

A multitude of biochemical compounds are involved in the enormous number of chemical reactions found in living organisms. They are also ultimately responsible for a seemingly infinite number of variations within a given species. All biochemical compounds rely significantly on weak attractive forces within and between their molecules to produce this variety. These intermolecular forces (often called van der Waals' forces) are much weaker than ionic, covalent or metallic bonding forces.

The properties of all small molecules are dependent on intermolecular forces. It is the properties of these small molecules that provide evidence for the existence of intermolecular forces and help us to understand the nature of these forces. If a gas is able to condense to a liquid, which can then be frozen to a solid, there must be an attraction between the molecules of the gas. Remember that, when a solid melts or a liquid boils, energy is needed. For example, water in a kettle will continue to boil only whilst the electricity is switched on. The temperature of the water is constant whilst the water is boiling, and the heating effect of energy from the electricity

is separating the water molecules from each other in the liquid to produce water vapour.

There are three types of intermolecular forces: instantaneous dipole–induced dipole forces, dipole–dipole forces and hydrogen bonds.

Instantaneous dipole–induced dipole forces

Even the noble-gas atoms must exert an attraction on each other. *Figure 3.17* shows the enthalpies of vaporisation of the noble gases plotted against the number of electrons present. (**Enthalpy of vaporisation** is the energy required to convert the liquid to a gas.) The trend in the enthalpy of vaporisation shows an increase from helium to xenon as the number of electrons increases. Alkanes (chapter 6, page 101) show a similar trend; their enthalpies of vaporisation also increase with increasing numbers of atoms in the molecules (and hence with increasing numbers of electrons). Both the noble gases and the alkanes have attractive forces between atoms and molecules, which are now known to depend on the number of electrons and protons present.

The forces arise because electrons in atoms or molecules are moving at very high speeds in orbitals. At any instant in time it is possible for more electrons to lie to one side of the atom or molecule. When this happens, an instantaneous electric dipole occurs. The momentary imbalance of electrons provides the negative

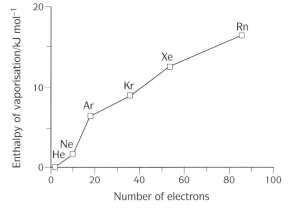

● *Figure 3.17* Enthalpies of vaporisation of the noble gases.

end of a dipole, with the atomic nucleus providing the positive end of the dipole. This instantaneous dipole produces an induced dipole in a neighbouring atom or molecule, which is hence attracted *(figure 3.18)*.

This is rather like the effect of a magnet (magnetic dipole) on a pin. The pin becomes temporarily magnetised and is attracted to the magnet. Intermolecular forces of this type are called **instantaneous dipole–induced dipole forces**. The strength of instantaneous dipole–induced dipole forces increases with the number of electrons and protons present.

Instantaneous dipole–induced dipole forces are the weakest type of attractive force found between atoms or molecules. They are responsible for the slippery nature of graphite *(figure 3.19)* and the volatility of bromine and iodine *(figure 3.20)*.

A polymer is a molecule built up from a large number of small molecules (called monomers). Low-density poly(ethene), LDPE, and high-density poly(ethene), HDPE, have differing properties because of the way the polymer molecules are packed *(figure 3.21)*. The HDPE molecules can pack much more closely as they are not branched. LDPE molecules are branched at intervals, which prevents them packing as closely.

Teflon is poly(tetrafluoroethene), PTFE. A model of part of a PTFE molecule is shown in *figure 3.22*. The instantaneous dipole–induced dipole forces between oil or grease and PTFE are much weaker than those present in the oil or grease. This gives rise to the polymer's non-stick properties.

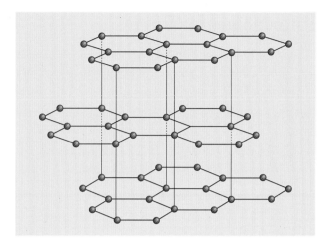

● *Figure 3.19* The structure of graphite. In the planar sheets of carbon atoms, all the bonding electrons are involved in covalent bonds. The sheets are held together by much weaker induced dipole forces. These forces are easily overcome, allowing the sheets to slide over each other (rather like a pack of cards). Graphite is often used as a lubricant.

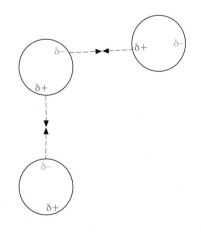

● *Figure 3.18* Induced dipole attractions.

● *Figure 3.20* Bromine **a** and iodine **b** exist as covalent molecules. They are both volatile, as only very weak instantaneous dipole–induced dipole forces need to be overcome to achieve vaporisation.

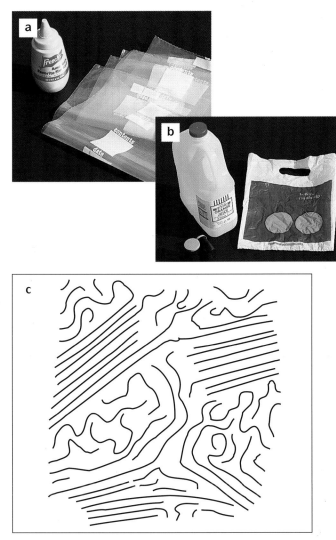

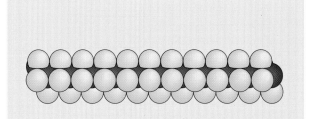

● *Figure 3.22* Model of PTFE.

Dipole–dipole forces

A Perspex rod may be given a charge of static electricity by rubbing it with a dry sheet of thin poly(ethene). If this is brought near a fine jet of water, the stream of water is attracted by the charge on the Perspex rod. This is shown in *figure 3.23*. (You can try this for yourself. Use a plastic comb and as fine a trickle of water from a tap as possible.)

The water molecules are attracted to the charged Perspex rod because they have a permanent electric dipole. A force of this type is called a **dipole–dipole force**. The dipole of water arises because of the bent shape of the molecule and the greater electron charge around the oxygen atom. The diagram shows the lone-pairs and electric dipole of a water molecule (note that the arrow head shows the negative end of the dipole).

● *Figure 3.21* Low-density and high-density poly(ethene).

a LDPE is made under high pressure with a trace of oxygen as catalyst. The product consists primarily of a tangled mass of polymer chains with some regions where the chains have some alignment.

b HDPE is made using catalysts developed by the Swiss chemist Ziegler and the Italian chemist Natta. (They received a Nobel Prize for their discoveries.) In HDPE, the polymer chains are arranged in a much more regular fashion. This increases the density of the material and makes it more opaque to light. As the molecules are closer together in HDPE, the induced dipole forces between the non-polar poly(ethene) molecules are greater and the tensile strength of the material is higher.

c Diagram of crystalline and non-crystalline regions in poly(ethene). LDPE has fewer of the crystalline regions than HDPE. In the crystalline regions, polymer chains (shown by lines in the diagram) lie parallel to each other.

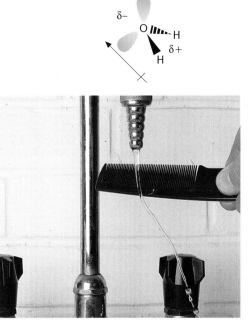

● *Figure 3.23* Deflection of water by an electrically charged plastic comb.

SAQ 3.7

The Perspex rod carries a positive charge. Which end of the water molecule is attracted to the rod? Why are no water molecules repelled by the rod? A poly(ethene) rod may be given a negative charge when rubbed with a nylon cloth. Will the charge on the poly(ethene) rod attract or repel a thin stream of water?

Many fabrics are made using poly(ester) fibres because of that polymer's strength. Production of poly(ester) fibres together with a section of a poly(ester) molecule are shown in *figure 3.24*.

SAQ 3.8

Copy the section of the poly(ester) chain shown in *figure 3.24* and mark on your copy the polar groups, showing the $\delta+$ and $\delta-$ charges. Draw a second section of poly(ester) chain alongside your first section and mark in the dipole–dipole forces with dotted lines. What is the effect of extruding the poly(ester) through spinnerets?

Water is peculiar

Figure 3.25 shows the enthalpies of vaporisation of water and other hydrides of Group VI elements.

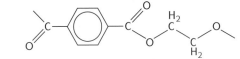

● **Figure 3.24**

a A photograph showing the production of poly(ester) fibre by melt spinning after extrusion through spinnerets and

b a section of the poly(ester) chain. The strength of poly(ester) fibre is due to the strong dipole–dipole forces between the ester groups.

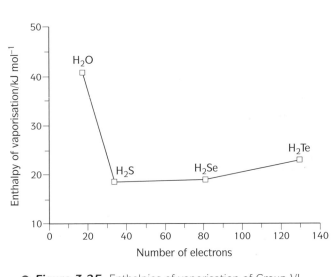

● **Figure 3.25** Enthalpies of vaporisation of Group VI hydrides.

SAQ 3.9

Explain the underlying increase in the enthalpy of vaporisation with increasing proton number. Estimate a value for water based on this trend. What is the significance of the much higher value observed for water?

The boiling point of water is also much higher than predicted by the trend in boiling points for other Group VI element hydrides. This trend would suggest that water should be a gas at room temperature and pressure. There are several more ways in which water behaves differently to most other liquids. For example, it has a very high surface tension and a high viscosity. Further, the density of ice is less than the density of water (*figure 3.26*). Most solids are denser than their liquids, as molecules usually pack closer in solids than in liquids.

Surface tension of water

You can demonstrate the high surface tension of water for yourself by floating a needle on water. Rinse a bowl several times with water. Fill the bowl with water. Place a small piece of tissue paper on the surface of the water. Now place a needle on the tissue. Leave it undisturbed. The paper will sink, leaving the needle floating. Now carefully add a few drops of washing-up liquid (which lowers the surface tension of water) and observe the effect.

● *Figure 3.26* Ice floats on water.

Hydrogen bonds

The peculiar nature of water is explained by the presence of the strongest type of intermolecular force – the hydrogen bond – (indicated on diagrams by dotted lines). Water is highly polar owing to the large difference in electronegativity between hydrogen and oxygen. The resulting intermolecular attraction between oxygen and hydrogen atoms on neighbouring water molecules is a very strong dipole–dipole attraction called a **hydrogen bond**. Each water molecule can form two hydrogen bonds to other water molecules. These form in the directions of the lone-pairs. In the liquid state, water molecules collect in groups. On boiling, the hydrogen bonds must be broken. This raises the boiling point significantly as the hydrogen bonds are stronger than the other intermolecular forces. Similarly the enthalpy of vaporisation is much higher than it would be if no hydrogen bonds were present.

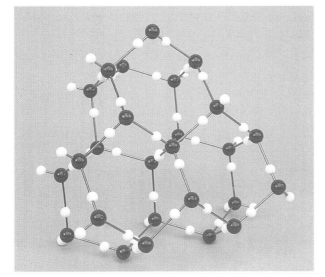

● *Figure 3.27* Model of ice.

In ice, a three-dimensional hydrogen-bonded lattice is produced. In this lattice, each oxygen is surrounded by a tetrahedron of hydrogen atoms bonded to further oxygen atoms. The structure is shown in *figure 3.27*.

SAQ 3.10

A diamond-type lattice is present in ice. The O ⸱⸱⸱ H hydrogen bond length is 0.159 nm and the O–H covalent bond length is 0.096 nm. When ice melts, some hydrogen bonds break and the density rises. Use *figure 3.27* and these values to explain why ice has a lower density than water.

The high surface tension of water is explained by the presence of a hydrogen-bonded network of water molecules at the surface. This network is sufficiently strong to enable a needle to be floated on the surface of water.

Within the bulk of water, small groups of molecules are attracted by hydrogen bonds. The hydrogen bonds are constantly breaking and re-forming at room temperature. As the temperature of water is raised towards the boiling point, the number of hydrogen bonds reduces. On boiling, the remaining hydrogen bonds are broken. Water vapour consists of widely separated water molecules.

SAQ 3.11

Why does a needle floating on water sink on the addition of washing-up liquid to the water?

SAQ 3.12

The boiling points for Group V element hydrides are as follows:

Hydride	Boiling point/K
ammonia, NH_3	240
phosphine, PH_3	185
arsine, AsH_3	218
stibine, SbH_3	256
bismuthine, BiH_3	295

Plot a graph of these boiling points against the relative molecular mass of the hydrides.

a Explain the steadily rising trend in the boiling points from phosphine to bismuthine.

b Explain why the boiling point of ammonia does not follow this trend.

Nylon

This synthetic polymer is an example of a poly(amide). It is similar to poly(ester) with the –O– link replaced by –NH–. The structure of a section of the polymer chain of one type of nylon is shown in *figure 3.28*.

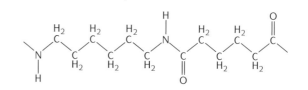

● **Figure 3.28** The structure of a section of nylon-6,6. Each building-block (monomer unit) contains six carbon atoms, hence the name nylon-6,6.

The –CO–NH– link is called an amide link. Hence the name poly(amide).

Nylon fibres are produced in the same way as poly(ester) fibres. Their high tensile strength is due to strong hydrogen bonds forming between an –NH– hydrogen atom and a C=O oxygen atom on a neighbouring polymer chain.

SAQ 3.13

Draw two short sections of nylon-6,6 polymer chain to show a hydrogen bond.

Not all the polymer chains lie close and parallel. When the fibres are stretched, the molecules straighten further but are held by the hydrogen bonds, which return the molecules to their original positions on release. The combination of strength and high elasticity are important properties in a climbing rope. If a climber falls, a nylon rope can stretch by up to half its length and stop the fall.

Hydrogen bonds play a very important part in the structures and properties of biochemical polymers. For example, protein chains often produce a helical structure, and the ability of DNA molecules to replicate themselves depends primarily on the hydrogen bonds, which hold the two parts of the molecules together in a double helix *(figure 3.29)*.

Table 3.4 shows the relative strengths of intermolecular forces and other bonds. Note that all the intermolecular forces are much weaker than the forces of attraction found in typical covalent bonds or in ionic bonding. Instantaneous dipole–induced dipole forces are weaker than dipole–dipole forces. Hydrogen bonds are about twice as strong as the other intermolecular forces.

Table 3.5 provides a summary of the pattern and variety of structures and bonding found among elements and compounds.

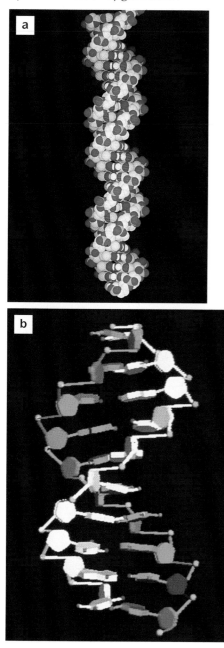

● **Figure 3.29** Photographs of models of biochemical polymers: **a** the α-helix formed by a protein molecule and **b** a section of the DNA molecule.

	Energy/kJ mol⁻¹
Instantaneous dipole–induced dipole, e.g. in xenon	15
Hydrogen bond, e.g. in water	22
O–H covalent bond in water	464
Ionic bonding, magnesium oxide	3791

● **Table 3.4** Relative strengths of intermolecular forces and bonds

46

	Type of structure					
	Ionic	**Giant lattices (Covalent)**	**Metallic**	**Macromolecular**	**Molecular Simple**	**Atomic**
Where this type of structure is found	compounds formed between metals and non-metals	Group IV elements and some of their compounds	metals	polymers	some elements and some compounds formed between non-metals	noble gases
Some examples	sodium chloride, magnesium oxide	diamond, graphite, silicon(IV) oxide	aluminium, copper	nylon, DNA	hydrogen H_2, chlorine Cl_2, methane, ammonia	helium, neon
Particles present	ions	atoms	positive ions and electrons	long-chain molecules	small molecules	atoms
Attractions that hold particles together	between oppositely charged ions	electrons in covalent bonds attract nuclei	delocalised sea of electrons attracts positive ions	various intermolecular forces between molecules, covalent bonds within molecule	various intermolecular forces between molecules, covalent bonds within molecule	intermolecular forces between atoms: instantaneous dipole–induced dipole only
Common physical state(s) at room temperature and pressure	solid	solid	solid	solid	solids, liquids and gases	gases
Melting and boiling points, enthalpies of vaporisation	high	very high	moderately high to high	moderate, may decompose	low	very low
Hardness	hard, brittle	very hard	hard, malleable	often soft, flexible	solids usually soft	
Electrical conductivity	conduct when molten or in aqueous solution	usually non-conductors	conduct when solid or molten	usually non-conductors	non-conductors	non-conductors
Solubility in water	many ionic compounds are soluble	insoluble (SiO$_2$ is very sparingly soluble)	insoluble, some react liberating hydrogen	mostly insoluble, natural polymers more likely to be soluble	usually insoluble unless very polar and capable of forming hydrogen bonds to water	sparingly soluble

● **Table 3.5** Summary of structure and bonding

SUMMARY

■ All bonding involves electrostatic attractive forces.

■ In ionic bonding, the attractive forces are between oppositely charged ions.

■ In a covalent bond (one electron from each atom) or a dative covalent bond (both electrons from one atom), the forces are between two atomic nuclei and pairs of electrons situated between them.

■ In metallic bonding, the forces are between delocalised electrons and positive ions.

■ Intermolecular attractive forces also involve electrostatic forces.

■ Intermolecular forces (hydrogen bonds, dipole–dipole and instantaneous dipole–induced dipole forces) are much weaker than ionic, covalent or metallic bonding forces.

■ Dot-and-cross diagrams enable ionic and covalent bonds to be described. Use of these diagrams with electron-pair repulsion theory enables molecular shapes to be predicted.

■ In molecules, atomic orbitals combine to produce σ and π molecular orbitals.

■ Physical properties and structures of elements and compounds may be explained in terms of kinetic theory and bonding *(table 3.5)*.

■ The reactivities of covalent compounds may be explained with reference to bond length, bond energy and bond polarity.

Questions

1 a Draw dot-and-cross diagrams to show the electronic configurations of
  (i) calcium chloride, $CaCl_2$,
  (ii) silicon tetrachloride, $SiCl_4$.
 b Use electron-pair repulsion theory to predict the shapes of the following molecules. Draw labelled diagrams to show your predicted shapes, marking the values of the bond angles.
  (i) phosphine, PH_3,
  (ii) sulphur hexafluoride, SF_6.
2 a Use **one** example in each case and, with the aid of diagrams, explain what is meant by
  (i) ionic bonding,
  (ii) covalent bonding,
  (iii) dative covalent bonding.
 b Describe and explain how the bonding in
  (i) ionic compounds,
  (ii) covalent compounds,
  (iii) metals,
  affects their physical properties.

Chemical energetics

1 explain that chemical changes involve transfers of energy *to* the surroundings (*exothermic* reactions) and *from* the surroundings (*endothermic* reactions);

2 understand that most energy transfers in chemical reactions are due to bonds being made and broken;

3 explain and use the terms *bond energy*, *standard enthalpy changes of reaction*, *of formation* and *of combustion* and *activation energy*;

4 explain how enthalpy changes may be calculated from experimental results, and how to use energy diagrams;

5 state and use Hess's law to construct simple energy cycles for determining enthalpy changes in reactions and average bond energies;

6 construct and interpret reaction pathway diagrams;

7 state what makes a substance a good fuel;

8 appreciate the problems of using fossil fuels, particularly the polluting effects of their products and the competing demands from their uses as raw materials;

9 recognise that there are alternatives to fossil fuels and that scientists play an important part in improving and developing these;

10 understand that enthalpy changes of formation of compounds may give a guide to their stability;

11 understand that, in general, enthalpy changes are not related to the rates of reactions;

12 appreciate the role of enthalpy changes in determining whether or not a process may occur naturally (without external interference).

All chemical reactions involve change. In flames, for example, we can see the changes caused by very fast reactions between the chemicals in burning materials and oxygen from the atmosphere *(figure 4.1)*. There are new substances, new colours

● *Figure 4.1*

and changes of state, but the most obvious changes in these reactions are the transfers of energy as light and heating of the surroundings. All life on Earth depends on the transfer of energy in chemical reactions. Plants need the energy from the sun for the production of carbohydrates by photosynthesis; animals gain energy from the oxidation of their food chemicals.

Energy transfer: exothermic and endothermic reactions

Most chemical reactions release energy *to* their surroundings. These reactions are described as **exothermic**. We recognise exothermic reactions most easily by detecting a rise in the temperature of the reaction mixture and the surroundings (the test-tube or beaker, the solvent, air, etc.). Examples of exothermic reactions are:

■ all reactions involving burning,
■ acids with metals,
■ water with 'quicklime' (calcium oxide) *(figure 4.2)*.

Some chemical reactions occur only while energy is transferred to them *from* an external source. These are **endothermic** reactions. The

● *Figure 4.2* Calcium oxide, before and after water is added. The exothermic reaction causes the solid to swell, crack and crumble as it changes to calcium hydroxide (slaked lime).

energy may be supplied directly by a flame or by electricity. An example *(figure 4.3)* is the decomposition by heating of calcium carbonate ('limestone') into calcium oxide and carbon dioxide:

$$CaCO_3(s) \longrightarrow CaO(s) + CO_2(g)$$

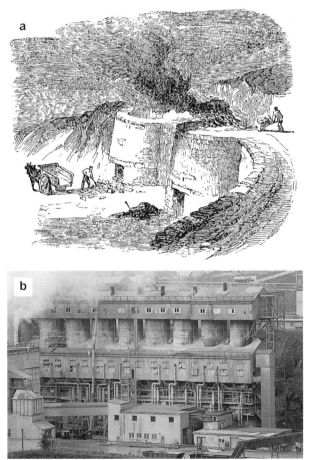

● *Figure 4.3* Calcium carbonate, as limestone or chalk, has been converted to calcium oxide (quicklime) for centuries, by strong heating in lime-kilns.
a Ancient lime-kilns. **b** Modern lime-kiln.

In some endothermic changes, no direct external heating is needed. When ammonium nitrate dissolves in water, energy is transferred from the surroundings – the beaker, bench and air. This causes such a large drop in temperature that water may freeze to ice on the outside of the beaker.

The most important endothermic reaction of all is photosynthesis in plants *(figure 4.4)*. Here the energy is supplied to the reactions in the cells by sunlight:

$$CO_2(g) + H_2O(l) + energy$$
$$\longrightarrow carbohydrate\ in\ leaves + O_2(g)$$

SAQ 4.1 _____
Classify the following processes as exothermic or endothermic: evaporation; crystallisation; making magnesium oxide from magnesium and air; making copper oxide from copper carbonate.

Energy is conserved

It is important to understand that energy is not being created by exothermic chemical reactions and it is not destroyed in endothermic reactions. Energy is transferred from the reacting chemicals to the surroundings or the other way around. The total energy of the whole system of reacting chemicals and the surroundings remains *constant*. This applies to any energy transfer and is summarised in

● *Figure 4.4* Photosynthesis in green leaves: the most essential chemical reaction of all.

the **law of conservation of energy**: Energy can neither be created nor destroyed.

You may also hear this universal law called the **first law of thermodynamics**, as thermodynamics is the science of transfers of energy.

Enthalpy, and enthalpy changes

Measurements of the energy transferred during chemical reactions must be made under controlled conditions. A special name is given to the energy exchange with the surroundings when it takes place at constant pressure. This name is **enthalpy change**.

Enthalpy is the total energy content of the reacting materials. It is given the symbol H.

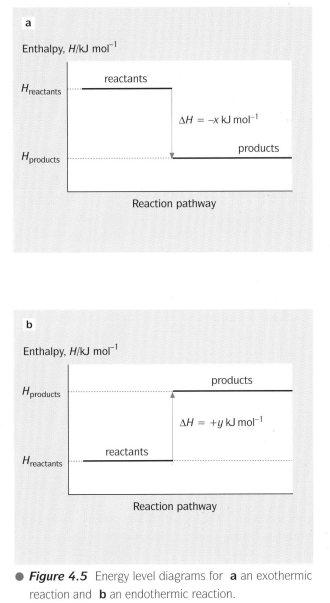

Enthalpy cannot be measured as such, but it is possible to measure the enthalpy change when energy is transferred to or from a reaction system and changes from one enthalpy to another.

Enthalpy change is given the symbol ΔH (Δ is the upper case of the Greek letter δ, pronounced 'delta', and it is often used in mathematics as a symbol for change). So

$$\Delta H = H_{\text{products}} - H_{\text{reactants}}$$

As ΔH is a measure of energy transferred to or from known amounts of reactants, the units are kilojoules per mole ($kJ\,mol^{-1}$).

We can illustrate enthalpy changes by energy level diagrams (*figure 4.5*). An exothermic enthalpy change is always given a negative value, as the energy is lost from the system to the surroundings. It is shown in *figure 4.5a* as

$$\Delta H = -x\,kJ\,mol^{-1}$$

For example, when methane burns:

$$CH_4(g) + 2O_2(g) \longrightarrow CO_2(g) + 2H_2O(l);$$
$$\Delta H = -890.3\,kJ\,mol^{-1}$$

This means that when one mole of methane burns completely in oxygen, 890.3 kilojoules of energy are transferred to the surroundings (*figure 4.6a*).

An endothermic enthalpy change is always given a positive value, as the energy is gained by the system from the surroundings. It is shown in (*figure 4.5b*) as

$$\Delta H = +y\,kJ\,mol^{-1}$$

For example, on heating calcium carbonate:

$$CaCO_3(s) \longrightarrow CaO(s) + CO_2(g);$$
$$\Delta H = +572\,kJ\,mol^{-1}$$

This means that an input of 572 kilojoules of energy is needed to break down one mole of calcium carbonate to calcium oxide and carbon dioxide (*figure 4.6b*).

Standard enthalpy changes: standard conditions

When we compare the enthalpy changes of various reactions we must use standard conditions, such as known temperatures, pressures, amounts and

● **Figure 4.5** Energy level diagrams for **a** an exothermic reaction and **b** an endothermic reaction.

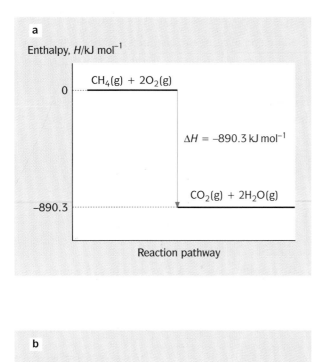

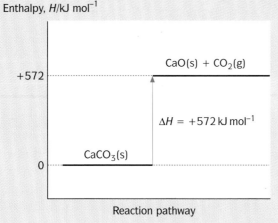

● *Figure 4.6* Energy level diagrams for **a** the combustion of methane and **b** the decomposition of calcium carbonate.

concentrations of reactants or products. This allows us to compare the standard enthalpy changes for reactions.

A standard enthalpy change for a reaction takes place under these standard conditions:

■ a pressure of 100 kilopascals (10^2 kPa);
■ a temperature of 298 K (25 °C);
■ the reactants and products must be in the physical states (solid, liquid or gas) that are normal for these conditions;
■ any solutions have a concentration of 1.0 mol dm^{-3}.

The complete symbol for a standard enthalpy change of reaction may be written as: $\Delta H^{\ominus}_{r,298}$ or as $\Delta_r H^{\ominus}_{298}$, the meanings of the symbols being:

■ $\ominus$ means standard and assumes a pressure of 100 kPa;
■ r is a general symbol for reaction and is changed to f for formation reactions or c for combustion reactions;
■ 298 means all reactants and products are in their physical states at a temperature of 298 K (25 °C), e.g. carbon dioxide is a gas at 298 K but water is a liquid.

Note that, as values for standard enthalpy changes are usually quoted at 298 K, it is common practice to omit 298 from the symbol.

Standard enthalpy change of reaction $\Delta H^{\ominus}_r$

This is defined as: the **standard enthalpy change of reaction** is the enthalpy change when amounts of reactants, as shown in the reaction equation, react together under standard conditions to give products in their standard states.

It is necessary to make clear which reaction equation we are using when we quote a standard enthalpy change of reaction. For example, the equation for the reaction between hydrogen and oxygen can be written in two different ways and there are different values for $\Delta H^{\ominus}_r$ in each case.

equation (i)
$$2H_2(g) + O_2(g) \longrightarrow 2H_2O(l);$$
$$\Delta H^{\ominus}_r = -572 \, kJ \, mol^{-1}$$
equation (ii)
$$H_2(g) + \tfrac{1}{2}O_2(g) \longrightarrow H_2O(l);$$
$$\Delta H^{\ominus}_r = -286 \, kJ \, mol^{-1}$$

Note that the value of $\Delta H^{\ominus}_r$ in (ii) is half that of $\Delta H^{\ominus}_r$ in (i).

Standard enthalpy change of formation ΔH_f

This is defined as: the **standard enthalpy change of formation** is the enthalpy change when one mole of a compound is formed from its elements under standard conditions; both compound and elements are in their standard states.

For example, water is formed in both equations (i) and (ii) above but only in equation (ii) is one mole of water formed. Thus equation (ii) shows that the value of $\Delta H_f^{\ominus}(H_2O) = -286\,kJ\,mol^{-1}$.

SAQ 4.2

Write balanced equations for the formation of **a** ethane (C_2H_6) and **b** aluminium oxide (Al_2O_3). Use a data book to add values for $\Delta H_f^{\ominus}$ in each case.

Standard enthalpy change of combustion $\Delta H_c^{\ominus}$

The **standard enthalpy change of combustion** is the enthalpy change when one mole of an element or compound reacts completely with oxygen under standard conditions.

For example, the standard enthalpy change of combustion of hydrogen is given by equation (ii) above:

$$H_2(g) + \tfrac{1}{2}O_2(g) \longrightarrow H_2O(l);$$
$$\Delta H_c^{\ominus} = -286\,kJ\,mol^{-1}$$

In practice it is not possible to achieve complete combustion under standard conditions. Measurements are taken under experimental conditions; then a value for the enthalpy change is determined and this is corrected to standard conditions through calculations.

SAQ 4.3

a What are the reaction equations for the combustion of (i) octane (C_8H_{18}) and (ii) ethanol (C_2H_5OH), including the values for $\Delta H_c^{\ominus}$ (use a data book)?

b Why is the $\Delta H_f^{\ominus}$ of water the same as the $\Delta H_c^{\ominus}$ of hydrogen?

Bond making, bond breaking and enthalpy change

A typical combustion reaction, such as the burning of methane is:

$$CH_4(g) + 2O_2(g) \longrightarrow CO_2(g) + 2H_2O(l);$$
$$\Delta H_c^{\ominus} = -890.3\,kJ\,mol^{-1}$$

or, drawing the molecules to show the bonds:

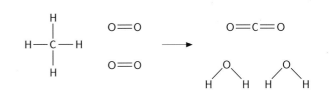

For this reaction to occur, some bonds must break and others form:

- bonds breaking $4 \times$ C–H and $2 \times$ O=O
- bonds forming $2 \times$ C=O and $4 \times$ H–O

The basis of understanding energy transfers during chemical reactions is a fairly simple rule: When bonds break, energy is absorbed (endothermic process). When bonds form, energy is released (exothermic process).

If the energy released by the formation of some bonds is greater than the energy absorbed by the breaking of other bonds, there will be a surplus of energy transferred to the surroundings. The overall reaction will be exothermic.

If the energy released by bond formation is less than the energy absorbed by bond breaking then, overall, energy must be transferred from the surroundings. The reaction will be endothermic.

In the case of the combustion of methane, after all the bond breaking and bond formation, the surplus energy transferred to the surroundings is 890.3 kJ for each mole of methane.

Bond energy

Chemists find that it is useful to measure the amount of energy needed to break a covalent bond, as this indicates the strength of the bond. They call it the **bond energy**. The values are always quoted as bond energy per mole (of bonds broken or made).

Consider the example of oxygen gas $O_2(g)$. The bond energy of oxygen is the enthalpy change for the process:

$$O_2(g) \longrightarrow 2O(g); \qquad \Delta H = +498\,kJ\,mol^{-1}$$

The symbol E is often used for bond energy per mole. It is related to particular bonds as $E(X–Y)$, where X–Y is a molecule . Thus $E(X–Y)$ is the same as ΔH for the dissociation process

$$X–Y(g) \longrightarrow X(g) + Y(g)$$

Typical values of bond energies per mole are:

Bond	$E(X–Y)/\text{kJ mol}^{-1}$
H–H	+436
C–C	+347
C=C	+612
C–H	+413
O=O	+498
O–H	+464
C–O	+336
C=O	+805

The values quoted in tables for bond energies per mole satisfy the following four conditions.

- They are all positive, as the changes during breaking of bonds are endothermic (energy is absorbed). The same quantities of energy would be released in an exothermic change when the bonds form.
- They are average values. The actual value of the bond energy for a particular bond depends upon which molecule the bond is in. For example, the C–C bond has slightly different strengths in ethane C_2H_6 and in propane C_3H_8, as it is affected by the other atoms and bonds in the molecules. The bond energy quoted in data books for C–C is an average of the values from many different molecules.
- They are compared for bonds in gaseous compounds only.
- They are very difficult to measure directly. They are usually calculated using data from measurements of enthalpy changes of combustion of several compounds.

SAQ 4.4

A book of data gives a value for the standard enthalpy change of combustion of hydrogen as $-285.8\,\text{kJ mol}^{-1}$. A value for the enthalpy change of formation of water, calculated from bond energies, is $-283.1\,\text{kJ mol}^{-1}$. Suggest why these values are slightly different.

Measuring energy transfers and enthalpy changes

Simple laboratory experiments can give us estimates of the energy transferred during some reactions. Enthalpy changes may then be calculated.

Enthalpy changes of combustion

Measurements of ΔH_c are important as they help to compare the energy available from the oxidation of different flammable liquids, which may be used as fuels.

The type of apparatus used for a simple laboratory method is shown in *figure 4.7*. A fuel, such as an alkane or alcohol, burns at the wick. Measurements are made of:

- the mass of cold water in the metal calorimeter (m g),
- the temperature rise of the water (ΔT K),
- the loss in mass of the fuel (y g).

It is known that 4.2 J of energy are needed to raise the temperature of 1 g of water by 1 K. (This is called the **specific heat capacity of water** and equals $4.2\,\text{J g}^{-1}\text{K}^{-1}$.)

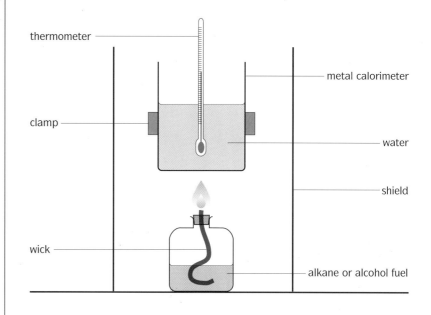

● **Figure 4.7** Apparatus used for approximate measurements of energy transferred by burning known masses of flammable liquids.

The specific heat capacity of a liquid is given the general symbol c. The energy required to raise m g of water by ΔT K is given by the general relationship:

energy transfer (as heating effect) = $m c \Delta T$ joules

Therefore, in the experiment, $m \times 4.2 \times \Delta T$ joules of energy are transferred during the burning of y grams of the fuel. Therefore, if one mole of the fuel has a mass of M grams, $m \times 4.2 \times \Delta T \times M/y$ joules of energy are transferred when one mole of the fuel burns. The answer will give an approximate value of the enthalpy change of combustion of the fuel in joules per mole ($J\,mol^{-1}$). Divide this answer by 1000 to find the value for ΔH_c in kilojoules per mole ($kJ\,mol^{-1}$).

We shall now look at an example. In an experiment using the simple apparatus above to find the enthalpy change of combustion of propanol (C_3H_7OH), the following measurements were made:

mass of water in the calorimeter (m) = 100 g
temperature rise of the water (ΔT) = 21.5 K
loss in mass of propanol fuel (y) = 0.28 g

We are given: A_r (H) = 1, A_r (C) = 12, A_r (O) = 16; and specific heat capacity of water $c = 4.2\,J\,g^{-1}\,K^{-1}$

The energy transferred as heat from the burning propanol is

$m c \Delta T$ = 100 × 4.2 × 21.5 joules
= 9030 joules

This is the energy transferred (heat produced) through burning 0.28 g of propanol. The mass of one mole of propanol is 60 g. Therefore energy transferred through burning one mole of propanol is

ΔH_c = 9030 × 60/0.28 joules per mole
= 193 500 joules per mole
= 1935 $kJ\,mol^{-1}$

From this experiment, the value for
ΔH_c (C_3H_7OH) = $-1935\,kJ\,mol^{-1}$.

SAQ 4.5

The value for $\Delta H_c^{\ominus}$ (C_3H_7OH) in a book of data is given as $-2010\,kJ\,mol^{-1}$. Suggest why the value calculated from the experimental results above is so much lower.

An improved apparatus: the flame calorimeter

The simple apparatus shown in *figure 4.7* is not efficient because energy from burning of the fuel is lost in heating the apparatus and surroundings. A more effective apparatus is shown in *figure 4.8*.

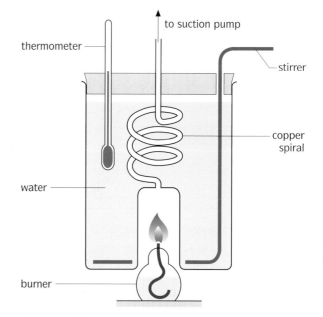

● *Figure 4.8* Flame calorimeter for measuring energy transfers during combustion of flammable liquids.

In using this apparatus we need to know its **heat capacity**. This is the energy needed to raise the temperature of the whole apparatus by 1 K. The heat capacity may be given by the manufacturer or calculated from measurements made using a fuel with known standard enthalpy change of combustion.

When the flame calorimeter is used, the energy transferred is found from:

energy transferred
= heat capacity of apparatus × ΔT

The 'unknown' ΔH_c is calculated as shown in the previous example.

Measuring enthalpy changes of other reactions

The experiments outlined above involved burning fuels. You may also undertake experiments in which the enthalpy changes are from reactions between chemicals in solutions. Here is an example.

We shall look at the enthalpy changes of neutralisation in the reaction between an acid and an alkali, e.g. hydrochloric acid plus sodium hydroxide solution:

$$HCl(aq) + NaOH(aq) \longrightarrow Na^+(aq) + Cl^-(aq) + H_2O(l)$$

The reaction that produces the enthalpy change here is shown more simply as:

$$H^+(aq) + OH^-(aq) \longrightarrow H_2O(l)$$

$Na^+(aq)$ and $Cl^-(aq)$ are **spectator ions** and take no part in the reaction producing the enthalpy change.

In such an experiment you would:

- use a heat-insulated vessel, such as a vacuum flask or a thick polystyrene cup, and stir the reactants;
- use known amounts of all reactants and known volumes of liquids – if one reactant is a solid, make sure you have an excess of solvent or other liquid reactant, so that all the solid dissolves or reacts;
- measure the temperature change by a thermometer reading to at least $0.2\,°C$ accuracy;
- calculate the energy transfers using the relationship

energy transferred (joules)
$$= mc\Delta T$$
= mass of liquid (g) × sp. heat cap. of aq. soln. $(J g^{-1}K^{-1})$ × temp. rise (K)

We shall now work through some typical results from an experiment. When $50\,cm^3$ of HCl(aq) are added to $50\,cm^3$ of NaOH(aq), both of concentration $1\,mol\,dm^{-3}$, in an insulated beaker, the temperature rose by $6.2\,K$. The acid and alkali are completely neutralised.

We may calculate the molar enthalpy change of neutralisation (for the reaction between hydrochloric acid and sodium hydroxide) as follows:

$50\,cm^3$ HCl(aq) + $50\,cm^3$ NaOH(aq)
$$= 100\,cm^3 \text{ solution}$$
mass of this solution (m) = 100 g
change in temperature (ΔT) = 6.2 K

We assume that the specific heat capacity (c) of the solution is the same as that for water $(4.2\,J g^{-1}K^{-1})$. Therefore the energy transferred (heat produced) by the reaction is

$$mc\Delta T = 100 × 4.2 × 6.2$$
$$= 2604 \text{ joules}$$

$50\,cm^3$ of HCl(aq) or NaOH(aq) of concentration $1\,mol\,dm^{-3}$ contain $50/1000\,mol =$ $5 × 10^{-2}\,mol$ of HCl or NaOH. Therefore the molar enthalpy of neutralisation, for the reaction between $1\,mol$ HCl and $1\,mol$ NaOH to give $1\,mol$ NaCl, is given by:

$$\Delta H_r = -2604/5 × 10^{-2} \text{ joules per mole}$$
$$= -52\,080 \text{ joules per mole}$$
$$= -52.08\,kJ\,mol^{-1}$$

When this reaction is carried out more accurately, the molar enthalpy change of neutralisation is calculated to be $\Delta H_r = -57.1\,kJ\,mol^{-1}$.

SAQ 4.6

Suggest why the molar enthalpy changes of neutralisation for the reactions of acids such as hydrochloric, sulphuric, or nitric with alkalis such as aqueous sodium hydroxide or potassium hydroxide are all very similar in value, at about $-57.2\,kJ\,mol^{-1}$.

Enthalpy changes by different routes: Hess's law

When we write a reaction equation, we usually show only the beginning and end, that is, the reactants and products. But there may be many different ways that the reaction actually occurs in between. The reaction may have different routes.

For example, consider a reaction system, with initial reactants A + B and final products C + D, in which two different routes (1 and 2) between A + B and C + D are possible (*figure 4.9*). What can be said about the enthalpy changes for the two different routes? Are they different too?

The answer to this question was first summarised in 1840 by Germain Hess and is now called **Hess's law**. There are several ways of stating Hess's law,

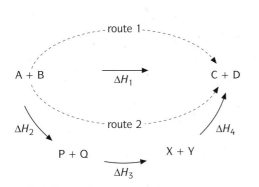

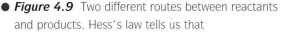

● **Figure 4.9** Two different routes between reactants and products. Hess's law tells us that

$$\Delta H_1 = \Delta H_2 + \Delta H_3 + \Delta H_4$$

but one concise form is: The total enthalpy change for a chemical reaction is *independent* of the route by which the reaction takes place.

In the case of our example above, Hess's law tells us that the enthalpy change for route 1 would equal the total of the enthalpy changes for route 2; that is

$$\Delta H_1 = \Delta H_2 + \Delta H_3 + \Delta H_4$$

The overall enthalpy change is affected only by the initial reactants and the final products, not by what happens in between.

Hess's law seems fairly obvious in the light of the more universal first law of thermodynamics (law of conservation of energy – see page 50). If different routes between the same reactants and products were able to transfer different amounts of energy, energy would be created or destroyed. We could make 'perpetual motion' machines *(figure 4.10)* and gain free energy for ever! Unfortunately, as in most aspects of life, you cannot get something for nothing.

Using Hess's law: energy cycles

Enthalpy changes that cannot be measured directly

For example, consider the formation of methane from carbon and hydrogen:

(a) $C(s) + 2H_2(g) \longrightarrow CH_4(g)$; $\Delta H_f^\ominus = ?$

This could be a very useful reaction for making methane gas starting with a plentiful supply of carbon such as coal or wood charcoal. Scientists

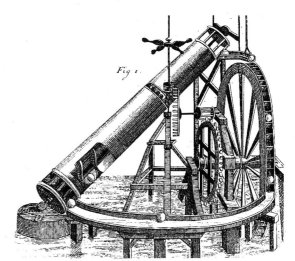

● **Figure 4.10** An attempt to design a mechanical perpetual motion machine. The heavy spheres cause the wheel to rotate. This operates the 'screw', which lifts the spheres back to the top of the wheel. Why does it not work?

are trying to find ways of making it occur directly and need to know the value of the enthalpy change of formation of methane. The best way is to use different routes, from reactants to product, with reactions that are known to occur.

Carbon, hydrogen and methane all burn in oxygen and the enthalpy changes of combustion of each can be measured.

(b) $C(s) + O_2(g) \longrightarrow CO_2(g)$;
$$\Delta H_c^\ominus = -393.5\,\text{kJ}\,\text{mol}^{-1}$$
(c) $H_2(g) + \frac{1}{2}O_2(g) \longrightarrow H_2O(l)$;
$$\Delta H_c^\ominus = -285.8\,\text{kJ}\,\text{mol}^{-1}$$
(d) $CH_4(g) + 2O_2(g) \longrightarrow CO_2(g) + 2H_2O(l)$;
$$\Delta H_c^\ominus = -890.3\,\text{kJ}\,\text{mol}^{-1}$$

One helpful way to calculate the enthalpy change for reaction (a) above starts with an **energy cycle,** which can be shown as a 'Hess's law triangle':

$$2O_2(g) + C(s) + 2H_2(g) \xrightarrow{\ (a)\ } CH_4(g) + 2O_2(g)$$
$$\text{(b) + 2(c)} \searrow \qquad \swarrow \text{(d)}$$
$$CO_2(g) + 2H_2O(g)$$

■ As the known enthalpy changes come from combustion reactions, we add oxygen to *both* sides of reaction (a). This does not alter the enthalpy change for reaction (a) itself.

■ The triangle shows two distinct routes between the same reactants and products.

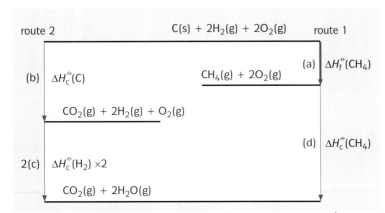

● **Figure 4.11** Energy level diagram to find the enthalpy change of formation of methane.

■ One route, (a) + (d), contains the 'unknown' enthalpy change for reaction (a), $\Delta H_f^{\ominus}(CH_4)$. The other route contains only known enthalpy changes for reactions (b) and (c).

We see that:

(a) + (d) = (b) + 2(c)

or   (a) = (b) + 2(c) − (d)

Thus:

$$\Delta H_f^{\ominus}(CH_4) = -393.5 + 2 \times (-285.8) - (-890.3)$$
$$= -393.5 - 571.6 + 890.3$$
$$= -74.8 \, kJ \, mol^{-1}$$

We may also display the energy cycle as a full energy level diagram (*figure 4.11*). This shows each stage of the energy cycle even more clearly. Enthalpy changes are represented by vertical lines with arrows: ↓ for exothermic changes, ↑ for endothermic changes, and ⇑ or ⇓ for unknown changes.

■ *Route 1*

Methane is formed ($\Delta H_f^{\ominus}$ unknown) and then oxidised ($\Delta H_c^{\ominus}$ known) (reactions (a) and (d)).

■ *Route 2*

Carbon and hydrogen are oxidised separately (reactions (b) and (c)). The enthalpy changes of combustion are known.

As Hess's law tells us (and the energy level diagram shows), the enthalpy changes for route 1 and route 2 are equal. We see that, as with the triangle above:

(a) + (d) = (b) + 2(c)

or   (a) = (b) + 2(c) − (d)

Thus:

$$\Delta H_f^{\ominus}(CH_4)$$
$$= \Delta H_c^{\ominus}(C(s)) + 2 \times \Delta H_c^{\ominus}(H_2) - \Delta H_c^{\ominus}(CH_4)$$
$$= (-393.5) + 2 \times (-285.8) - (-890.3)$$
$$= -74.8 \, kJ \, mol^{-1}$$

Using Hess's law to find average bond energies

We shall consider an example: finding the average bond energy of C–H bonds in methane, E(C–H).

First we should recognise that the average bond energy of C–H bonds in methane is the energy needed to break all the bonds in a mole of CH_4 molecules, divided by 4.

We can draw the energy cycle as a triangle or as an energy level diagram.

■ *Energy cycle as triangle*

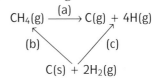

Reaction (a) is the breaking of four C–H bonds in methane molecules to form separate atoms. The enthalpy change of atomisation $\Delta H_{at}^{\ominus}(CH_4)$ is the unknown we are trying to find. Reaction (b) is the formation of methane from its elements. The enthalpy change $\Delta H_f^{\ominus}(CH_4) = -74.8 \, kJ \, mol^{-1}$. Reaction (c) is the atomisation of the elements carbon and hydrogen. The enthalpy changes of atomisation $\Delta H_{at}^{\ominus}(C(s)) = +715 \, kJ \, mol^{-1}$ and $\Delta H_{at}^{\ominus}(H_2(g)) = +218 \, kJ \, mol^{-1}$. The **enthalpy change of atomisation** is defined as the enthalpy change when one mole of gaseous atoms is formed from an element under standard conditions.

We should note that *four* moles of hydrogen atoms are formed from $2H_2(g)$. We see that

(a) + (b) = (c)

(a) = (c) − (b)

Then

$$\Delta H_{at}^{\ominus}(CH_4)$$
$$= \Delta H_{at}^{\ominus}(C(s)) + 4 \times \Delta H_{at}^{\ominus}(H_2(g)) - \Delta H_f^{\ominus}(CH_4)$$
$$= (+715) + 4 \times (+218) - (-74.8)$$
$$= +1661.8 \, kJ \, mol^{-1}$$

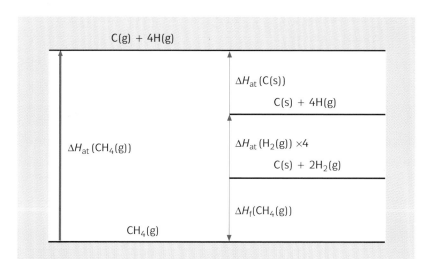
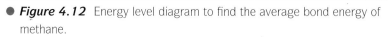

● *Figure 4.12* Energy level diagram to find the average bond energy of methane.

● *Figure 4.13* Gases from oilfields are often disposed of by being burnt as controllable 'flares'. This is a waste of gas but the costs of collection, storage and transportation are higher than the income available from selling the gas for other uses.

Thus the average bond energy of C–H bonds in methane is

$$E(\text{C–H}) = +1661.8/4 = +415.5 \, \text{kJ mol}^{-1}$$

■ *Energy cycle as energy level diagram*
The energy level diagram (*figure 4.12*) displays the same enthalpy changes for the reactions mentioned above. It shows perhaps more clearly that:

$$\Delta H_{\text{at}}^{\ominus}(\text{CH}_4) = \Delta H_{\text{at}}^{\ominus}(\text{C(s)}) + 4 \times \Delta H_{\text{at}}^{\ominus}(\text{H}_2(\text{g})) - \Delta H_{\text{f}}^{\ominus}(\text{CH}_4)$$

We would reach the same conclusion, i.e. that
$$E(\text{C–H}) = +415.5 \, \text{kJ mol}^{-1}.$$

Fuels

Many substances burn in reactions with oxygen, with transfer of energy to the surroundings. Only those used on a large scale, however, are properly described as fuels. Oxidation of chemicals in the fuels coal, petroleum and gas provides over 90% of the energy used in most industrialised countries; hydroelectricity and nuclear power together supply about 9%.

Fuel	Formula	Relative molecular mass	Energy released per mole/kJ mol^{-1}	Energy released per kilogram /kJ kg^{-1}
Carbon (coal)	C(s)	12	−393	−32 750
Methane	CH$_4$(g)	16	−890	−55 625
Octane	C$_8$H$_{18}$(l)	114	−5 512	−48 350
Methanol	CH$_3$OH(l)	32	−715	−22 343
Hydrogen	H$_2$(g)	2	−286	−143 000

● *Table 4.1* Comparison of fuels in terms of energy released

What makes a good fuel?

The essential reaction for any chemical fuel is:

fuel + oxygen (or other oxidiser)
→ oxidation products
+ energy transfer

Though different fuels are needed for different purposes the ideal characteristics include the following.

■ *A fuel should react with an oxidiser to release large amounts of energy*
It is interesting to compare fuels on the basis of energy per unit amount of material (mole) and energy per unit mass (kilogram) (*table 4.1*). Remember that fuels are usually purchased in kilograms or tonnes, not in moles.

SAQ 4.7

From the data in *table 4.1*, compare hydrogen with methane. Why are the values for the energy released per kilogram so different when compared with the energy released per mole?

■ *A fuel must be oxidised fairly easily, ignite quickly and sustain burning without further intervention*
Gaseous or easily vaporised fuels usually perform well, as they mix easily and continuously with air/oxygen, which helps the reaction. Solid fuels (coal) are sometimes powdered for use in large industrial furnaces.

■ *A fuel should be readily available, in large quantities and at a reasonable price*
The availability and price of oil, for example, affect national economies so much that governments can fall and countries go to war when these change. The price of any fuel includes many factors: the costs of finding it; extraction, refining and transportation; all the company overheads, such as buildings, salaries and advertising; fuel taxes levied by governments; and the capital costs of the equipment needed to burn it. During the 1960s Britain changed the main gas supply from 'coal gas' (mainly hydrogen and carbon monoxide) to 'natural gas' (methane). This required a large-scale and expensive programme of adapting gas burners in industries and homes to suit the slower burning rate of methane. The advantages were that large supplies of methane were becoming available from gas-fields near to the British coast and that methane was thought to be a much 'cleaner' and safer fuel than the coal gas produced in dirty gas-works in most towns *(figure 4.14)*.

■ *A fuel should not burn to give products that are difficult to dispose of, or are unpleasant or harmful*
This is a considerable problem for most fuels (see below), as hydrogen is the only fuel with a safe, non-polluting product from its oxidation reaction to water.

■ *A fuel should be convenient to store and transport safely and without loss*
Over the ages, people have tackled many problems of fuel storage, from how to keep wood dry to how to keep liquid oxygen extremely cold and safe for space flight *(figure 4.15)*. If gases such as methane and hydrogen are to be used as alternatives to petrol in vehicles, the problems of storage of large amounts of gas must be solved. People are worried about storing these gases under high pressure in cylinders. Scientists are developing some interesting ways, however, of storing hydrogen as its solid compounds, such as the hydrides of metals: $FeTiH_2$ or $LaNi_5H_7$ or

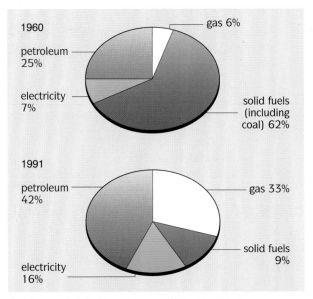

● **Figure 4.14** Changing use of fuel in Britain, 1960–91. Use of coal has greatly declined as methane gas is used for domestic and industrial energy supply, and many more gas-fuelled power stations for generating electricity are built.

1960
gas 6%
petroleum 25%
electricity 7%
solid fuels (including coal) 62%

1991
petroleum 42%
gas 33%
solid fuels 9%
electricity 16%

● **Figure 4.15** A space shuttle is propelled by fuels including liquid oxygen. Note the spherical storage tank for fuel on the right-hand side of the picture.

$MgNiH_4$. These hydrides release hydrogen when warmed gently and they may enable safe hydrogen-fuelled motor transport.

SAQ 4.8

a Why is oxygen transported into space in liquid form instead of as gas?

b Why are large quantities of liquid or gaseous fuels often stored in spherical tanks?

Problems with chemical fuels

Reliance upon the main chemical fuels coal, oil and gas is increasingly a matter of worldwide concern.

These fuels are 'fossil fuels', formed over millions of years. They are, in effect, non-renewable resources, yet we are consuming them extremely quickly. It is predicted that most of the Earth's oil reserves will be depleted over the next hundred years. Britain's oil- and gas-fields will disappear long before that, if used at the present rate.

The fossil fuels also happen to be the raw materials that supply the feedstock for most of our chemical industry. They may be processed by distillation, cracking and re-forming to yield the carbon-based compounds which are made into the polymers, medicines, solvents, adhesives, etc., that modern society would find difficult to replace (see chapter 6). For how long can we afford to carry on burning the feedstock?

Oxidation of the carbon-based compounds in fuels produces vast amounts of carbon dioxide (CO_2). At one time carbon dioxide was considered to be a relatively harmless gas. Now it is known to be a major contributor to the 'greenhouse effect', which causes an increase in atmospheric temperatures. Some governments are so concerned about this effect, which could bring about disastrous climatic change, that many means of reducing carbon dioxide levels in the atmosphere are being considered. Britain has set a target of reducing CO_2 emissions by 35% of the 1992 levels by the year 2000. The simplest solution would be an outright ban on the use of coal, oil and methane. Governments are understandably reluctant to take such drastic action, as national economies have

● *Figure 4.16* The oil tanker *Braer* broke open and spilled large amounts of oil around the Shetland Islands in 1993.

become so dependent on these fuels. However, we may see increasing 'carbon taxes' (extra taxes levied upon use of carbon-compound fuels) and other means of restricting their use.

Spillage of fuel often causes great damage to local environments (*figure 4.16*). This damage ranges from streams and ponds polluted by leaky fuel tanks to major disasters when oil tankers break open. There can be immense loss of animal and plant life and enormous costs of cleaning up.

Inefficient burning of carbon-based fuels in defective furnaces and domestic gas fires and in poorly tuned engines produces the very poisonous gas, carbon monoxide. Instead of:

$$C(s) + O_2(g) \longrightarrow CO_2(g)$$

partial oxidation gives:

$$2C(s) + O_2(g) \longrightarrow 2CO(g)$$

Inhalation of carbon monoxide may cause death, as it interferes with the transport of oxygen in the bloodstream (see chapter 5, page 94). Other dangerous gases produced by the burning of fuels include nitrogen oxides and sulphur oxides, which form strongly acidic solutions in water (hence 'acid rain') (*figure 4.17*). A large variety of compounds, including carcinogens, appear in the smoke from burning coal and wood.

SAQ 4.9

What are the reactions of nitrogen(IV) oxide (NO_2) and the sulphur oxides (SO_2 and SO_3) with water? Write equations for these reactions.

● *Figure 4.17* These trees in Germany were killed by the effects of acid rain, caused mainly by the sulphur oxides produced from burning coal.

Alternatives to fossil fuels

Biofuels

Plants can be grown to be used *directly* as fuels, e.g. wood. Plants can also be grown for *conversion* into fuels, e.g. sugar from sugar cane is easily fermented into ethanol. This can be used directly as an alternative to petrol (*figure 4.18*) or mixed with petrol as 'gasohol'. There is increasing use of natural oils, such as sunflower oil, as part of diesel fuels.

Waste products (animal and plant) can be allowed to decay in 'digesters' to produce methane.

■ *Advantages*: renewable; helps to reduce waste; used with simple technology.
■ *Disadvantages*: not large enough supply to replace fossil fuels at present rates of use.

● *Figure 4.18* This is a 'gasohol' fuel station. Gasohol is petrol with 10–22% of ethanol. In Brazil, 100% ethanol from fermented sugar is often used in a fuel known there as 'alcóol'.

Methanol (CH₃OH)

This simple alcohol can be made quite cheaply from methane. It is often used in racing cars (*figure 4.19*).

■ *Advantages*: methanol burns cleanly and completely; little carbon monoxide is produced.
■ *Disadvantages*: methanol is more toxic than ethanol; it provides much less energy per litre than petrol; mixtures of methanol and petrol absorb water and car engines may corrode.

● *Figure 4.19* This 'Indycar', driven by Nigel Mansell, is fuelled by methanol.

Nuclear fuels

Fission: Energy is released when the nuclei of atoms of isotopes of uranium U-235 or plutonium undergo fission (splitting) in a chain reaction (*figure 4.20*). Very large amounts of energy are available from this process. The energy is normally used in power stations to heat water to drive electricity-generating steam turbines.

■ *Advantages*: no carbon, nitrogen or sulphur oxides as polluting by-products; good supply of 'fuel', as U-238 can be converted into plutonium in breeder reactors.
■ *Disadvantages*: radioactive waste products are difficult to store and treat; safety systems to contain radioactivity are very costly.

Fusion: Energy is released when deuterium and tritium 'fuse' to form helium:

$$_1^2\text{H} + {}_1^3\text{H} \longrightarrow {}_2^4\text{He} + {}_0^1\text{n}$$

■ *Advantages*: potentially almost limitless as an energy supply as the 'fuels' come from water.
■ *Disadvantages*: no fusion reactors are yet producing energy at economic rates· they are extremely costly.

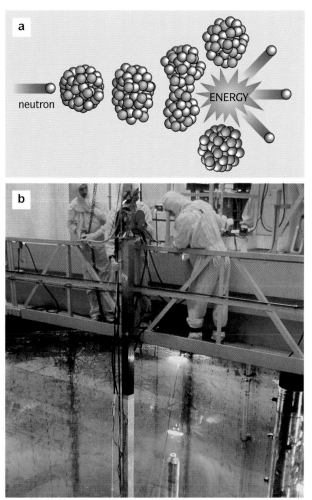

● **Figure 4.20** Nuclear energy.

a Nuclear fission: a neutron colliding with a uranium nucleus causes fission and the release of energy and more neutrons.

b Fuel rods containing uranium-235 being loaded into a nuclear reactor. The top of the reactor core is kept under 11 metres of water to protect the workers from the intense radiation.

● **Figure 4.21** This wind-farm in Spain includes many wind turbines for generating electricity.

Moving air: wind

The energy of moving air is transferred into the motion of windmills and wind turbines (*figure 4.21*). Much science and technology is being devoted to improving the efficiency of the wind machines, and they soon may provide over 10% of the UK energy needs.

- ■ *Advantages*: renewable; pollution- and waste-free; can be used in locality where energy is needed.
- ■ *Disadvantages*: high initial expense for large-scale generation of electricity; not a reliable source in calm weather; large 'wind-farms' have environmental impact, noise and visual.

Moving water

Hydroelectricity: Water stored behind dams or from waterfalls can be released through turbines and generate electricity or be used directly to turn wheels in mills (*figure 4.22*). Hydroelectricity is a major source of power in many countries.

Waves: The motion of waves is used to cause oscillating motion in various devices and to generate electricity (*figure 4.22*).

● **Figure 4.22**

a A hydroelectric power station is sited below the storage lake and dam.

b This device, on a sea inlet in Islay, uses the motion of waves to generate electricity. Other wave motion devices are used out at sea.

Tides: Incoming tides in river estuaries fill up large water stores behind barrages across the river. The water can be released through turbines to generate electricity.

■ *Advantages*: renewable; quite predictable; pollution- and waste-free; can be used on large scale.

■ *Disadvantages*: costly to install; environmental impact of dams and barrages.

Sunlight: solar heating and photovoltaics

Solar panels, which are panels of solar heat collectors, are used to heat water in parts of the world where sunshine is plentiful *(figure 4.23)*.

Photovoltaic cells convert light into electricity *(figure 4.23)*. In future, large satellites may generate electricity and beam energy by microwave to Earth:

■ *Advantages*: renewable; pollution-free with no waste products.

● *Figure 4.23*
a Solar water heaters on a roof top in Kathmandu, Nepal.
b A lighthouse in Shetland that uses photovoltaic cells to charge storage batteries.

■ *Disadvantages*: low sunlight levels in UK; none at night; photovoltaics have high initial costs; very large arrays needed for large-scale production of electricity.

Geothermal: hot rocks

Some distance below the surface of the Earth, the temperature is high (about 85 °C at 2 km below). Water pumped into wells in the hot rock zone is heated; the extracted hot water can be used to heat buildings *(figure 4.24)*.

■ *Advantages*: almost unlimited source.

■ *Disadvantages*: not widely available; expensive initially; technological problems.

● *Figure 4.24* Geothermal power stations are widely used in Iceland where hot rocks are near the surface. The four wells in this station provide enough steam to drive a power plant producing 100 megawatts of thermal energy and 2.7 megawatts of electricity. The steam is also used to heat cold water, which is then piped to the capital, Reykjavik, for heating and washing.

Hydrogen

Many scientists believe that we should run a 'hydrogen economy'. Hydrogen can be extracted quite cheaply from water by electrolysis. Much scientific and technological effort is being spent on effective storage and transport systems.

■ *Advantages*: no pollution, as water is the only waste product from burning hydrogen in air; available in large quantities.

■ *Disadvantages*: regarded as too dangerously explosive by many people *(figure 4.25)*; difficult to store and use for transport or in domestic situations.

● *Figure 4.25* The fate of the airship *Hindenburg* in 1937. Hydrogen was not used as fuel but to keep the airship buoyant. This and similar tragedies have made people very cautious about the use of hydrogen as a fuel for transport, but with modern technology it can be used at least as safely as petrol.

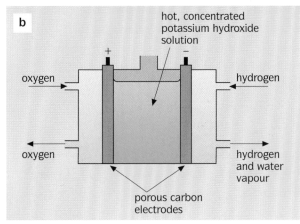

● *Figure 4.26*

a This vehicle is powered by a number of rechargeable lead–acid batteries, seen underneath.

b A simple fuel cell using the hydrogen–oxygen reaction. The gases must be supplied continuously to the electrodes, so a fuel cell is not a 'store' of electricity. This cell provides a voltage of 1.23 V and can be designed to give 70% efficiency in converting the energy of the reaction to electricity.

Electricity from chemical cells

Cells work by using oxidation and reduction reactions (redox systems) in which electrons are transferred. Cells act as convenient stores of electricity *(figure 4.26)*. There is much research into batteries (collections of cells) that will provide energy in sufficient quantities to power cars and lorries. The familiar lead–acid batteries, used in many delivery vans in towns, may be replaced in future by other batteries using, for example, sodium and sulphur.

Fuel cells are of great interest *(figure 4.26)*. In these, redox reactions between hydrogen and oxygen, or alcohols and oxygen, take place over catalysts. Fuel cells are very clean and efficient, and are used in small spacecraft. They have not yet been developed for very large-scale generation of electricity.

Activation energy: reaction pathway diagrams

Petrol burns extremely quickly, so why does it not ignite as soon as it is mixed with air in a car engine? Fortunately for us all, ignition needs a spark from the spark plugs. A mixture of hydrogen and oxygen gases is also apparently quite stable when left to itself; nothing would happen during your lifetime or indeed many lifetimes. But a single small spark will set off an explosively fast reaction between the gases *(figure 4.25)*. Many reaction systems behave this way, with no obvious change until there is an initial input of energy.

The reason becomes fairly clear if you consider what happens as the gases react. First, the molecules must come into contact. Then bonds in the molecules must break, and only then can the products start to form. Energy is not released from the reacting system until that product-formation stage.

The reaction needs some initial input of energy to help the process of bond stretching and breaking in the reacting molecules. The minimum energy needed to make a reaction take place is called the **activation energy** for the reaction. In the hydrogen and oxygen reaction the energy can be supplied by a single spark. That starts the reaction with a few molecules; thereafter the activation energy needed to keep the reaction going is supplied by the formation of products in the reaction itself.

Reaction pathways may be illustrated by diagrams (*figure 4.27*). The activation energy is shown as a 'hill' or 'energy barrier' on the reaction pathway diagram. The reacting chemicals must gain enough energy to overcome the energy barrier before they can form products. *Figure 4.27* also shows how the activation energies for endothermic reactions are usually much higher than for exothermic reactions. The enthalpy change of reaction supplies the necessary activation energy in exothermic reactions, after the initial input. All the activation energy for endothermic reactions must be supplied by an external energy source.

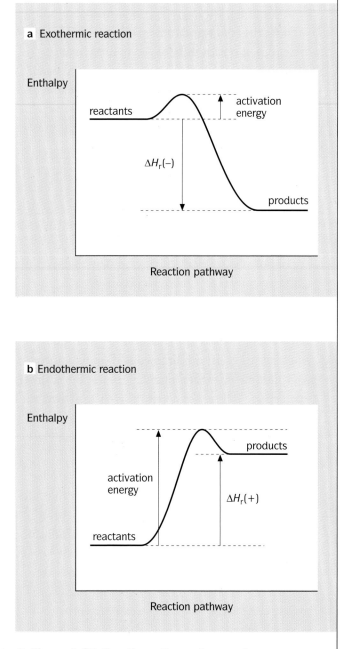

● *Figure 4.27* Reaction pathway diagrams for **a** an exothermic and **b** an endothermic reaction, showing the activation energy and the enthalpy change of reaction in each case.

SAQ 4.10

Draw reaction pathway diagrams for the reactions involved in the burning of methane and the action of heat on limestone. What are the main differences?

$\Delta H_f^\ominus$ as a guide to the stability of compounds

Some compounds decompose (break down) easily when they are heated. Others are more stable and are little affected even at high temperatures. Chemists are interested in studying how chemicals change under different conditions, and they find it helpful to be able to compare and make predictions about the stability of compounds. Are they more likely to decompose at lower or higher temperatures? How is this related to their known enthalpy changes of formation? Any predictions and hypotheses should, of course, be tested by the reality of evidence from experiments.

Compare the following compounds – they are all oxides of metals:

aluminium oxide, Al_2O_3 $\Delta H_f^\ominus = -1669 \text{ kJ mol}^{-1}$
copper(II) oxide, CuO $\Delta H_f^\ominus = -155 \text{ kJ mol}^{-1}$
silver oxide, Ag_2O $\Delta H_f^\ominus = -30.6 \text{ kJ mol}^{-1}$
gold oxide, Au_2O_3 $\Delta H_f^\ominus = +80.3 \text{ kJ mol}^{-1}$

Aluminium oxide is a very stable compound. It is so resistant to strong heating that it is used to make firebricks for high-temperature furnaces. It is the main chemical in the very stable gemstones ruby and sapphire.

Copper(II) oxide is quite stable but decomposes slowly to copper and oxygen on strong heating above 600°C.

Silver oxide is stable at room temperatures but decomposes to silver and oxygen on only gentle heating around 300 °C.

Gold oxide is very unstable and breaks down on gentle heating. It cannot be made by direct reaction between gold and oxygen and is difficult to prepare. As gold is not affected by oxygen in the atmosphere, gold does not tarnish and keeps its shiny metallic surface (*figure 4.28*).

This evidence supports the idea of using $\Delta H_f^\ominus$ values as a guide to the stability of compounds during heating. A high negative value of $\Delta H_f^\ominus$ for a compound indicates that a large amount of energy is released to the surroundings when it is formed from its elements. In the reverse reaction, if the same large amount of energy is transferred *into* the compound, it should break down to its elements. A compound with a positive or low negative value of $\Delta H_f^\ominus$ should break down more easily. We can predict that compounds with high negative $\Delta H_f^\ominus$ values are more stable during heating than compounds with positive or low negative $\Delta H_f^\ominus$ values.

We must not assume, however, that all compounds with positive $\Delta H_f^\ominus$ values behave as if they are unstable and decompose quickly and easily into their elements. A compound such as benzene (C_6H_6) with $\Delta H_f^\ominus = +49 \, kJ \, mol^{-1}$ exists in an apparently stable condition and can be boiled without decomposing to its elements.

SAQ 4.11

The enthalpy changes of formation of four hydroxides are shown below. Predict the order of stability to heating of these compounds, placing the most stable first.

Compound	$\Delta H_f^\ominus \, kJ \, mol^{-1}$
$Zn(OH)_2$	−642
$Fe(OH)_2$	−568
$Ca(OH)_2$	−987
$Cu(OH)_2$	−448

Enthalpy change ΔH and rates of reaction

While $\Delta H_f^\ominus$ values give some helpful indications about the stability of compounds, they cannot be used to predict the *rate* of reactions. $\Delta H_r^\ominus$ values tell us only about the difference in enthalpy between the beginning and end of a reaction and nothing about what happens in between (remember Hess's law). They give no information about the mechanism of how the reaction took place. The rate of a reaction is affected by factors such as the concentrations of reactants, the temperature and anything that affects the size of the activation energy. So do not assume that a large, exothermic $\Delta H_r^\ominus$ means that a reaction will be fast; it may be fast, but then again it may not!

● **Figure 4.28** The beautiful gold mask of an Egyptian Pharaoh, untarnished after 3000 years.

Consider the oxidation of iron. This has a large, exothermic enthalpy change of reaction:

$$2Fe(s) + 3O_2(g) \longrightarrow Fe_2O_3(s);$$
$$\Delta H_r^\ominus = -822 \, kJ \, mol^{-1}$$

This reaction is fast when powdered iron burns in air, but it is slow when iron rusts on your car or bicycle (*figure 4.29*). $\Delta H_r^\ominus$ is the same in both cases; it does not help us to predict the rate of oxidation of iron under different conditions.

ΔH as a guide to the feasibility of chemical reactions

Most systems, whether chemical or physical, tend to lose energy during changes – objects fall, springs uncoil, exothermic reactions heat the surroundings, and so on. The greater the energy transferred away from these systems, the more stable they become. This means that a large negative $\Delta H_r^\ominus$ value for any

● *Figure 4.29*

a Powdered iron oxidising very quickly in a 'sparkler' firework.

b The oxidation of iron to 'rust' is slow but destructive, as it wastes much valuable metal.

reaction indicates that the reaction is likely to occur (it is 'feasible') under some conditions.

That is not the whole story, however. We also know that endothermic reactions occur by taking in energy. These reactions happen even if their products are less stable than the reactants. There must be additional factors controlling the feasibility of chemical reactions. Enthalpy changes can be helpful for predicting feasibility, but using them on their own is just too simple.

The other major factor involves **entropy changes**. Discussion of entropy and entropy changes is outside the scope of this book, but, if you wish to enquire further, ask about entropy and another of the great laws of science – the second law of thermodynamics.

SUMMARY

■ Chemical reactions are often accompanied by transfers of energy to or from the surroundings, mainly as heat. In exothermic reactions, energy is transferred away from the reacting chemicals; in endothermic reactions, energy is gained by the reacting chemicals.

■ Changes in energy of reacting chemicals at constant pressure are known as enthalpy changes (ΔH). Exothermic enthalpy changes are shown as negative values ($-$) and endothermic enthalpy changes are positive values ($+$).

■ Standard enthalpy changes are compared under standard conditions of pressure, temperature, concentration and physical states.

■ Standard enthalpy changes of formation $\Delta H_f^\ominus$ and of combustion $\Delta H_c^\ominus$ are defined in terms of one mole of compound formed or of one mole of element or compound reacting completely with oxygen; their units are $kJ\,mol^{-1}$

■ Bond breaking is an endothermic process; bond making is an exothermic process.

■ Bond energy is a measure of the energy required to break a bond. The values quoted are usually average bond energies, as the strength of a bond between two particular atoms is different in different molecules.

■ Enthalpy changes may be calculated from measurements involving temperature change in a liquid, using the relationship:

enthalpy change = mass of liquid
    × specific heat capacity of liquid
    × temperature change.
$$\Delta H = mc\Delta T$$

■ Hess's law states that 'the total enthalpy change for a chemical reaction is independent of the route by which the reaction takes place'.

■ The principle of Hess's law may be used to calculate enthalpy changes for reactions that do not occur directly and cannot be found by experiment.

■ All reactions require some initial input of energy to start the process of bond breaking. The minimum energy is called the **activation energy** of the reaction.

■ The larger the exothermic (negative) values of $\Delta H_f^\ominus$ for a compound, the more stable it is likely to be when heated. Endothermic (positive) or low exothermic values of $\Delta H_f^\ominus$ indicate low stability.

■ Fossil fuels are a valuable, non-renewable resource, and society will have to decide future consumption related to their use as raw materials, while scientists improve and develop new fuels and alternative energy sources.

■ ΔH values give some guide to reaction feasibility, but do not give any indication of the rate of reaction.

Questions

1 Using bond energy data (page 54), calculate the enthalpy change of combustion of ethanol (C_2H_5OH) to carbon dioxide and water. Why does this differ from the value obtained directly from an experimental measurement?

2 Use energy cycles (in the form of triangles or energy level diagrams) to find the following:

   a the enthalpy change of formation of ethene (C_2H_4);

   b the average bond energy of ammonia (NH_3)

   [The data needed for the calculations are given in the chapter, except for:

   $\Delta H^{\ominus}_{at}(N_2(g)) = +473\,kJ\,mol^{-1}$;

   $\Delta H^{\ominus}_{f}(NH_3(g)) = -46.2\,kJ\,mol^{-1}$.]

3 What are the relative merits of using hydrogen and octane as fuels for motor vehicles?

4 If you were asked to find compounds to make materials that could withstand high temperatures, what sort of thermochemical data would you use in your search? Explain your answer with examples.

Periodic patterns

Introduction to periodicity

Patterns of chemical properties and atomic masses

If you were given samples of all the elements (some are shown in *figure 5.1*) and the time to observe their properties, you would probably find many ways of arranging them. You could classify them by their states at a particular temperature (solids, liquids or gases) or as metals and non-metals; you might find patterns in their reactions with oxygen or water or other chemicals. Would you consider trying to link these properties to the relative atomic masses of the elements?

● *Figure 5.1* A few of the 109 known elements.

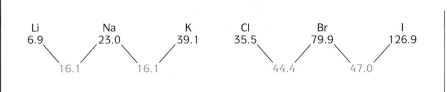

● **Figure 5.2** Two of Döbereiner's 'triads'.

If you have studied the metallic elements lithium, sodium and potassium, you will know that they have similar reactions with oxygen, water and chlorine, and form similar compounds. The rates of their reactions show that sodium comes between lithium and potassium in reactivity. Now look at their relative atomic masses:

Li   Na   K
6.9   23   39.1

The relative atomic mass of sodium is the average of the relative atomic masses of lithium and potassium. There is a pattern here which is also shown by other group of elements in threes – chlorine, bromine and iodine, for example. The 'middle' element has the average properties and average relative atomic mass of the other two. This pattern was first recorded by the German chemist Johann Döbereiner (1780–1849) as his 'Law of Triads' *(figure 5.2)*. At the time, however, it was little more than a curiosity, as too few elements were known and values for atomic masses were uncertain.

Later in the century, more elements were known and atomic masses could be measured more accurately. A British chemist, John Newlands (1837–98), suggested that, when the elements were arranged in order of increasing atomic mass, 'the eighth element, starting from a given one, is a kind of repetition of the first, like the eighth note in an octave of music'.

Newlands presented his ideas for a 'Law of Octaves' to a meeting of the Chemical Society in 1866 *(figure 5.3)*. They were not well received. Unfortunately, his 'octaves' only seemed to apply to the first 16 elements. He had not allowed space in his table for the possibility of new elements to be discovered.

Despite the Chemical Society's sceptical reception of Newlands' ideas, we now know that he had found the important pattern of **periodicity**. This means that the properties of elements have a regularly recurring or 'periodic' relationship with their relative atomic masses.

Mendeleev's periodic table

The greatest credit for producing chemistry's most famous organisa-tion of elements – 'the Periodic Table' – is always given to Dmitri Mendeleev (1834–1907) from Russia.

Mendeleev arranged the elements, just as Newlands had, in order of increasing relative atomic

a

b

CHEMICAL NEWS, }
March 9, 1866. }

Table II.—*Elements arranged in Octaves.*

No.	No.	No.	No.	No.	No.	No.	No.
H 1	F 8	Cl 15	Co & Ni 22	Br 29	Pd 36	I 42	Pt & Ir 50
Li 2	Na 9	K 16	Cu 23	Rb 30	Ag 37	Cs 44	Os 51
G 3	Mg 10	Ca 17	Zn 24	Sr 31	Cd 38	Ba & V 45	Hg 52
Bo 4	Al 11	Cr 19	Y 25	Ce & La 33	U 40	Ta 46	Tl 53
C 5	Si 12	Ti 18	In 26	Zr 32	Sn 39	W 47	Pb 54
N 6	P 13	Mn 20	As 27	Di & Mo 34	Sb 41	Nb 48	Bi 55
O 7	S 14	Fe 21	Se 28	Ro & Ru 35	Te 43	Au 49	Th 56

● **Figure 5.3**

a John Newlands.

b This is the table Newlands presented to the Chemical Society in 1866 in a paper entitled 'The Law of Octaves, and the Causes of Numerical Relations among the Atomic Weights'. Note that some elements have symbols that we do not use today, e.g. G and Bo. What are these elements?

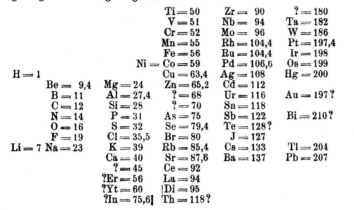

a

Ueber die Beziehungen der Eigenschaften zu den Atomgewichten der Elemente. Von D. Mendelejeff. — Ordnet man Elemente nach zunehmenden Atomgewichten in verticale Reihen so, dass die Horizontal-reihen analoge Elemente enthalten, wieder nach zunehmendem Atomge-wicht geordnet, so erhält man folgende Zusammenstellung, aus der sich einige allgemeinere Folgerungen ableiten lassen.

```
                      Ti = 50     Zr =  90     ? = 180
                      V  = 51     Nb =  94     Ta = 182
                      Cr = 52     Mo =  96     W  = 186
                      Mn = 55     Rh = 104,4   Pt = 197,4
                      Fe = 56     Ru = 104,4   Ir = 198
                  Ni = Co = 59    Pd = 106,6   Os = 199
                      Cu = 63,4   Ag = 108     Hg = 200
H = 1        Be =  9,4   Mg = 24  Zn = 65,2    Cd = 112
       Be =  9,4   Mg = 24   Zn = 65,2   Cd = 112
       B  = 11     Al = 27,4  ? = 68     Ur = 116     Au = 197?
       C  = 12     Si = 28    ? = 70     Sn = 118
       N  = 14     P  = 31    As = 75    Sb = 122     Bi = 210?
       O  = 16     S  = 32    Se = 79,4  Te = 128?
       F  = 19     Cl = 35,5  Br = 80    J  = 127
Li = 7 Na = 23     K  = 39    Rb = 85,4  Cs = 133     Tl = 204
                   Ca = 40    Sr = 87,6  Ba = 137     Pb = 207
                    ? = 45    Ce = 92
                   ?Er = 56   La = 94
                   ?Yt = 60   !Di = 95
                   ?In = 75,6| Th = 118?
```

● *Figure 5.4*

a Mendeleev's first published periodic table in the *Zeitschrift für Chemie* in 1869. Note that the elements with similar properties (e.g. Li, Na, K) are in horizontal rows in this table.

b This photograph shows a late version of Mendeleev's periodic table on the building where he worked in St Petersburg. Elements with similar properties are now arranged vertically in groups.

mass *(figure 5.4)*. At the time (late 1860s) over 60 elements were known, and he saw that there was some form of regularly repeating pattern of properties.

Mendeleev made several crucial decisions that ensured the success of his first periodic table. The most important decisions were the following.

■ He left spaces in the table so that similar elements could always appear in the same Group.

■ He said that the spaces would be filled by elements not then known. Furthermore, he predicted what the properties of these elements might be, based on the properties of known elements in the same Group. He made predictions, for example, about the element between silicon and tin in Group IV. This element was only discovered about 15 years later. Mendeleev had called it 'eka-silicon'; it is now known as germanium *(table 5.1)*.

SAQ 5.1

From *table 5.1*, how well do you think Mendeleev's predicted properties for eka-silicon compare with the known properties of germanium?

A theory or model is most valuable when it is used to explain and predict. Mendeleev's periodic table was immensely successful. By linking the observed periodicity in the properties of elements with the

Property	Mendeleev's predictions for 'eka-silicon'	Germanium
Appearance	light-grey solid	dark-grey solid
Atomic mass	72	72.59
Density/g cm⁻³	5.5	5.35
Oxide formula	eka-SiO₂	GeO₂
Oxide density	4.7	4.2
Chloride density	1.9 (liquid)	1.84 (liquid)
Chloride b.p./°C	<100	84

● *Table 5.1* Comparison of Mendeleev's predictions for eka-silicon with known properties of germanium

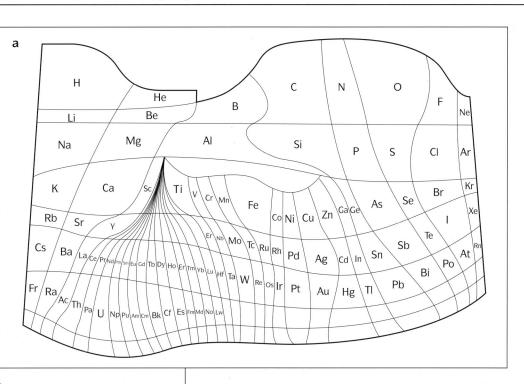

atomic theory of matter, the table helped to organise and unify the science of chemistry and led to much further research. It has been greatly admired ever since. It was even able to cope with the discovery of a whole new group of elements, now called 'the noble gases' (helium to radon), though these had not been predicted by Mendeleev.

Atomic structure and periodicity

In 1913 the British scientist Henry Moseley was able to show that the real sequence in the Periodic Table is not the order of relative atomic masses. The sequence is the order of proton (atomic) numbers – the numbers of protons in the nuclei of atoms of the elements (see chapter 1). This sequence of elements by proton numbers is close to the sequence by relative atomic masses, but not exactly the same.

SAQ 5.2

a What is the relationship between proton numbers and relative atomic masses?

b Why are the relative atomic mass values for tellurium (Te) and iodine (I; J in Mendeleev's table) the 'wrong' way around in the Periodic Table, whereas their proton numbers fit the Table?

Moseley's work was about the nature of the nucleus and led to the correct sequence of elements. It did not, however, answer questions about the periodic variations in physical and chemical properties. This is because these properties depend much more upon the numbers and distributions of electrons in atoms.

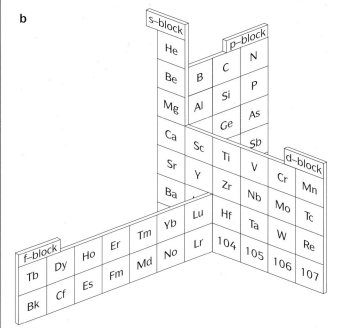

● **Figure 5.5** Two rather unusual versions of the Periodic Table:
a the elements according to relative abundance and
b a three-dimensional, four-vaned model.

Versions of the Periodic Table

Chemists have enjoyed displaying the Periodic Table in many different ways (for two versions, see *figure 5.5*). You may be able to invent some new versions.

s-Block — d-Block — p-Block

Period	I	II						Group					III	IV	V	VI	VII	0
1								1.0 H Hydrogen 1										4.0 He Helium 2
2	6.9 Li Lithium 3	9.0 Be Beryllium 4											10.8 B Boron 5	12.0 C Carbon 6	14.0 N Nitrogen 7	16.0 O Oxygen 8	19.0 F Fluorine 9	20.2 Ne Neon 10
3	23.0 Na Sodium 11	24.3 Mg Magnesium 12											27.0 Al Aluminium 13	28.1 Si Silicon 14	31.0 P Phosphorus 15	32.1 S Sulphur 16	35.5 Cl Chlorine 17	39.9 Ar Argon 18
4	39.1 K Potassium 19	40.1 Ca Calcium 20	45.0 Sc Scandium 21	47.9 Ti Titanium 22	50.9 V Vanadium 23	52.0 Cr Chromium 24	54.9 Mn Manganese 25	55.9 Fe Iron 26	58.9 Co Cobalt 27	58.7 Ni Nickel 28	63.5 Cu Copper 29	65.4 Zn Zinc 30	69.7 Ga Gallium 31	72.6 Ge Germanium 32	74.9 As Arsenic 33	79.0 Se Selenium 34	79.9 Br Bromine 35	83.8 Kr Krypton 36
5	85.5 Rb Rubidium 37	87.6 Sr Strontium 38	88.9 Y Yttrium 39	91.2 Zr Zirconium 40	92.9 Nb Niobium 41	95.9 Mo Molybdenum 42	– Tc Technetium 43	101 Ru Ruthenium 44	103 Rh Rhodium 45	106 Pd Palladium 46	108 Ag Silver 47	112 Cd Cadmium 48	115 In Indium 49	119 Sn Tin 50	122 Sb Antimony 51	128 Te Tellurium 52	127 I Iodine 53	131 Xe Xenon 54
6	133 Cs Caesium 55	137 Ba Barium 56	La to Lu	178 Hf Hafnium 72	181 Ta Tantalum 73	184 W Tungsten 74	186 Re Rhenium 75	190 Os Osmium 76	192 Ir Iridium 77	195 Pt Platinum 78	197 Au Gold 79	201 Hg Mercury 80	204 Tl Thallium 81	207 Pb Lead 82	209 Bi Bismuth 83	– Po Polonium 84	– At Astatine 85	– Rn Radon 86
7	– Fr Francium 87	– Ra Radium 88	Ac to Lr	– Unq Unnilquadium 104	– Unp Unnilpentium 105	– Unh Unnilhexium 106	– Uns Unnilseptium 107	– Uno Unniloctium 108	– Une Unnilennium 109									

Key: *a* X Name *b* — *a* = relative atomic mass; X = symbol; *b* = proton number

f-Block

139 La Lanthanum 57	140 Ce Cerium 58	141 Pr Praseodymium 59	144 Nd Neodymium 60	– Pm Promethium 61	150 Sm Samarium 62	152 Eu Europium 63	157 Gd Gadolinium 64	159 Tb Terbium 65	163 Dy Dysprosium 66	165 Ho Holmium 67	167 Er Erbium 68	169 Tm Thulium 69	173 Yb Ytterbium 70	175 Lu Lutetium 71
– Ac Actinium 89	– Th Thorium 90	– Pa Protactinium 91	– U Uranium 92	– Np Neptunium 93	– Pu Plutonium 94	– Am Americium 95	– Cm Curium 96	– Bk Berkelium 97	– Cf Californium 98	– Es Einsteinium 99	– Fm Fermium 100	– Md Mendelevium 101	– No Nobelium 102	– Lr Lawrencium 103

● ***Figure 5.6*** The Periodic Table of the elements.

The Periodic Table most often seen is shown in *figure 5.6* (and also in the appendix). Its main features are:

- the vertical Groups of elements, labelled I, II, III, up to VII; the noble gases are not called Group VIII but Group 0;
- the horizontal Periods labelled 1, 2, 3, etc.

Blocks of elements in the Periodic Table

Chemists find it helpful to identify 'blocks' of elements by the type of electron orbital most affecting the properties. These are shown on the Periodic Table in *figure 5.6*.

- Groups I and II elements are in the **s-block**.
- Groups III to VII and Group 0 (except He) are in the **p-block**.
- The transition elements (except lanthanoid and actinoid elements) are included in the **d-block**.

Periodic patterns of physical properties of elements

We shall now look in more detail at the physical properties of elements and their relationships with the electronic configurations of atoms.

Summary of structure and bonding of first 36 elements

Figure 5.7 shows details of the structures and bonding of elements 1 to 36, hydrogen (H) to krypton (Kr).

First ionisation energies

How first ionisation energies vary with proton number

The **first ionisation energy** of an element gives a measure of the energy required to remove one

H₂(g) mols																	He(g) atoms
Li(s) metal	Be(s) metal											B(s) giant mol	C(s) giant mol	N₂(g) mols	O₂(g) mols	F₂(g) mols	Ne(g) atoms
Na(s) metal	Mg(s) metal											Al(s) metal	Si(s) giant mol	P₄(s) mols	S₈(s) mols	Cl₂(g) mols	Ar(g) atoms
K(s) metal	Ca(s) metal	Sc(s) metal	Ti(s) metal	V(s) metal	Cr(s) metal	Mn(s) metal	Fe(s) metal	Co(s) metal	Ni(s) metal	Cu(s) metal	Zn(s) metal	Ga(s) metal	Ge(s) metal	As(s) giant mol	Se(s) mol	Br₂(l) mols	Kr(g) atoms

● **Figure 5.7** Structures of elements 1 (hydrogen, H) to 36 (krypton, Kr).

electron from every atom in a mole of atoms of that element. The first ionisation energies of the first 36 elements in the Periodic Table are shown in *figure 5.8*. Their variation with proton number is displayed in the *figure 5.9*. The most significant features of the graph are:

■ the 'peaks' are all occupied by elements of the same Group (Group 0, the noble gases) and the 'troughs' by the Group I elements (the alkali metals);

■ there is a general increase in ionisation energy across a Period, from the Group I elements to the Group 0 elements, but the trend is uneven;

■ the first ionisation energies of the elements 21 (scandium) to 29 (copper) (the d-block elements of Period 4) vary much less than other series of elements.

How are these periodic variations in first ionisation energies to be explained in terms of the model of atomic structure and electronic configurations outlined in chapter 1?

Consider some examples:

fluorine, element 9, has the configuration
$1s^2\ 2s^2\ 2p^5$

neon, element 10, has the configuration
$1s^2\ 2s^2\ 2p^6$

sodium, element 11, has the configuration
$1s^2\ 2s^2\ 2p^6\ 3s^1$

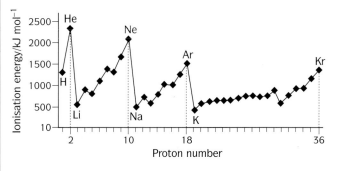

● **Figure 5.9** The first ionisation energies of elements 1 to 36, plotted against proton number.

H 1310																	He 2370
Li 519	Be 900											B 799	C 1090	N 1400	O 1310	F 1680	Ne 2080
Na 494	Mg 736											Al 577	Si 786	P 1060	S 1000	Cl 1260	Ar 1520
K 418	Ca 590	Sc 632	Ti 661	V 648	Cr 653	Mn 716	Fe 762	Co 757	Ni 736	Cu 745	Zn 908	Ga 577	Ge 762	As 966	Se 941	Br 1140	Kr 1350

● **Figure 5.8** The first ionisation energies of elements 1 to 36, measured in kilojoules per mole (kJ mol⁻¹).

As you see in *figure 5.9*, the ionisation energy of neon is higher than that of fluorine; sodium's ionisation energy is much lower. The main differences in the atoms of these elements are:

- the numbers of protons in their nuclei, and hence their positive nuclear charges, are different;
- the outer occupied orbital in both fluorine and neon is in the 2p subshell but sodium has an electron in the next shell, in its 3s orbital;
- neon has a completely filled outer shell, fluorine has one electron fewer than a complete shell and sodium has one electron more than a complete shell.

These differences between the atoms lead us to the factors that influence their first ionisation energies.

Factors influencing first ionisation energies

The three strongest influences on the first ionisation energies of elements are the following:

- *The size of the positive nuclear charge*
  This charge affects all the electrons in an atom. The increase in nuclear charge with proton number will tend to cause an increase in ionisation energies.
- *The distance of the electron from the nucleus*
  It has been found that, if F is the force of attraction between two objects and d is the distance between them, then

  F is proportional to $1/d^2$
      (the 'inverse square law')

  This **distance effect** means that all forces of attraction decrease rapidly as the distance between the attracted bodies increases. Thus the attractions between a nucleus and electrons decrease as the quantum numbers of the shells increase. The further the shell is from the nucleus, the lower are the ionisation energies for electrons in that shell.
- *The 'screening' or 'shielding' effect by electrons in filled inner shells*
  All electrons are negatively charged and repel each other. Electrons in the filled inner shells repel electrons in the outer shell and reduce the effect of the positive nuclear charge. This is called the **screening effect** (sometimes known as the 'shielding effect'). The greater the screening effect upon an electron, the lower is the energy required to remove it and thus the lower the ionisation energy.

We shall now apply these ideas to the three elements, 9, 10, and 11 – fluorine, neon and sodium.

The outer electrons in both fluorine and neon atoms are in the 2p orbitals. This means that the 'distance' effect and the 'screening' effect are similar. However, the nuclear charge in a neon atom is larger and attracts the 2p electrons more strongly. This causes the first ionisation energy of neon to be higher than that of fluorine.

The outer electron of sodium is in the 3s orbital, as the 2p orbitals are full. The ionisation energy of sodium is much lower than that of neon, even though a sodium atom has a larger nuclear charge. This shows how the combined effects, of increased distance and of screening, reduce the effective nuclear charge. The 3s electron in a sodium atom is further from the nucleus than any 2p electrons. It is also screened from the attractions of the nuclear charge by two complete inner shells ($n = 1$ and $n = 2$). The electrons in shell $n = 2$ are screened only by the electrons in one shell ($n = 1$).

First ionisation energies across a Period

From *figure 5.9* you will see that there is a general trend of increasing ionisation energies across a Period. There are, however, variations. Look, for example, at elements 3, 4 and 5, lithium ($1s^2\ 2s^1$), beryllium ($1s^2\ 2s^2$) and boron($1s^2\ 2s^2\ 2p^1$). We might have predicted that boron would have the highest ionisation energy of the three; in fact, it is beryllium. Experimental evidence such as this leads to a further assumption about electron configurations: it is easier to remove electrons from p orbitals than from s orbitals in the same shell. Thus the 2p electron in boron is easier to remove than one of the 2s electrons. Though the nuclear charge in boron is larger than in beryllium, boron has the lower first ionisation energy.

Now look at the other elements in Period 2:

	Carbon	*Nitrogen*	*Oxygen*
atomic number	6	7	8
electronic config.	$1s^2\ 2s^2\ 2p^2$	$1s^2\ 2s^2\ 2p^3$	$1s^2\ 2s^2\ 2p^4$
box config. for 2p	[↑][↑][ ]	[↑][↑][↑]	[↑↓][↑][↑]

	Fluorine	*Neon*
atomic number	9	10
electronic config.	$1s^2\ 2s^2\ 2p^5$	$1s^2\ 2s^2\ 2p^6$
box config. for 2p	[↑↓][↑↓][↑]	[↑↓][↑↓][↑↓]

In the general trend across the Period, we might expect the ionisation energy of oxygen to be higher than that of nitrogen. In fact, the ionisation energy of nitrogen is the higher of the two. Nitrogen has three electrons in the p orbitals, each of them unpaired; oxygen has four electrons, with two of them paired. The repulsion between the electrons in the pair makes it easier to remove one of them and to ionise an atom of oxygen, even though the nuclear charge is larger than in an atom of nitrogen.

The general trend, of increasing ionisation energies across a Period, is re-established in atoms of fluorine and neon, by the effect of larger nuclear charge.

SAQ 5.3

In terms of their electronic configurations, explain the relative first ionisation energies of :

a sodium, magnesium and aluminium;

b silicon, phosphorus and sulphur.

First ionisation energies in Groups

Elements are placed in Groups in the Periodic Table, as they show many similar physical and chemical properties. Note how elements in Groups occupy similar positions on the plot of first ionisation energy against proton number *(figure 5.9)*. This is evidence that the elements in Groups have similar electronic configurations in their outer orbitals. For example:

Group I (alkali metals, Li–Cs)
    all have one (s^1) electron in their outer orbitals

Group II (alkaline-earth metals, Be–Ba)
    all have two (s^2) electrons in their outer orbitals

Group VII (halogens, F–At)
    all have seven ($s^2\ p^5$) electrons in their orbitals

The first ionisation energies generally decrease down a vertical Group, with increasing proton number. This shows the combined

result of several factors. With increasing proton number, in any Group:

■ the positive nuclear charge increases;

■ the distance of the outer electrons from the nucleus increases with each new shell;

■ the screening effect of the filled inner electron shells increases as the number of inner shells grows.

The distance and screening effects together are able to reduce the effect of the increasing nuclear charges from element to element down any Group.

SAQ 5.4

Helium has the highest first ionisation energy in the Periodic Table. Suggest which element is likely to have the lowest first ionisation energy and explain why.

Trend of first ionisation energies across Period 4

Period 4 is significantly different from Periods 2 and 3. The d-block (including the transition elements) appears after element 20 (calcium). A 'normal' periodic trend is renewed only at element 31 (gallium), up to element 36 (krypton). Look at the electronic configurations in *table 1.4* on page 13. We see that potassium and calcium have electrons in the 4s orbital but none in the 3d orbitals. From scandium to zinc, electrons add to the 3d orbitals, leaving the 4s occupied. Both 3d and 4s are full at zinc. The next electron adds to a 4p orbital in gallium; the 4p orbitals are full in krypton.

The first ionisation energies across Period 4, for potassium and calcium, then for gallium to krypton, follow a similar pattern to the trend across Period 3. The trend of outer electronic configurations is also similar.

The trend across the d-block elements is different and is affected by the following factors:

- across the elements Sc to Zn the outer electrons are in the 4s orbital;
- the nuclear charge attractions upon the 4s electrons increase from element to element;
- the distance effect is fairly constant, as electrons are added only to inner 3d orbitals;
- the screening effect of the unfilled 3d subshell is low, but repulsive forces between 3d and 4s electrons increase as the 3d electrons increase in number.

The effects are fairly evenly balanced and the overall result is a small general increase in first ionisation energies (with slight variations) as far as zinc.

First ionisation energies and reactivity of elements

Ionisation energies give a measure of the energy required to remove electrons from atoms and form positive ions. The lower the first ionisation energy of an element, the more easily the element forms positive ions during reactions:

$$M(g) \longrightarrow M^+(g) + e^-$$

This is the main reason for the metallic nature of the elements on the 'left' of the Periodic Table (Groups I, II and III) and increasingly metallic nature of elements down all Groups.

- In elements with low first ionisation energies, one or more electrons are relatively free to move from atom to atom in the metallic bonding of the structure.
- The characteristic chemical properties of metallic elements include the formation of positive ions (see page 84 for examples). In the reactions of metals with oxygen, chlorine or water, for example, formation of positive ions is one of several stages

involving enthalpy changes. The elements with low first ionisation energies usually do react more quickly and vigorously. In any Period, the Group I elements (alkali metals) have the lowest first ionisation energies and are the most reactive metals. They also have lower first ionisation energies going 'down' the Group, with increasing proton number, and become much more reactive.

The factors that affect the values of ionisation energies thus also influence the reactivities of many elements.

Periodic patterns of atomic radii

The size of an atom cannot be measured precisely as their electron shells do not define a clear outer limit. However, one measure of the size of an atom is its 'atomic radius'. This can be either the 'covalent radius' or the 'metallic radius' *(figure 5.10)*. **Covalent radius** is half of the distance between the nuclei of neighbouring atoms in molecules. **Metallic radius** is half of the distance between the nuclei of neighbouring atoms in metallic crystals. The covalent radius can be measured for most elements and is usually what is meant when we use the term **atomic radius**.

Atomic radii of elements 1 to 36 are shown in *figure 5.11*. When atomic (covalent) radii are plotted against proton numbers for the first 36 elements, the graph appears as in *figure 5.12*. The noble gases are not included as they do not have covalent radii.

SAQ 5.5

Why do the noble gases not have any measured covalent radii?

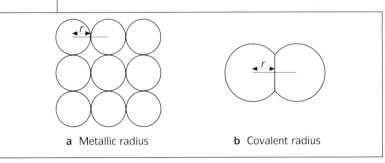

a Metallic radius   **b** Covalent radius

● *Figure 5.10* Metallic and covalent radii.

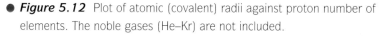

H 0.037																	He –
Li 0.123	Be 0.089											B 0.080	C 0.077	N 0.074	O 0.074	F 0.072	Ne –
Na 0.157	Mg 0.136											Al 0.125	Si 0.117	P 0.110	S 0.104	Cl 0.099	Ar –
K 0.203	Ca 0.174	Sc 0.144	Ti 0.132	V 0.122	Cr 0.117	Mn 0.117	Fe 0.116	Co 0.116	Ni 0.115	Cu 0.117	Zn 0.125	Ga 0.125	Ge 0.122	As 0.121	Se 0.117	Br 0.114	Kr –

● *Figure 5.11* The atomic (covalent) radii of elements 1 to 36, measured in nanometres (nm).

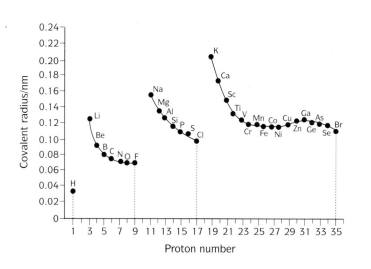

● *Figure 5.12* Plot of atomic (covalent) radii against proton number of elements. The noble gases (He–Kr) are not included.

Note the relative positions of the elements in any one Group, such as Group I (alkali metals) or Group VII (halogens), and across the Periods 2 and 3. The trends *(figure 5.13)* show that atomic radii:

■ increase down a Group;

■ decrease across a Period;

■ after some decrease, are relatively constant across the transition elements, titanium to copper.

Note that the trends in atomi radii are generally in the opposite direction to the trends in first ionisation energies. As atomic radii become larger, first ionisation energies become smaller. In any one atom, both trends are due to the same combined effects of:

■ the size of the nuclear charge;

■ the distance of the outer electron shell from the nucleus;

■ the screening effect of filled inner electron shells upon the outer shell.

Down any one Group, the nuclear charges increase, but the distance and screening effects increase even more, as extra electron shells are added. The overall result is an increase in atomic radii.

Across Periods 2 and 3, the nuclear charges increase from element to element. The distance and screening effects remain fairly constant, because electrons are added to the same outer shell. As the increasing attraction pulls the electrons closer to the nuclei, the radii of the atoms decrease.

Across Period 4, we see a decrease in atomic radii in the first few elements. Then most of the d-block elements have atomic radii that are relatively close in size. After a slight increase for zinc and gallium, there is a slight decrease from germanium to bromine. The combined effects of nuclear charge, distance of the 4s orbitals, and

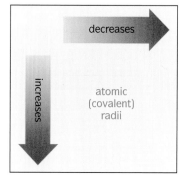

● *Figure 5.13* Trends of atomic (covalent) radii.

H 20																	He 4
Li 1604	Be 2750											B 4200	C 5100	N 77	O 90	F 85	Ne 27
Na 1163	Mg 1390											Al 2720	Si 2950	P 554	S 718	Cl 239	Ar 87
K 1039	Ca 1765	Sc 2750	Ti 3550	V 3650	Cr 2915	Mn 2314	Fe 3160	Co 3150	Ni 3110	Cu 2855	Zn 1181	Ga 2510	Ge 3100	As 886	Se 958	Br 331	Kr 120

● **Figure 5.14** Boiling points of elements 1 to 36, measured in kelvin (K).

repulsions between 3d and 4s electrons are approximately in balance. This is why atomic radii values of the transition elements are relatively similar.

Periodic patterns of boiling points for elements 1 to 36

The variation in boiling points is shown in *figures 5.14* and *5.15*. In any boiling liquid, particles are entering the vapour phase in large numbers. If the forces of attraction between the particles are strong, the boiling point is high; if the forces are weak, the boiling point is low.

Note that the 'peaks' of the graph are occupied by elements from the same Group – carbon and silicon from Group IV. Their extremely high boiling points are due to the strong covalent bonds between atoms of these elements, which exist in the giant molecular lattice structure and persist, to some extent, in the liquid phase. These bonds are broken when the elements boil. Atoms, singly or in groups, separate into the vapour phase.

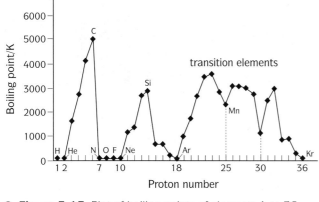

● **Figure 5.15** Plot of boiling points of elements 1 to 36 against proton numbers.

The 'troughs' are occupied by elements that consist of diatomic molecules (H_2, N_2, O_2, F_2, Cl_2, Br_2) or single atoms (He, Ne, Ar, Kr). The forces of attraction between the particles are very weak, even in the liquid phase, and are readily broken. The diatomic molecules or atoms are easily separated from each other as the temperature rises.

Elements in Groups I, II and III occupy similar positions on the rising parts of the curve. Most of the elements in these Groups are metals, and the rising boiling points show that their metallic bonding persists into the liquid phase. The metallic bonding is stronger on moving from Group I to Group II to Group III, as there are more outer-shell electrons available to be mobile and take part in the bonding.

In Period 4, the d-block elements, scandium to copper, have very high boiling points. They are all metals of high density due to small atomic radii and close-packed structures. This leads to particularly strong interatomic, metallic bonding, which must involve the 3d electrons as well as the 4s. Their boiling points are much higher than the s-block metals, potassium and calcium. Zinc has a surprisingly low boiling point, compared with the previous d-block metals. It does not have such strong metallic bonding, due mainly to its electronic configuration of full 3d and 4s orbitals, $[Ar]3d^{10} 4s^2$. You can see why chemists do not include zinc among the transition elements.

SAQ 5.6

Why do both phosphorus (P_4) and sulphur (S_8) occupy low positions on the boiling-point curve but are higher than chlorine?

H																	He
–																	–
Li	Be											B	C	N	O	F	Ne
0.108	0.25											10^{-12}	7×10^{-4}	–	–	–	–
Na	Mg											Al	Si	P	S	Cl	Ar
0.218	0.224											0.382	2×10^{-10}	10^{-17}	10^{-23}	–	–
K	Ca	Sc	Ti	V	Cr	Mn	Fe	Co	Ni	Cu	Zn	Ga	Ge	As	Se	Br	Kr
0.143	0.218	0.015	0.024	0.04	0.078	0.054	0.010	0.16	0.145	0.593	0.167	0.058	2.2×10^{-8}	0.029	0.08	10^{-18}	–

● **Figure 5.16** Electrical conductivities of elements 1 to 36, measured in 10^8 siemens per metre ($10^8\,Sm^{-1}$, or $10^{-8}\,\Omega^{-1}\,m^{-1}$).

Periodic patterns of electrical conductivities

Electrical conductivities are measured in units called 'siemens per metre' (Sm^{-1}). Siemens are the reciprocal of the units of electrical resistance (ohms, Ω), $S = \Omega^{-1}$. *Figure 5.16* shows the known values of electrical conductivities, in units of $10^8\,Sm^{-1}$, for elements up to bromine. Conductivity values give an indication of how easily electrons move through the element. Metallic elements thus have higher electrical conductivities than molecular elements.

SAQ 5.7

a Why do electrical conductivities increase from Group I to Group III elements in Period 3?

b Why are the electrical conductivities of d-block transition elements relatively high, compared with most p-block elements?

Elements of Period 3 with oxygen and chlorine

Sodium metal reacts rapidly with oxygen. Its surface is quickly coated in a layer of sodium oxide when it is freshly exposed to air. This is why sodium is normally stored under oil.

$$4Na(s) + O_2(g) \longrightarrow 2Na_2O(s)$$
sodium oxide

Sodium also burns with a distinctive yellow flame after heating in air or oxygen. A mixture of white oxides is formed, sodium oxide (as above) and sodium peroxide.

$$2Na(s) + O_2(g) \longrightarrow Na_2O_2(s)$$
sodium peroxide

Sodium also burns when heated in chlorine, to form the familiar crystalline 'common salt', sodium chloride:

$$2Na(s) + Cl_2(g) \longrightarrow 2NaCl(s)$$

Both the oxides and the chloride of sodium consist of ionic lattices.

Magnesium metal is normally covered with a layer of its oxide. It burns rapidly in air or oxygen with a brilliant whitish flame *(figure 5.17)*. This reaction is much used in fireworks and warning flares. White, crystalline magnesium oxide is formed.

$$2Mg(s) + O_2(g) \longrightarrow 2MgO(s)$$

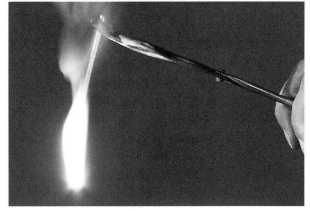

● **Figure 5.17** Magnesium burning in air. The reaction was used in the first photographic flash, and is still used in fireworks and flares.

Magnesium also burns in chlorine to form white, crystalline magnesium chloride:

$$Mg(s) + Cl_2(g) \longrightarrow MgCl_2(s)$$

Both magnesium oxide and magnesium chloride consist of ionic lattices.

Aluminium metal is normally coated with a thin, tough layer of its oxide, which forms very rapidly whenever aluminium is freshly exposed to air. It burns, when powdered, to form more of the white, crystalline aluminium oxide:

$$4Al(s) + 3O_2(g) \longrightarrow 2Al_2O_3(s)$$

The oxide layer on aluminium can be made thicker by an electrolytic process known as **anodising** . Aluminium objects such as cooking pans are made the anode in a cell with dilute sulphuric acid as the electrolyte. The thicker layer protects the metal even more effectively. Aluminium reacts rapidly when heated in chlorine to give the whitish solid aluminium chloride:

$$2Al(s) + 3Cl_2(g) \longrightarrow 2AlCl_3(s)$$

This is an easily vaporised solid, with polar covalent bonding. In the vapour phase it consists of molecules of Al_2Cl_6.

Silicon burns in oxygen, when powdered, to form the white solid oxide, silicon dioxide (silica), which has a giant covalent lattice:

$$Si(s) + O_2(g) \longrightarrow SiO_2(s)$$

Silicon reacts when heated in chlorine to form the colourless volatile liquid, silicon tetrachloride, which consists of covalently bonded molecules:

$$Si(s) + 2Cl_2(g) \longrightarrow SiCl_4(l)$$

Phosphorus reacts very rapidly with oxygen and will ignite without any external heating when exposed to air *(figure 5.18)*. It must be stored under water. In a limited supply of oxygen the main product is the white solid, phosphorus(III) oxide:

$$P_4(s) + 3O_2(g) \longrightarrow P_4O_6(s)$$

With plentiful oxygen, the main product is the white solid, phosphorus(V) oxide:

$$P_4(s) + 5O_2(g) \longrightarrow P_4O_{10}(s)$$

● *Figure 5.18* Phosphorus burning in air. Phosphorus ignites very easily and is used to start the flame on a match.

Both of these oxides consist of molecules, with covalent bonding. Phosphorus combines directly with dry chlorine to give the colourless, volatile liquid, phosphorus trichloride:

$$P_4(s) + 6Cl_2(g) \longrightarrow 4PCl_3(l)$$

With excess chlorine, phosphorus trichloride is converted to the pale yellow solid, phosphorus pentachloride:

$$PCl_3(l) + Cl_2(g) \longrightarrow PCl_5(s)$$

Liquid phosphorus trichloride and vaporised phosphorus pentachloride consist of covalently bonded molecules. Solid phosphorus pentachloride, however, contains ions PCl_4^+ and PCl_6^-.

Sulphur burns easily in air and oxygen, with a blue flame, to form the gas, sulphur dioxide.

$$S(s) + O_2(g) \longrightarrow SO_2(g)$$

Sulphur dioxide reacts with oxygen, when passed over a heated platinum catalyst, to give sulphur trioxide:

$$2SO_2(g) + O_2(g) \rightleftharpoons 2SO_3(g)$$

This reaction is important on an industrial scale. Large amounts of sulphur trioxide are produced to react with water, giving sulphuric acid:

$$SO_3(g) + H_2O(l) \longrightarrow H_2SO_4(aq)$$

Both $SO_2(g)$ and $SO_3(g)$ consist of covalently bonded molecules. For more details about their reactions with water, see page 85.

Chlorine does form oxides but not by direct reaction with oxygen. Some details about chlorine oxides appear in the following sections.

Argon is extremely unreactive and has not yet been persuaded to form any oxides.

The main oxides and chlorides of elements 1 to 36

Figure 5.19 shows the formulae of the oxides and chlorides of elements 1 to 36. There are clear trends:

- The formulae of the compounds show periodic variations; that is, they show a repeating (and thus a fairly predictable) pattern, with increasing proton number. These observations were among the evidence for the concept of periodicity, used by the early developers of the Periodic Table.
- Left to right across the 'typical' Periods 2 and 3, and across Period 4 without the d-block elements, there is a trend from crystalline, ionically bonded compounds to increasingly molecular, covalently bonded compounds.
- Within Groups, compounds have similar formulae. This is particularly clear for elements in Groups I, II and III, which have only one chloride each. There is a larger variety among the molecular oxides and chlorides of Group IV to Group VII.
- The d-block transition elements, but not scandium or zinc, have more than one oxide or chloride. (This is discussed more fully later, on page 90.)

Oxidation numbers/oxidation states

When you look at the formulae of many compounds you see that there are differences in the ratios of the atoms that combine with each other – MgO and Al_2O_3, for example. Chemists have devised various ways for comparing the 'combining ability' of individual elements. One term, much used in the past, but less so nowadays, is **valency** meaning 'strength'. The more useful measure is **oxidation number**. This is a numerical

Main-group elements (Periods 1–4)

Period	Group I	Group II	Group III	Group IV	Group V	Group VI	Group VII
1	H_2O(l), H_2O_2(l), HCl(g)						
2	Li_2O(s), $LiCl$(s)	BeO(s), $BeCl_2$(s)	B_2O_3(s), BCl_3(l)	CO_2(g), CCl_4(l)	N_2O(g), NO(g), NO_2(g), —	O_2(g), —	F_2O(g), —
3	Na_2O(s), Na_2O_2(s), $NaCl$(s)	MgO(s), $MgCl_2$(s)	Al_2O_3(s), $AlCl_3$(s)	SiO_2(s), $SiCl_4$(l)	P_4O_6(s), P_4O_{10}(s), PCl_3(l), PCl_5(s)	SO_2(g), SO_3(g), S_2Cl_2(l)	Cl_2O(g), ClO_2(g), Cl_2O_7(l), Cl_2(g)
4	K_2O(s), KO_2(s), KCl(s)	CaO(s), $CaCl_2$(s)	Ga_2O(s), Ga_2O_3(s), $GaCl_3$(s)	GeO_2(s), $GaCl_4$(l)	As_4O_6(s), As_2O_5(s), $AsCl_3$(l)	SeO_3(s), —	—, $BrCl$(g)

d-block elements (Period 4)

Sc	Ti	V	Cr	Mn	Fe	Co	Ni	Cu	Zn
Sc_2O_3(s), $ScCl_3$(s)	TiO_2(s), $TiCl_4$(l)	V_2O_3(s), VO_2(s), V_2O_5(s), VCl_2(s), VCl_3(s)	Cr_2O_3(s), CrO_3(s), $CrCl_2$(s), $CrCl_3$(s)	MnO(s), MnO_2(s), Mn_2O_3(s), Mn_3O_4(s), $MnCl_2$(s)	FeO(s), Fe_2O_3(s), $FeCl_2$(s), $FeCl_3$(s)	CoO(s), Co_3O_4(s), $CoCl_2$(s)	NiO(s), $NiCl_2$(s)	Cu_2O(s), CuO(s), $CuCl$(s), $CuCl_2$(s)	ZnO(s), $ZnCl_2$(s)

● **Figure 5.19** The formulae of the oxides and chlorides of elements 1 to 36.

value associated with atoms or ions of each element in a compound. Some chemists prefer the term **oxidation state**. The only difference between this and oxidation number is that we say an atom '*has* an oxidation number of +2' but 'is *in* an oxidation state of +2'. Oxidation numbers (abbreviated ox. no.) are used more often.

There are rules for determining the values of oxidation numbers.

■ Oxidation numbers are usually calculated as the number of electrons that atoms have to lose, gain or share, when they form ionic or covalent bonds in compounds.

■ The oxidation number of uncombined elements (that is, not in compounds) is always zero. For example, each atom in $H_2(g)$ or $O_2(g)$ or $Na(s)$ or $S_8(s)$ has an oxidation number of zero; otherwise, the numbers are always given a sign, + or −.

■ For a monatomic ion, the oxidation number of the element is simply the same as the charge on the ion. For example:

ion	Na^+	Ca^{2+}	Cl^-	O^{2-}
ox. no.	+1	+2	−1	−2

■ In a chemical species (compound or ion), with atoms of more than one element, the most electronegative element is given the negative oxidation number. Other elements are given positive oxidation numbers. (For an explanation of the term 'electronegative', see page 36.) For example, in the compound disulphur dichloride, S_2Cl_2, chlorine is more electronegative than sulphur. The two chlorine atoms each have an oxidation number of −1, and thus the two sulphur atoms each have the oxidation number of +1.

■ The oxidation number of hydrogen in compounds is always +1, except in metal hydrides (e.g. NaH), when it is −1.

■ The oxidation number of oxygen in compounds is always −2, except in peroxides (e.g. H_2O_2), when it is −1, or in OF_2, when it is +2.

■ The sum of all the oxidation numbers in a neutral compound is zero. In an ion, the sum equals the overall charge. For example, the sum of the oxidation numbers in $CaCl_2$ is 0; the sum of the oxidation numbers in OH^- is −1.

Some examples of determining oxidation numbers will now be shown:

In CO_2 the ox. no. of each O atom is −2, giving a total of −4
CO_2 is neutral
the ox. no. of C is +4

In $MgCl_2$ the ox. no. of Mg is +2
the ox. no. of each Cl is −1

In NO_3^- the ox. no. of each O is −2
total for O_3 is −6
the overall charge on the ion is −1
therefore ox. no. of N in NO_3^- is +5

SAQ 5.8

What is the oxidation number of: C in CO_3^{2-}; Al in Al_2Cl_6?

Oxidation numbers across Period 3

Look at the formulae of the oxides and chlorides of elements in Period 3 in *figure 5.19*. In these compounds, the oxygen and chlorine are more electronegative than the other elements. This means that, across the Period, the elements have positive oxidation numbers in their oxides and chlorides. An account of oxidation numbers by Groups is given below.

■ *Group I*
Sodium forms only the ion Na^+ and has the ox. no. +1.

■ *Group II*
Magnesium forms only the ion Mg^{2+} and has the ox. no. +2.

■ *Group III*
Aluminium forms the ion Al^{3+} or shares three electrons and has ox. no. +3.

■ *Group IV*
Silicon shares four electrons and has the ox. no. +4.

■ *Group V*
Phosphorus has several ox. no. with the highest at +5. In P_4O_6 (phosphorus(III) oxide) and PCl_3 (phosphorus trichloride), it shares three electrons per P atom and has ox. no. of +3. In P_4O_{10} (phosphorus(V) oxide) and PCl_5 (phosphorus pentachloride), it shares five electrons per P atom and has an ox. no. of +5.

■ *Group VI*

Sulphur has several ox. no. with the highest at +6 . In S_2Cl_2 (disulphur dichloride) it shares one electron per S atom and has an ox. no. of +1. In SCl_2 (sulphur dichloride) it shares two electrons and has an ox. no. of +2. In SO_2 (sulphur dioxide) it shares four electrons and has an ox. no. of +4. In SO_3 (sulphur trioxide) it shares six electrons and has an ox. no. of +6.

■ *Group VII*

Chlorine has several ox. no. with the highest at +7. In Cl_2O (dichlorine oxide or chlorine(I) oxide) it has an ox. no. of +1. In ClO_2 (chlorine dioxide or chlorine(IV) oxide) it has an ox. no. of +4. In Cl_2O_7 (chlorine(VII) oxide) it has an ox. no. of +7.

Action of water with elements and compounds of Period 3

The action of water with these elements and compounds is summarised in *table 5.2*.

Note on acidity and alkalinity

Acidity, alkalinity or neutrality of solutions depend upon the relative concentrations of hydrogen ions, $H^+(aq)$, and hydroxide ions, $OH^-(aq)$:

■ excess $H^+(aq)$ gives acidic solutions of pH below 7;

■ excess $OH^-(aq)$ gives alkaline solutions of pH above 7;

■ equal concentrations of $H^+(aq)$ and $OH^-(aq)$ give neutral solutions of pH 7.

Compounds that do not react with water may still be classified as **acidic** if they react with alkalis, or **basic** if they react with acids. If they react with both acids and alkalis, they are described as **amphoteric**.

Action of water with the elements of Period 3

Sodium melts, floats and fizzes in a rapid, exothermic reaction with cold water (*figure 5.20*). Hydrogen is evolved and a solution of sodium

Element	Na	Mg	Al	Si	P	S	Cl	Ar
Element + water	vigorous H_2 evolved	slow/cold fast/steam H_2 evolved	slow	none	none	none	some dissolves	none
pH of solution	14 strongly alkaline	9–11 weakly alkaline	–	–	–	–	2–5 acidic	–
Formulae of oxides	$Na_2O(s)$ $Na_2O_2(s)$	$MgO(s)$	$Al_2O_3(s)$	$SiO_2(s)$	$P_4O_{10}(s)$ $P_4O_6(s)$	$SO_3(g)$ $SO_2(g)$	$Cl_2O_7(l)$ $Cl_2O(g)$	–
Oxides + water	dissolves and reacts	slightly soluble	no reaction	no reaction	dissolves and reacts	dissolves and reacts	dissolves and reacts	–
pH of solution	14 strongly alkaline	9 slightly alkaline	–	–	1 strongly acidic	1 strongly acidic	1 strongly acidic	
Formulae of chlorides	$NaCl(s)$	$MgCl_2(s)$	$AlCl_3(s)$	$SiCl_4(l)$	$PCl_3(l)$ $PCl_5(s)$	$S_2Cl_2(l)$	$Cl_2(g)$	–
Chlorides + water	dissolves; no obvious reaction		reaction with water : HCl fumes produced				some Cl_2 dissolves	–
pH of solution	7 neutral	6.5 slightly acidic	3 acidic	2 acidic	2 acidic	2 acidic	2 acidic	–

● **Table 5.2** Action of water with the elements of Period 3 and their oxides and chlorides

hydroxide remains.

$$2Na(s) + 2H_2O(l)$$
$$\longrightarrow 2Na^+(aq) + 2OH^-(aq) + H_2(g)$$

The solution is highly alkaline, owing to the large excess of OH^- ions formed. This is why the chemical family containing sodium is called the 'alkali metals'. The first ionisation energy of sodium is relatively low (see page 9). Atoms in the metal form sodium ions (Na^+) rapidly during the reaction, when the single 3s electron is removed.

Magnesium reacts very slowly with cold water. A little hydrogen and magnesium hydroxide are formed over a few days.

$$Mg(s) + 2H_2O(l)$$
$$\longrightarrow Mg^{2+}(aq) + 2OH^-(aq) + H_2(g)$$

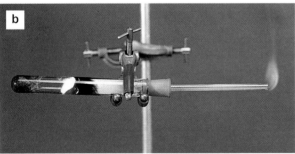

● **Figure 5.20**

a Sodium reacting with water. Note how the exothermic reaction has raised the temperature above the melting point of sodium.

b Apparatus to show the reaction of magnesium with steam. The steam is generated by heating material soaked in water at the left-hand end of the test-tube.

The aqueous solution is weakly alkaline. When water, as steam, is passed over heated magnesium, there is a rapid reaction (*figure 5.20*). Hydrogen is released and magnesium oxide remains.

$$Mg(s) + H_2O(g) \longrightarrow MgO(s) + H_2(g)$$

Aluminium appears, at first, not to react with water at all. This is because the outer layer is not aluminium metal in contact with water, but a thin, strongly bonded layer of aluminium oxide. The oxide layer protects the metal underneath from attack by water. We can use aluminium as a strong, light metal for construction in buildings, ships, aircraft and cooking vessels only because of the tough, comparatively unreactive, oxide layer (*figure 5.21*). The oxide layer may be removed from aluminium using mercury or its compounds. Then aluminium shows that it is quite a reactive metal with water and aluminium hydroxide forms on the surface. Mercury and its compounds are not welcome around any aluminium construction!

● **Figure 5.21** This shopping mall in Saudi Arabia is made almost entirely of aluminium. Do not spill any mercury if you go shopping there!

Silicon, **phosphorus** and **sulphur** do not react with water.

Chlorine reacts slowly with water forming chloric(I) acid (hypochlorous acid). This decomposes readily to oxygen and hydrochloric acid.

$$Cl_2(g) + H_2O(l)$$
$$\longrightarrow H^+(aq) + Cl^-(aq) + HClO(aq)$$
$$2HClO(aq) \longrightarrow 2H^+(aq) + 2Cl^-(aq) + O_2(g)$$

SAQ 5.9

Why are alkaline materials added occasionally to swimming pools treated with chlorine?

Oxides of Period 3 elements with water

Across Period 3 there is a general trend from the formation of a strongly alkaline solution by the ionic oxide in Group I (Na_2O), to the formation of increasingly acidic solutions by the molecular oxides of Groups V to VII. Between these extremes lie the basic oxide of Group II (MgO), the insoluble amphoteric oxide of Group III (Al_2O_3) and the insoluble but acidic oxide of Group IV (SiO_2).

Oxides of sodium and magnesium

Sodium oxide has an ionic lattice structure of Na^+ and O^{2-} ions. Water can separate the ions in the lattice and react with the oxide ions. This gives an excess of hydroxide ions in the aqueous solution, which is strongly alkaline.

$$(Na^+)_2O^{2-}(s) + H_2O(l) \longrightarrow 2Na^+(aq) + 2OH^-(aq)$$
$$\text{aqueous sodium hydroxide}$$

Magnesium oxide has strong ionic bonding in the crystal structure and only reacts very slowly with water to form a suspension of magnesium hydroxide.

$$MgO(s) + H_2O(l) \longrightarrow Mg(OH)_2(s)$$

This is slightly alkaline. It is used in some 'antacids', such as 'Milk of Magnesia' to treat indigestion caused by excess acid in the stomach.

Oxides of aluminium and silicon

Aluminium oxide has a very stable crystal structure. The small, highly charged Al^{3+} ions are so strongly attracted to the O^{2-} ions that the oxide ion's electrons are partially shared with the aluminium ions. This gives the bonding some covalent character and the bonds are very strong. Water has hardly any effect upon such a structure – the solubility is extremely low.

Silicon dioxide (silica) has a stable network structure with strong covalent bonds. The solubility in water is extremely low. This is why sand does not dissolve away rapidly in the sea.

Oxides of phosphorus, sulphur and chlorine

The reactions of the Group V to Group VII molecular oxides with water give an excess of hydrogen ions and hence acidic solutions in each case. For example:

$$P_4O_{10}(s) + 6H_2O(l) \longrightarrow 4H_3PO_4(aq)$$
$$\rightleftharpoons 4H^+(aq) + 4H_2PO_4^-(aq)$$
$$\text{aqueous phosphoric(v) acid}$$

$$SO_2(g) + H_2O(l) \longrightarrow H_2SO_3(aq)$$
$$\rightleftharpoons H^+(aq) + HSO_3^-(aq)$$
$$\text{aqueous sulphurous acid}$$

Sulphur dioxide appears in the atmosphere when the sulphur compounds that are present in many fossil fuels burn in air. Its reaction with water, to form sulphurous acid solution, which is quickly oxidised to sulphuric acid, contributes to the problem of 'acid rain'.

The reaction of sulphur trioxide with water is important on an industrial scale as it produces the essential chemical, sulphuric acid:

$$SO_3(g) + H_2O(l) \longrightarrow H_2SO_4(aq)$$

The reactions of the chlorine oxides are:

$$Cl_2O_7(l) + H_2O(l) \longrightarrow 2HClO_4(aq)$$
dichlorine heptoxide   chloric(VII) acid

$$Cl_2O(g) + H_2O(l) \longrightarrow 2HClO(aq)$$
dichlorine oxide   chloric(I) acid (hypochlorous acid)

Chlorides of Period 3 elements with water

All the chlorides of Period 3 elements dissolve readily in water. Across the Period there is a general trend of increasing speed of reaction and increasing acidity of the solutions.

Chlorides of sodium and magnesium

The ionic crystal lattices of sodium chloride and magnesium chloride dissolve easily in water. This releases the hydrated ions of sodium or magnesium and chloride ions into solution. For example:

$$NaCl(s) + H_2O(l) \longrightarrow Na^+(aq) + Cl^-(aq)$$

Sodium chloride solution is neutral (pH = 7). Aqueous magnesium chloride solution is faintly acidic (pH = 6.5). This is due to an effect of magnesium ions on water, which releases some hydrogen ions from water molecules.

Aluminium chloride

The structure of aluminium chloride is molecular and the bonding is polar covalent. Anhydrous aluminium chloride 'fumes' in moist air by releasing hydrogen chloride.

$$AlCl_3(s) + 3H_2O(l)$$
$$\longrightarrow Al(OH)_3(s) + 3HCl(g)$$

In plenty of water, aluminium chloride dissolves rapidly and exothermically, giving fumes of hydrogen chloride and a strongly acidic solution. The aqueous solution contains hydrated aluminium ions and chloride ions.

$$AlCl_3(s) + water$$
$$\longrightarrow Al^{3+}(aq) + 3Cl^-(aq)$$

The very small, highly charged aluminium ions affect the surrounding water molecules and many hydrogen ions are released, increasing the acidity of the solution.

Chlorides of silicon, phosphorus and sulphur

The molecular, covalent chlorides of silicon, phosphorus and sulphur react very rapidly and exothermically with water. The reactions produce oxides of the elements and hydrogen chloride. Much of the hydrogen chloride dissolves in the water to give an excess of aqueous hydrogen ions

and strongly acidic solutions. For example:

$$SiCl_4(l) + 2H_2O(l) \longrightarrow SiO_2(s) + 4H^+(aq) + 4Cl^-(aq)$$

silicon dioxide   hydrochloric acid

$$PCl_3(l) + 3H_2O(l) \longrightarrow H_3PO_3(aq) + 3H^+(aq) + 3Cl^-(aq)$$

phosphoric acid   hydrochloric acid

$$2S_2Cl_2(l) + 2H_2O(l) \longrightarrow 3S(s) + SO_2(g) + 4H^+(aq) + 4Cl^-(aq)$$

hydrochloric acid

Transition elements

The term 'transition elements' is used for a particular set of elements in the Periodic Table. They are part of the set of 'd-block elements', whose electronic configurations change, with increasing proton number, by addition of electrons to their d subshells. The transition elements in Period 4 are also often called the '*first-row* transition elements' as they are in the first row of the d-block.

The Period 4 part of the d-block contains ten elements from scandium (21) to zinc (30). Scandium and zinc are not typical members of the set, as their properties show significant differences from the other elements, titanium (22) to copper (29). This is why most chemists do not regard scandium and zinc as transition elements.

Transition elements are now generally agreed to be d-block elements that can form one or more stable ions which have incompletely filled d orbitals.

The Period 4 (first-row) transition elements are thus elements 22 to 29, titanium to copper.

Electronic configurations of Period 4 transition elements

The electronic configurations of some of the d-block elements from scandium to zinc are shown in detail in chapter 1 (page 13). Two examples are:

iron, Fe (26 electrons) $1s^2\ 2s^2\ 2p^6\ 3s^2\ 3p^6\ 3d^6\ 4s^2$
copper, Cu (29 electrons) $1s^2\ 2s^2\ 2p^6\ 3s^2\ 3p^6\ 3d^{10}\ 4s^1$

The distribution among the five d orbitals is seen in the 'box' configuration below, where [Ar] represents $1s^2\ 2s^2\ 2p^6\ 3s^2\ 3p^6$:

The configuration of copper, with full 3d orbitals and a single 4s electron, may seem strange. It appears that the symmetrical charge distribution of the completely full 3d orbitals is more stable (has lower energy) than partially filled 3d orbitals and a full 4s.

Iron and copper both form two ions with different charges:

the iron(II) ion is $\quad Fe^{2+}$ $[Ar]3d^6$ (loss of two 4s electrons)

the iron(III) ion is $\quad Fe^{3+}$ $[Ar]3d^5$ (loss of two 4s and one 3d electrons)

the copper(I) ion is $\quad Cu^+$ $[Ar]3d^{10}$ (loss of one 4s electron)

the copper(II) ion is $\quad Cu^{2+}$ $[Ar]3d^9$ (loss of one 4s and one 3d electrons)

Characteristics of transition elements

The main characteristics of Period 4 (first-row) transition elements are as follows:

- They are all metals with high melting points, boiling points and densities compared with other metals such as sodium, potassium or magnesium.
- Their atomic radii, ionic radii and first ionisation energies show only small variations compared with the trends for elements across Period 3 and s-block and p-block elements in Period 4.
- In their ions and compounds they can exist in a variety of oxidation states.
- They form complex ions with many different ligands (for explanation of the term *ligand*, see page 92).
- Many of their complex ions are coloured.
- The elements themselves and their ions can act as catalysts for many reactions. These reactions are often of industrial and biological importance.

Trends in some atomic properties of transition elements

Atomic radii

There is a small decrease from titanium to chromium; then the radii are almost equal up to copper (*figure 5.22*). The variations in the atomic

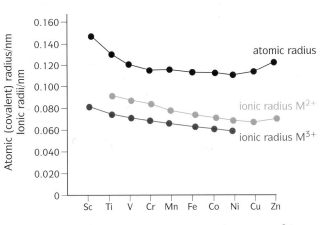
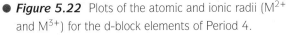

● **Figure 5.22** Plots of the atomic and ionic radii (M^{2+} and M^{3+}) for the d-block elements of Period 4.

radii of elements are due to the combination of effects explained on page 79.

Ionic radii

We shall compare only ions of charge M^{2+} and M^{3+}. The effect of increasing nuclear charge upon the 3d electrons in the ions causes a small decrease in ionic radii of all ions across the Period 4 transition elements (*figure 5.22*).

First ionisation energies

The general trend in first ionisation energies of the elements shows a small increase from titanium to copper (*figure 5.23*). The variation is much less than across the elements of Period 3. The same effects that produce the trend of a slight reduction in atomic radii also cause the trend of a small increase in first ionisation energies.

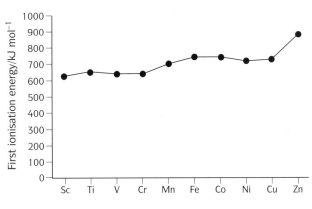

● **Figure 5.23** Plot of the first ionisation energy for the d-block elements of Period 4.

Variable oxidation numbers/states of transition elements

In discussion of the transition elements, we shall use the term 'oxidation state'. Most of the transition elements are able to lose or share electrons from the 4s orbital and some electrons from the 3d orbitals. This leads to a variety of oxidation states for different ions and compounds. *Table 5.3* below shows the variety of oxidation states for the Period 4 transition elements. Scandium and zinc are included for comparison.

Redox: oxidation and reduction

The term **redox** is used for the simultaneous processes of *red*uction and *ox*idation. Originally oxidation and reduction were related only to reactions of oxygen and hydrogen. They now include any reactions in which electrons are transferred.

For example, consider what happens when iron reacts with oxygen and chlorine.

 (i) with oxygen:
  $$4Fe(s) + 3O_2(g) \longrightarrow 2Fe_2O_3(s)$$
(ii) with chlorine:
  $$2Fe(s) + 3Cl_2(g) \longrightarrow 2FeCl_3(s)$$

In both of these reactions, each iron atom has lost three electrons and changed oxidation state from 0 in Fe(s) to +3 in $Fe_2O_3(s)$ and $FeCl_3(s)$.

$$Fe \longrightarrow Fe^{3+} + 3e^-$$
ox. no. $\qquad 0 \qquad +3$

This is oxidation. In all **oxidation** reactions, atoms of an element in a chemical species lose electrons and increase their oxidation numbers.

In reaction (i) above, the oxygen atoms each gain two electrons and change oxidation state from 0 in $O_2(g)$ to -2 in $Fe_2O_3(s)$.

$$O_2 + 4e^- \longrightarrow 2O^{2-}$$
ox. no. of atoms $\quad 0 \qquad\qquad -2$

Element	Sc $3d^1 4s^2$	Ti $3d^2 4s^2$	V $3d^3 4s^2$	Cr $3d^5 4s^1$	Mn $3d^5 4s^2$	Fe $3d^6 4s^2$	Co $3d^7 4s^2$	Ni $3d^8 4s^2$	Cu $3d^{10} 4s^1$	Zn $3d^{10} 4s^2$
									+1	
		+2	+2	+2	+2	+2	+2	+2	+2	+2
	+3	+3	+3	+3	+3	+3	+3	+3	+3	
		+4	+4	+4	+4	+4	+4	+4		
			+5	+5	+5	+5	+5			
				+6	+6	+6				
					+7					
Oxides										
+1									Cu_2O	
+2					MnO	FeO	CoO	NiO	CuO	ZnO
+3	Sc_2O_3	Ti_2O_3	V_2O_3	Cr_2O_3		Fe_2O_3	Co_2O_3			
+4		TiO_2			MnO_2					
+5			V_2O_5							
+6				CrO_3						
+7					Mn_2O_7					
Chlorides										
+1									CuCl	
+2				$CrCl_2$	$MnCl_2$	$FeCl_2$	$CoCl_2$	$NiCl_2$	$CuCl_2$	$ZnCl_2$
+3	$ScCl_3$	$TiCl_3$	VCl_3	$CrCl_3$	$MnCl_3$	$FeCl_3$				
+4		$TiCl_4$								
+5										
+6										

● **Table 5.3** Oxidation states of the d-block elements in Period 4. The most common oxidation states are shown underlined.

Similarly, in reaction (ii), chlorine atoms each gain one electron and change oxidation state from 0 to −1.

$$Cl_2 + 2e^- \longrightarrow 2Cl^-$$
ox. no. of atoms   0   −1

These are processes of **reduction**. In all reduction reactions, atoms of an element in a chemical species gain electrons and decrease their oxidation numbers.

We call reactions, such as (i) and (ii) above, redox reactions, as both oxidation and reduction take place at the same time. Any chemical system in which the oxidised and reduced forms of a chemical species exist is a **redox system**. The chemical that *gains* electrons acts as an **oxidising agent**; the chemical that *loses* electrons acts as a **reducing agent**.

Redox systems and transition elements

Transition elements can exist in different oxidation states. In many of their reactions they change from one oxidation state to another by losing or gaining electrons, that is, by oxidation or reduction. Three examples of redox systems are now described:

- *iron(II) ions and iron(III) ions*: $Fe^{2+}(aq)/Fe^{3+}(aq)$
  These ions are converted from one to the other by loss or gain of electrons.

  $$Fe^{2+}(aq) \rightleftharpoons Fe^{3+}(aq) + e^-$$

- *Manganate(VII) ions and manganese(II) ions*: MnO_4^-/Mn^{2+}
  An aqueous solution of potassium manganate(VII), $KMnO_4$ (sometimes known as potassium permanganate), contains manganate(VII) ions, $MnO_4^-(aq)$, and has a purple colour. It is a powerful oxidising agent and, in an acidified solution, is reduced to manganese(II) ions, $Mn^{2+}(aq)$. Each manganese atom in MnO_4^- changes its oxidation state from +7 to +2 in Mn^{2+} by gaining five electrons.

  $$MnO_4^-(aq) + 8H^+(aq) + 5e^- \\ \longrightarrow Mn^{2+}(aq) + 4H_2O(l)$$

- *Dichromate(VI) ions and chromium(III) ions*: $Cr_2O_7^{2-}(aq)/Cr^{3+}(aq)$
  A solution of potassium dichromate(VI), $K_2Cr_2O_7$, contains dichromate(VI) ions, $Cr_2O_7^{2-}(aq)$, and has an orange colour. In acidified solution it is a powerful oxidising agent and the dichromate(VI) ions are reduced to chromium(III) ions, $Cr^{3+}(aq)$. Each chromium atom in $Cr_2O_7^{2-}$ changes its oxidation state from +6 to +3 in Cr^{3+} by gaining three electrons.

$$Cr_2O_7^{2-}(aq) + 14H^+(aq) + 6e^- \\ \longrightarrow 2Cr^{3+}(aq) + 7H_2O(l)$$

Using redox systems

The redox systems described above may be used for chemical analysis. The purple colour of $MnO_4^-(aq)$ is changed to colourless $Mn^{2+}(aq)$ by soluble reducing agents in acidified solutions. Similarly the orange colour of $Cr_2O_7^{2-}(aq)$ changes to green $Cr^{3+}(aq)$. These colour changes are used as tests for soluble reducing gases such as sulphur dioxide, SO_2, and hydrogen sulphide, H_2S. The well known alcohol, ethanol, C_2H_5OH, is oxidised to the aldehyde, ethanal, CH_3CHO, by warm acidified potassium dichromate(VI). The orange to green colour change has been used as the basis of the 'breathalyser' test for detecting ethanol levels in breath *(figure 5.24)*.

Both potassium manganate(VII) and potassium dichromate(VI) are used for more accurate quantitative analysis of chemicals.

For example, the quantity of 'soluble iron' in 'iron tablets' may be measured by titration of $KMnO_4$, of known concentration, with an acidified

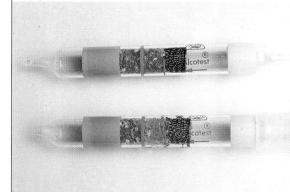

● *Figure 5.24* A redox reaction at work. Alcohol (ethanol) in exhaled air changes the colour of the acidified potassium dichromate crystals from yellow to green. This colourful detector has now been replaced by electronic breathalysers.

solution of the tablets *(figure 5.25)*. The tablets contain soluble iron(II) sulphate and release $Fe^{2+}(aq)$ ions into solution. In acid conditions the $Fe^{2+}(aq)$ ions are oxidised to $Fe^{3+}(aq)$ by the $MnO_4^-(aq)$ ions and the MnO_4^- ions are reduced to $Mn^{2+}(aq)$. As the manganate(VII) solution is added to the iron(II) solution, the purple colour of $MnO_4^-(aq)$ ions disappears. When the purple colour just appears in excess the redox reaction is complete. The reaction equation is found by adding the two 'half-equations' for oxidation and reduction. Five electrons are transferred.

(i) oxidation half-equation:
$$5Fe^{2+}(aq) \longrightarrow 5Fe^{3+}(aq) + 5e^-$$

(ii) reduction half-equation:
$$MnO_4^-(aq) + 8H^+(aq) + 5e^-$$
$$\longrightarrow Mn^{2+}(aq) + 4H_2O(l)$$

Full redox equation:
$$MnO_4^-(aq) + 8H^+(aq) + 5Fe^{2+}(aq)$$
$$\longrightarrow Mn^{2+}(aq) + 5Fe^{3+}(aq) + 4H_2O(l)$$

The reacting volumes may be measured accurately by burette (MnO_4^-) and pipette (Fe^{2+}). With these volumes and a known concentration of $KMnO_4$, the concentration of $Fe^{2+}(aq)$ ions in the solution of tablets may be calculated.

● *Figure 5.25* Measuring the concentration of iron(II) ions in a solution of 'iron tablets' by titration with potassium manganate(VII).

SAQ 5.10

Concentrations of iron(II) in compounds may be measured by the redox reaction of $Fe^{2+}(aq)$ ions with dichromate(VI) ions in acidified conditions. What are the oxidation and reduction half-equations and the full redox equation?

Reactions of transition elements to form complex ions

Everyone studying chemistry knows that copper sulphate is blue. A little more investigation shows that solutions of many copper salts in water are also blue. If ammonia solution is added, however, the solution changes to a very deep blue.

The pale blue colour of aqueous solutions of copper compounds is due to the presence of the hydrated copper ion $Cu^{2+}(aq)$. This is a complex ion $[Cu(H_2O)_6]^{2+}$ in which six water molecules are attached to each copper ion in an octahedral arrangement *(figure 5.26)*.

$[Cu(H_2O)_6]^{2+}$ is a typical complex ion. In general, complex ions have a central metal cation surrounded by a number of ligands, which are molecules or negative ions. **Ligands** must contain atoms with non-bonded electron-pairs (lone-pairs), which can be used for bonding by sharing with the central cation in a coordinate (dative covalent) bond. Coordinate bonds are shown as arrows in the diagram of the hydrated copper complex ion.

Water (H_2O) and ammonia (NH_3) are typical ligands. Oxygen and nitrogen atoms have non-bonded electron pairs in these compounds. When ammonia solution is added to a copper salt solution, ammonia molecules replace four of the water ligands

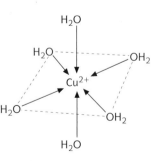

● *Figure 5.26* The complex ion $[Cu(H_2O)_6]^{2+}$. The H_2O molecules are 'ligands' surrounding the copper(II) ion in an octahedral arrangement.

to give the complex ion $[Cu(NH_3)_4(H_2O)_2]^{2+}$ (*figure 5.27b*).

$$[Cu(H_2O)_6]^{2+}(aq) + 4NH_3(aq)$$
hexaaquacopper(II)
pale blue

$$\longrightarrow [Cu(NH_3)_4(H_2O)_2]^{2+}(aq) + 4H_2O(l)$$
tetraamminecopper(II)
dark blue

Water and ammonia are neutral ligands. Other ligands include negative ions such as chloride ions (Cl^-), cyanide ions (CN^-) and thiocyanate ions (SCN^-). When potassium thiocyanate is added to a pale yellow solution containing iron(III) ions, a deep blood-red solution is formed (*figure 5.27c*). The change in colour is due to an exchange of ligands (SCN^- for H_2O) in the complex ion containing iron(III).

$$[Fe(H_2O)_6]^{3+}(aq) + SCN^-(aq)$$
hexaaquairon(III) ion
pale yellow

$$\longrightarrow [Fe(SCN)(H_2O)_5]^{2+}(aq) + H_2O(l)$$
pentaaquathiocyanatoiron(III) ion
blood red

Note that the replacement of a neutral water molecule ligand by a negative thiocyanate ion ligand changes the overall charge of the complex ion from 3+ to 2+.

The names of these complex ions look rather complicated, but it will help to remember that:

■ 'tetra' means four; 'penta' means five; 'hexa' means six;

■ 'ammine' means ammonia molecules; 'aqua' means water molecules; 'thiocyanato' means thiocyanate ions;

■ in cationic (positively charged) complex ions, the metal ion keeps its normal name and oxidation number, e.g. iron(III) or copper(II);

■ in anionic (negatively charged) complex ions, the metal changes its name to a Latin form with an -ate ending, e.g. the complex ion $[CuCl_4]^{2-}$ is the tetrachlorocuprate(II) ion, and the complex ion $[Fe(CN)_6]^{3-}$ is the hexacyanoferrate(III) ion.

Coloured ions of transition elements

The Period 4 transition elements, titanium to copper, have a variety of coloured ions (*figure 5.27a*). This is due to the effect of ligands upon the orbitals of the metal cation. Typical examples of coloured ions in aqueous solution are shown in *table 5.4*.

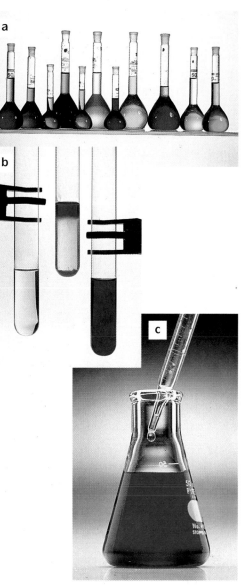

● *Figure 5.27* Some of the strongly coloured solutions of compounds of transition elements.

a From left to right, these solutions contain ions in the order listed in *table 5.4*.

b The change of colour, from pale blue to dark blue, as ammonia solution is added to copper(II) sulphate in water.

c This solution contains the complex ion $[Fe(SCN)(H_2O)_5]^{2+}_{(aq)}$.

Titanium	Vanadium	Chromium	Manganese	Iron	Cobalt	Nickel	Copper
$Ti^{3+}(aq)$ violet	$V^{3+}(aq)$ green	$Cr^{3+}(aq)$ green	$Mn^{2+}(aq)$ pale pink	$Fe^{3+}(aq)$ yellow	$Co^{2+}(aq)$ pink	$Ni^{2+}(aq)$ green	$Cu^{2+}(aq)$ blue
	$VO^{2+}(aq)$ blue	$Cr_2O_7^{2-}(aq)$ orange	$MnO_4^-(aq)$ purple				

● *Table 5.4* Coloured ions of transition elements

The colours of ions are often used to detect transition elements in solution. For example, the deep blue of the copper–ammonia complex ion, $[Cu(NH_3)_4(H_2O)_2]^{2+}$ is used to detect copper. The blood red $[Fe(SCN)(H_2O)_5]^{2+}$ detects iron(III) ions. Cobalt has a chloro complex ion $CoCl_4^{2-}$ that is blue. In water the blue colour changes to the pink of the hydrated cobalt(II) ion $[Co(H_2O)_6]^{2+}$. This change is used as a simple test for the presence of water.

Ligand exchange

When ammonia solution is added to hydrated copper ions, ammonia molecules replace four of the water molecules. This is **ligand exchange**. An important, indeed dangerous, example of ligand exchange occurs in our own bodies. Our blood contains the complex chemical haemoglobin. The essential working part of haemoglobin is a molecule called haem and at the centre of haem is an iron(II) ion Fe^{2+}, coordinated to four nitrogen atoms *(figure 5.28)*. Haemoglobin acts as an agent for transporting oxygen or carbon dioxide in the blood by bonding the oxygen or carbon dioxide weakly to the Fe^{2+}.

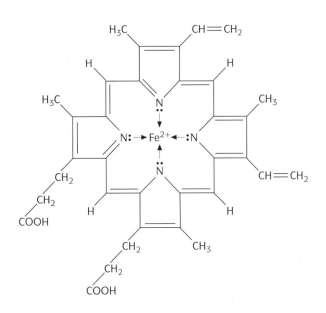

● *Figure 5.28* The haem group in haemoglobin. This is attached to a larger complex protein molecule. Note the Fe^{2+} ion at the centre, coordinated to four nitrogen atoms. It can also accept electrons from other donors such as oxygen or, unfortunately, carbon monoxide.

Unfortunately both oxygen and carbon dioxide are easily replaced by a stronger ligand such as carbon monoxide. Molecules of CO attach themselves to the haem and cannot easily be removed. The carbon monoxide thus prevents the haem molecules from transporting oxygen from the lungs and affects the transport of carbon dioxide to the lungs. Carbon monoxide acts as an effective and rapid poison. People die every year from the effects of inhaling carbon monoxide from defective gas fires. The carbon monoxide in cigarette smoke and exhaust fumes from motors using carbon-based fuels is damaging to health *(figure 5.29)*.

● *Figure 5.29* The visible emissions from car exhausts are not the most dangerous pollutants. Carbon monoxide and nitrogen oxides are invisible but cause more harm.

Transition elements and their compounds as catalysts

Much of the modern chemical industry depends upon catalysts to increase the rate of production. Transition elements and their compounds provide many important industrial catalysts. Some examples are listed below.

■ Titanium(IV) chloride, $TiCl_4$, is used to catalyse the important polymerisation of ethene to poly(ethene) better known as 'Polythene'.

$$nC_2H_4 \longrightarrow (-CH_2-CH_2-)_n$$

■ Vanadium(V) oxide, V_2O_5, is used for the contact process for making sulphur trioxide.

This is the first stage in the production of sulphuric acid.

$$2SO_2(g) + O_2(g) \rightleftharpoons 2SO_3(g)$$
$$SO_3(g) + H_2O(l) \longrightarrow H_2SO_4(l)$$

■ Iron as the metal or oxide, Fe_2O_3, is used in the Haber process for making ammonia.

$$N_2(g) + 3H_2(g) \rightleftharpoons 2NH_3(g)$$

■ Many transition elements, usually as their ions, are important as catalysts in very small quantities in biological systems. Here they are called 'trace' elements. We would not survive without small quantities of chromium, manganese, iron, cobalt, nickel and copper helping to keep enzymes working in our bodies.

SUMMARY

■ Early periodic patterns (regularly repeating variations) in the properties of elements were based on the elements in order of their relative atomic masses. The modern Periodic Tables are based on the elements in order of their proton (atomic) numbers.

■ A Group in the Periodic Table contains elements with the same outer-shell electronic configuration but very different proton numbers; the elements and their compounds have many similar chemical properties.

■ Periods in the Periodic Table are sequences of elements, differing by one proton and one electron, from Group I to Group 0.

■ Periodic variations may be observed across Periods in physical properties such as ionisation energies, atomic radii, boiling points and electrical conductivities.

■ The main influences on ionisation energies and atomic radii are: the size of the positive nuclear charge; the distance of the electron from the nucleus; the screening effect on outer electrons by electrons in filled inner shells.

■ Ionisation energies decrease down a Group and tend to increase across a Period; atomic radii increase down a Group and tend to decrease across a Period.

■ Across a Period (left to right, from Group I to Group VII), the structures of the elements change from giant metallic, through giant molecular to simple molecular. Group 0 elements consist of individual atoms.

■ Chemically, the elements change from reactive metals, through less reactive metals and less reactive non-metals to reactive non-metals. Group 0 contains the extremely unreactive noble gases.

■ There are periodic variations in the formulae and properties of oxides and chlorides of elements, from ionic compounds in Group I to molecular covalent compounds in Group VII.

■ Across Period 3, the trend in the reactions of the elements and their oxides and chlorides with water shows decreasing pH in the solutions formed.

■ The atoms or ions of each element in a compound may be assigned an oxidation number. The rules for assigning the numbers are on page 84.

■ First-row (Period 4) transition elements have incompletely filled 3d orbitals in one or more ions. Their outer orbital, 4s, is filled as $4s^2$, except in their ions. Cr and Cu are unusual in having only one electron in the 4s orbital.

■ The characteristic properties of transition elements, titanium to copper, are that they: are metals; have variable oxidation numbers/states; form complex ions with different ligands; often have coloured solid compounds and ions in solutions; will often act as catalysts.

■ The atomic radii, ionic radii and first ionisation energies of transition elements show low variations compared with other sequences of elements in the Periodic Table.

■ In redox reactions, oxidising agents gain electrons and are reduced; reducing agents lose electrons and are oxidised.

Questions

1 A chemistry book claims that 'all transition elements are in the d-block of the Periodic Table but not all d-block elements are transition elements'. Explain, with examples, what this statement means, including what is meant by a **d-block element** and a **transition element**.

2 The label on a bag of garden fungicide says that the bag contains (among other chemicals) a quantity of 'complex copper compounds'.
   a How would you describe in more detail what is meant by a **complex copper compound**?

   b Give **two** examples of complex copper ions and their formulae.
   c How would you attempt to prove the presence of copper compounds in the mixture of garden chemicals?

3 Explain: a why vanadium, chromium and manganese can exist in several oxidation states; b why the first ionisation energies and atomic radii of transition elements do not vary so much as those of the other elements in Period 4.

Carbon compounds: Introduction to organic chemistry

1 name examples of alkanes, alkenes and arenes, and use displayed and structural formulae to recognise or represent these hydrocarbons;

2 use and explain the terms *isomerism*, *structural isomers* and *cis–trans isomerism*, *saturated* and *unsaturated compounds*, *functional group*, *free radical*, *photochemical reaction*, *substitution reaction* and *electrophilic addition reaction*;

3 describe the structure of C–C and C=C bonds in terms of σ and π bonds;

4 describe the model of delocalisation of electrons for benzene;

5 explain the use of crude oil as a source of both aliphatic and aromatic hydrocarbons, and describe how cracking or re-forming can be used to obtain more useful low-molecular-mass hydrocarbons from larger hydrocarbon molecules or other, less directly useful, molecules;

6 show awareness of the reasons for the trend towards the use of unleaded petrols;

7 describe and explain the chemistry of alkenes as shown by **a** combustion, **b** oxidation, **c** addition of hydrogen, water or bromine and **d** polymerisation.

8 explain the mechanism of the electrophilic addition reaction between bromine and alkenes;

9 describe the relative inertness of benzene compared with ethene in electrophilic addition reactions;

10 describe the characteristics of addition polymerisation using poly(ethene) and poly(phenylethene) as examples;

11 show awareness of the difficulties of disposal of poly(alkenes), for example through non-biodegradability or combustion;

12 show awareness of the value to society of the work of chemists in the research, development and production of organic chemicals;

13 explain the shape of, and bond angles in, the ethane, ethene and benzene molecules in terms of σ and π bonds, and predict the shapes of, and bond angles in, other related molecules.

Introduction to the chemistry of carbon compounds

Carbon forms a much greater number and variety of compounds than any other element. Reasons for this include the following.

■ Carbon readily bonds to itself and to most other elements, including metals.

■ Carbon can bond in a variety of ways giving rise to chains, rings and even cages of carbon atoms.

Compounds that contain only carbon and hydrogen atoms are known as hydrocarbons (*figure 6.1*). Organic chemistry includes the study of hydrocarbons and of compounds containing other elements as well as carbon and hydrogen. As single carbon–carbon and carbon–hydrogen bonds are relatively unreactive, the reactions of these compounds are typically those involving particular functional groups. Examples of functional groups include carbon–carbon double bonds (page 106), arene rings (page 111) and hydroxyl and halogen groups.

Organic compounds are also classified as either aliphatic or aromatic. **Aromatic** compounds contain one or more arene rings. They are called aromatic compounds as they have distinctive, usually pleasant, smells. All other organic

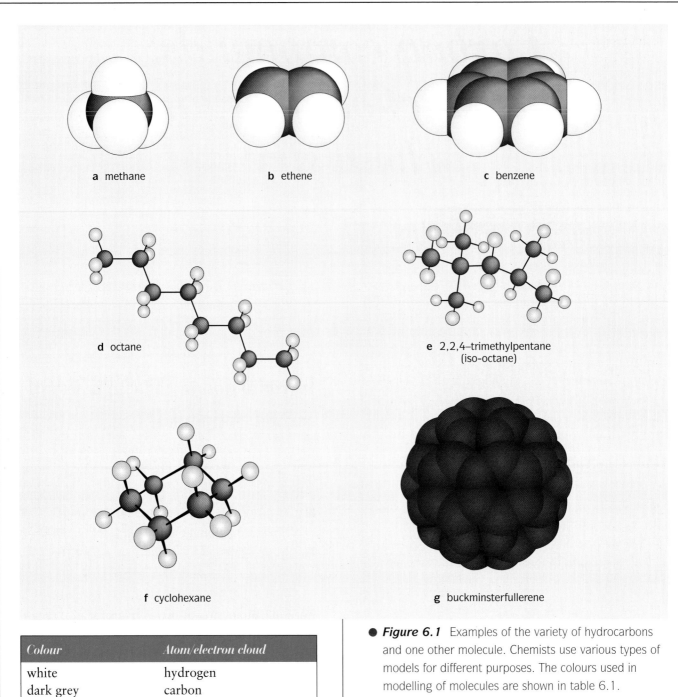

a methane

b ethene

c benzene

d octane

e 2,2,4–trimethylpentane (iso-octane)

f cyclohexane

g buckminsterfullerene

Colour	Atom/electron cloud
white	hydrogen
dark grey	carbon
red	oxygen
blue	nitrogen
green	chlorine
yellow-green	fluorine
orange-brown	bromine
brown	iodine
violet	phosphorus
pale yellow	sulphur
yellow ochre	boron
pink	lone-pair electron clouds
green	π-bond electron clouds

● **Table 6.1** Colours used in molecular modelling

● **Figure 6.1** Examples of the variety of hydrocarbons and one other molecule. Chemists use various types of models for different purposes. The colours used in modelling of molecules are shown in table 6.1.

a-c These hydrocarbons are shown as space-filling models. Such models show the region of space occupied by the atoms and the surrounding electrons.

d-f These hydrocarbons are shown as ball-and-stick models, which enable bonds between atoms to be clearly seen.

g Buckminsterfullerene is not a hydrocarbon but an allotrope of carbon (diamond and graphite are other allotropes), a spherical C_{60} molecule. It is named after the architect who designed geodesic domes. Another model of it is shown on the cover of this book.

compounds are aliphatic. Hence alkanes and alkenes are **aliphatic** compounds, whilst benzene is an aromatic compound.

Different formulae and isomerism

Types of formulae

As well as using different types of models to help visualise molecules, chemists also use different formulae. These include the following.

■ *Molecular formula*
  This simply shows the number of atoms of each element present in the molecule, e.g. the molecular formula of hexane is C_6H_{14}.

■ *Structural formula*
  This shows how the atoms are joined together in a molecule. The structural formula of hexane is $CH_3CH_2CH_2CH_2CH_2CH_3$. More information is conveyed. Hexane is seen to consist of a chain of six carbon atoms; the carbon atoms at each end are joined to one carbon and three hydrogen atoms; the carbon atoms between the two ends are joined to two hydrogen and two carbon atoms.

■ *Displayed formula*
  This shows all the bonds and all the atoms. The displayed formula of hexane is:

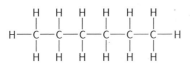

  Displayed formulae are also called full structural formulae. One of their disadvantages is that they are a two-dimensional representation of molecules which are three-dimensional. Compare the displayed formula for hexane with the model in *figure 6.2a*.

■ *Skeletal formula*
  This shows the carbon skeleton only. Hydrogen atoms on the carbon atoms are omitted. Carbon atoms are not labelled. Other types of atom are shown as in a structural formula. Skeletal

formulae are frequently used to show the structures of cyclic hydrocarbons. The skeletal formula of hexane is:

Isomerism

The atoms of hexane can be joined together in five different ways. Try building models of these using six carbon atoms and 14 hydrogen atoms. You should obtain the models shown in *figure 6.2*. Note that these models all have the same molecular formula. Compounds with the same molecular formula but with different structural formulae are known as **structural isomers**.

Naming organic compounds

The names given in *figure 6.2* are the systematic names for the structural isomers of hexane. Such names precisely describe the structure of a molecule and enable chemists to communicate

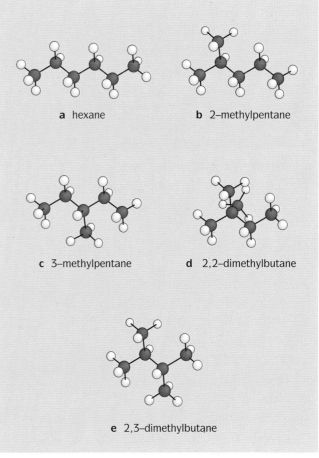

● *Figure 6.2* Models and systematic names of C_6H_{14}.

clearly. International rules have been agreed for the systematic naming of most compounds. The basic rules for naming hydrocarbons are as follows:

1   The number of carbon atoms in the longest chain provides the stem of the name. Simple alkanes consist entirely of unbranched chains of carbon atoms. They are named by adding -ane to this stem as shown in *table 6.2*.

2   Branched-chain alkanes are named in the same way. The name given to the longest continuous carbon chain is then prefixed by the names of the shorter side-chains. The same stems are used with the suffix -yl. Hence CH_3- is methyl (often called a methyl group). In general, such groups are called alkyl groups. The position of an alkyl group is indicated by a number. The carbon atoms in the longest carbon chain are numbered from one end of the chain. Numbering starts from the end that produces the lowest possible numbers for the side chains. For example

$$CH_3CHCH_2CH_2CH_3$$
$$|$$
$$CH_3$$

is 2-methylpentane, not 4-methylpentane.

3   Each side-chain must be included in the name. If there are several identical side-chains, the name is prefixed by di-, tri-, etc. For example 2,2,3-trimethyl- indicates that there are three methyl groups, two on the second and one on the third carbon atom of the longest chain. Note that numbers are separated by commas, whilst a number and a letter are separated by a hyphen.

4   Where different alkyl groups are present, they are placed in alphabetical order as in 3-ethyl-2-methylpentane.

5   Compounds containing a ring of carbon atoms are prefixed by cyclo-. Cyclohexane is represented as

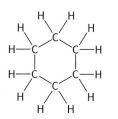

displayed formula   skeletal formula

6   Hydrocarbons may contain alkene or arene groups. These are represented as follows:

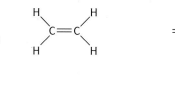

alkene: ethene

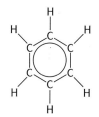

arene: benzene

displayed formulae   skeletal formulae

Hydrocarbons containing one double bond are called alkenes. The same stems are used but are followed by -ene. The position of an alkene double bond is indicated by the lower number of the two carbon atoms involved. This number is placed between the stem and -ene. Hence $CH_3CH=CHCH_3$ is but-2-ene. The simplest arene is benzene. When an alkyl group is attached to a benzene ring, a number is not needed as all

Structural formula	Number of carbon atoms in longest chain	Stem	Name
CH_4	1	meth-	methane
C_2H_6	2	eth-	ethane
C_3H_8	3	prop-	propane
C_4H_{10}	4	but-	butane
C_5H_{12}	5	pent-	pentane
C_6H_{14}	6	hex-	hexane
C_7H_{16}	7	hept-	heptane
C_8H_{18}	8	oct-	octane
C_9H_{20}	9	non-	nonane
$C_{10}H_{22}$	10	dec-	decane
$C_{20}H_{42}$	20	eicos-	eicosane

● **Table 6.2** Naming simple alkanes

carbon atoms are equivalent. Two or more groups will require a number. For example:

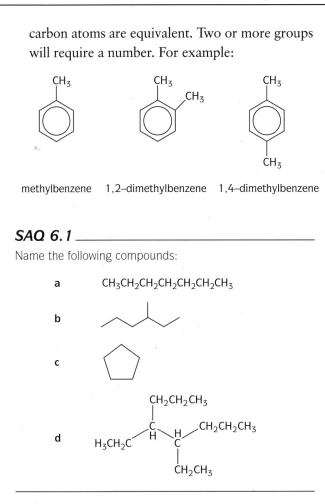

methylbenzene   1,2–dimethylbenzene   1,4–dimethylbenzene

SAQ 6.1

Name the following compounds:

a $CH_3CH_2CH_2CH_2CH_2CH_2CH_3$

b

c

d

SAQ 6.2

Draw displayed formulae for the following compounds:
a 2,2,3-trimethylbutane; **b** cyclobutane;
c 3-ethylpent-2-ene; **d** ethylbenzene.

Alkanes

Sources

The fossil deposits of crude oil and natural gas have been the primary source of alkanes throughout the twentieth century. Much of the wealth of the industrialised world can be ascribed to this one-off exploitation of a natural resource. The vast majority of these deposits have been used to provide fuel for heating, electricity generation and transport. Smaller, but significant, proportions have been used to produce lubricants and to provide a source of hydrocarbons for the chemical process industry. In the UK, the chemical and petrochemical industries are by far the biggest contributors

● *Figure 6.3* Californian crude is rich in cycloalkanes!

towards a positive balance in the value of our trade with the rest of the world. The UK chemical industry employs approximately 5% of our workforce and produces about 9% of total industrial output. More than 41% of its sales are exports.

Naphtha is the fraction of crude oil that is the most important source of chemicals for the chemical process industry. Other fractions and natural gas are of lesser importance.

Crude oil is a complex mixture of hydrocarbons. The composition of oil from different places varies considerably. Three main series of hydrocarbons are present: aromatics, cycloalkanes and alkanes. At a given boiling point, the densities of these decrease in the order aromatic > cycloalkanes > alkanes. This provides a method for comparing the composition of different oils. Naphthenic oils are high in aromatics and cycloalkanes; paraffinic oils are high in alkanes (and hence wax).

A primary fractional distillation column (*figure 6.4*) is designed to separate oil of a particular

● *Figure 6.4* The skyline of an oil refinery is dominated by fractional distillation columns.

composition. After primary distillation, the different hydrocarbon fractions are treated in a variety of different ways. These include processes such as vacuum distillation (to separate less-volatile components such as arenes), desulphurisation (to remove sulphur) and cracking. Cracking involves heating the oil fraction with a catalyst. Under these conditions, high-molecular-mass alkanes are broken down into lower-molecular-mass alkanes as well as alkenes. The alkenes provide a very important feedstock to the chemical industry for making a wide range of products (page 110). Both C–C and C–H bonds are broken in the process. As the bond breaking is a random process, a variety of products, including hydrogen, are possible, and some of the intermediates can react to produce branched-chain alkane isomers. For example a possible reaction equation for decane is

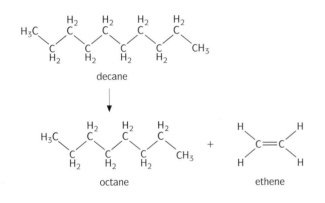

decane

↓

octane + ethene

SAQ 6.3

Write balanced equations showing the structural formulae for some of the possible products formed on cracking pentane.

In the catalytic cracker (*figure 6.5*) the hot, vaporised oil fraction and the catalyst behave as a fluid. The seething mixture is called a 'fluidised bed'. Modern catalysts are based on a type of clay known as a zeolite. In the past, catalysts were discovered by a 'hit-and-miss' process, but it is becoming possible to use computers to design some catalysts such as zeolites. *Figure 6.6* shows a diagram of zeolite Y, used in the catalytic cracker. Some of the hydrocarbon mixture is broken down to carbon, which blocks the pores of the catalyst. The fluidised bed of catalyst is easily pumped into

● *Figure 6.5* A catalytic cracker occupies the bulk of the central part of this photograph.

a regeneration chamber where the carbon coke is burnt off in air at a high temperature, allowing the catalyst to be recycled.

Problems with petrol

Increasing the quantity

Primary distillation of crude oil produces a gasoline fraction that is called 'straight-run' petrol. There is insufficient of this fraction to satisfy the demand for petrol, so naphtha fractions are cracked to produce more gasoline. Petrol produced by cracking is called 'crackate'.

Improving the grade

Around the world, petrol is often graded – 'Normal', 'Premium' or 'Super'. Such grades refer to a range of quality. Early in motoring history, tetra(ethyl)lead was found to be a cheap and easily produced additive that raised the quality of petrol.

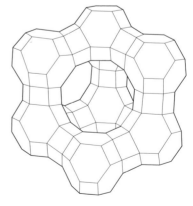

● *Figure 6.6* A computer graphic showing the framework of zeolite Y.

This had an additional advantage of providing further lubrication within the engine, extending its life. Tetra(ethyl)lead together with 1,2-dibromoethane has been added to petrol for many years. (The 1,2-dibromoethane decomposes in the engine, the bromine atoms combining with the lead to produce insoluble lead(II) bromide. This is often seen as a white deposit inside the exhaust pipes of cars that use leaded petrol.)

Changing to unleaded petrol

In the early 1970s concern about the environmental effects of lead began to increase. In particular, evidence was accumulating which suggested that its presence was affecting the intelligence of young children. Despite the evidence and arguments put forward by chemists such as Professor D. Bryce-Smith of Reading University, it was a further ten years before unleaded fuel started to become available in the UK. The major petrol companies said that they could supply unleaded fuel with the required octane number, but it was not until the UK Government made the price of unleaded fuel less than that of leaded fuel that motorists started using it in any significant quantity. The change was also hampered by some car manufacturers who were slow to develop engines that could run on the new fuel.

Unleaded petrol requires more branched alkanes in order to improve its quality. Aromatics such as benzene can also be used for this purpose. Use of benzene has raised a new problem, as it is a dangerous carcinogen. In 1992, when measurements of air pollutants were made in the centre of Cambridge, benzene was detected for the first time as well as ozone and the oxides of nitrogen.

Isomerisation and re-forming provide two routes to increasing the supply of branched alkanes.

Isomerisation involves heating the straight-chain isomers in the presence of a platinum catalyst.

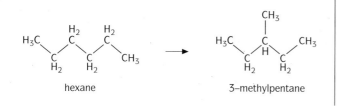

hexane   3–methylpentane

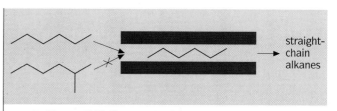

● **Figure 6.7** Shape selectivity by a zeolite catalyst – separation of isomers by a molecular sieve.

The resulting mixture of straight- and branched-chain isomers then has to be separated. This is done by using a molecular sieve, which is another type of zeolite that has pores through which the straight-chain isomers can pass *(figure 6.7)*. The branched-chain isomers are too bulky and thus are separated off; the straight-chain molecules are recycled to the reactor.

Re-forming involves the conversion of alkanes to cycloalkanes, or of cycloalkanes to arenes. Re-forming reactions are catalysed by bimetallic catalysts. For example, a cluster of platinum and rhenium atoms is very effective at dehydrogenating methylcyclohexane to methylbenzene:

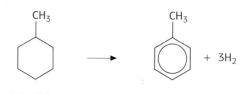

methylcyclohexane   methylbenzene

A catalyst containing clusters of platinum and iridium atoms enables conversion of straight-chain alkanes to arenes:

hexane   benzene

Properties of alkanes

The geometry of alkane molecules is based on the tetrahedral arrangement of four covalent (σ) bonds round each carbon atom. The σ bonds lie between a carbon and either hydrogen or other carbon atoms. All bond angles are 109°. The molecules can rotate freely about each carbon–carbon single bond. This freedom to rotate allows a great degree of flexibility to alkane chains.

Alkanes are remarkably inert compounds. Although they make excellent fuels, their oxidation reactions have high activation energies and require a significant input of energy before ignition. This energy input may come from a spark, as in the internal combustion engine, or from the match used to light a bunsen burner. One of the reasons for this inertness is the relatively high bond energies of C–H and C–C bonds (see page 54).

SAQ 6.4

a Use the bond energies on page 54 to calculate:

   (i) the enthalpy change for
$$CH_4(g) + 2O_2(g) \rightarrow C(g) + 4H(g) + 4O(g);$$

   (ii) the enthalpy change for
$$C(g) + 4H(g) + 4O(g) \rightarrow CO_2(g) + 2H_2O(g);$$

   (iii) the percentage of the energy released in (ii) that is used to break the bonds in (i).

b Explain this percentage in terms of the bonds broken and calculate the enthalpy change for
$$CH_4(g) + 2O_2(g) \rightarrow CO_2(g) + 2H_2O(g).$$

c $\Delta H_c[CH_4(g)]$ is $-890.3\,kJ\,mol^{-1}$. Give **two** reasons why this differs from your answer in **b**.

A second, very important, reason for the inertness of alkanes arises from their lack of polarity. As carbon and hydrogen have very similar electronegativities, alkanes are non-polar molecules. Consequently, alkanes are not readily attacked by common chemical reagents. Most reagents that you have met are highly polar compounds. For example, water, acids, alkalis, and many oxidising and reducing agents are polar and usually initiate reactions by attraction to polar groups in other compounds. Such polar reagents do not react with alkanes.

Some non-polar reagents will react with alkanes. The most important of these are the halogens, which, in the presence of ultraviolet light, will *substitute* hydrogen atoms in the alkane with halogen atoms. For example, when chlorine is mixed with methane and exposed to sunlight, chloromethane is formed.

$$CH_4(g) + Cl_2(g) \longrightarrow CH_3Cl(g) + HCl(g)$$

Because the reaction requires ultraviolet light it is a **photochemical reaction**.

Further substitution is possible, producing in turn dichloromethane, trichloromethane and tetra-chloromethane. Other halogens such as bromine produce similar products. You will meet several important types of organic reaction; **substitution reactions** are one of these reaction types.

SAQ 6.5

a Write balanced equations for the stepwise formation of dichloromethane, trichloromethane and tetra-chloromethane from chloromethane and chlorine.

b Draw structural formulae for all the possible products from the reaction of bromine with ethane in ultraviolet light. Name each product.

Mechanism of the substitution of alkanes by halogens

The overall equation for a reaction gives no clue as to the stages involved between reactants and products. The sequence of stages is known as the **mechanism** of a reaction. The energy of ultraviolet light is sufficient to break the Cl–Cl bond. When this happens, two chlorine atoms are formed, each having seven electrons in their outer shell. When a covalent bond is broken so that the electrons are shared between the atoms involved, the process is called **homolytic fission**. (When a covalent bond undergoes **heterolytic fission**, both electrons are transferred to one atom. This produces two ions of opposite charge, e.g. $HCl \rightarrow H^+ + Cl^-$.)

Homolytic fission is often represented using half-headed curly arrows as follows.

$$Cl\frown\!\!\!\frown Cl(g) \longrightarrow Cl\bullet(g) + Cl\bullet(g)$$

The *half-headed* curly arrow shows the movement of *one electron* from the bond to a chlorine atom. When drawing curly arrows, it is important that the arrow starts at the electron to be moved and ends at the point to which the electron moves. The dot in Cl• indicates the presence of an unpaired electron on a chlorine atom.

The chlorine atoms produced in this way are very reactive. They may recombine to form a chlorine molecule, Cl_2, or they may react with another molecule such as an alkane. Either way, they pair with another electron and achieve a full outer shell of eight electrons. As the homolytic fission of a chlorine molecule must occur before any chloromethane can be formed, it is known as the **initiation** step.

The reaction of a chlorine atom with a methane molecule produces hydrogen chloride and a $CH_3\cdot$ fragment. The carbon atom in this $CH_3\cdot$ fragment also has seven electrons in its outer shell. Both the chlorine atom and the $CH_3\cdot$ fragment have one unpaired electron. Such molecular fragments or atoms with one unpaired electron are known as **free radicals**. In general, free radicals are highly reactive. They are shown in reactions with a dot to represent the unpaired electron. A methyl free radical can react with a chlorine molecule to produce chloromethane and a new chlorine atom. These reaction steps are:

$$Cl\cdot(g) \; + \; H{-}CH_3(g) \longrightarrow CH_3\cdot(g) \; + \; HCl(g)$$

$$\qquad\qquad\qquad\qquad\qquad \text{methyl} \qquad\quad \text{hydrogen}$$
$$\qquad\qquad\qquad\qquad\qquad \text{radical} \qquad\quad\; \text{chloride}$$

$$CH_3\cdot(g) \; + \; Cl{-}Cl(g) \longrightarrow CH_3Cl(g) \; + \; Cl\cdot(g)$$

$$\qquad\qquad\qquad\qquad\qquad \text{chloromethane}$$

Again half-headed curly arrows show the movement of the single electrons. These two steps enable the reaction to continue. In the first step a chlorine free radical is used up. The second step releases a new chlorine free radical, which can allow repetition of the first step. Reaction will continue for as long as there is a supply of methane molecules and undissociated chlorine molecules. The two steps constitute a chain reaction and are known as the **propagation** steps of the reaction.

Reaction to form chloromethane and hydrogen chloride will cease when the supply of reagents is depleted. There is a variety of possible **termination** steps. These include recombination of chlorine free radicals to form chlorine molecules. Alternatively, two methyl free radicals can combine to form an ethane molecule.

$$Cl\cdot(g) \; + \; Cl\cdot(g) \longrightarrow Cl_2(g)$$

$$CH_3\cdot(g) \; + \; CH_3\cdot(g) \longrightarrow C_2H_6(g)$$

$$\qquad\qquad\qquad\qquad\qquad\quad \text{ethane}$$

As the number of free radicals in a reaction mixture is very small, the amount of ethane formed will be negligible compared with the amount of chloromethane.

These, or any other, termination steps will remove a free radical and disrupt the propagation steps, thus stopping the chain reaction.

The four steps involved in the formation of chloromethane and hydrogen chloride from methane and chlorine constitute the mechanism of this reaction. As the reaction is a substitution involving free radicals, it is known as a **free-radical substitution**.

Alkenes

Alkenes are used to make many chemicals that feature prominently in modern life. Poly(ethene), usually called by its ICI tradename 'Polythene', is probably familiar to most people on Earth. Formed by the polymerisation of ethene, it is an alkane with a very long chain of carbon atoms. As an alkane, it has very strong, non-polar C–C and C–H bonds, which make it very resistant to both chemical and biological attack. It can be destroyed by burning and is very slowly broken down by oxygen free radicals produced by ultraviolet radiation in sunlight. Other important products from ethene include those shown in *table 6.3*.

Chemists have played their part in making new discoveries and finding ways to make compounds desired by society. A good example is tetra(ethyl)lead (see also page 102). In the 1920s the popularity of the motor car as a means of transport was rising. It was at this time that motor racing also began to attract a large following. This interest led to a desire for faster cars. Engineers and chemists were called upon to develop more powerful engines and more efficient fuels.

Ethane-1,2-diol, CH$_2$OHCH$_2$OH	Used in anti-freeze and one of the two compounds used to make poly(ester)s such as Terylene (ICI trademark)
1,2-Dichloroethane, CH$_2$ClCH$_2$Cl	Used to make chloroethene (vinyl chloride), which is polymerised to poly(chloroethene) (polyvinylchloride or PVC)
1,2-dibromoethane, CH$_2$BrCH$_2$Br	An additive to leaded petrol
Tetra(ethyl)lead, (C$_2$H$_5$)$_4$Pb	The lead additive in petrol; an organic lead compound soluble in petrol
Ethanol, C$_2$H$_5$OH	For use as a solvent (not for alcoholic drinks!)

● **Table 6.3** Some products from ethene

Tetra(ethyl)lead was found to give an improved performance in engines with a higher compression ratio. It consequently became an additive to petrol despite concerns expressed in Parliament at the time regarding the toxicity of lead. The introduction of leaded petrol is an interesting example of the way in which consumers can influence development of a new product. When such a product is subsequently found to be undesirable, consumers may be to blame, not just the companies, engineers and scientists who responded to our desires!

Simple alkenes are hydrocarbons that contain one carbon-carbon double bond. The simplest alkene is ethene, CH$_2$=CH$_2$.

SAQ 6.6

Draw a dot-and-cross diagram for ethene. Predict the shape of the molecule and give estimates of the bond angles.

Bonding in alkenes: σ *and* π *bonds*

In chapter 3, we saw how electrons in molecules occupy σ and π molecular orbitals. A σ orbital lies predominantly along the axis between two nuclei. It may be regarded as being formed by

overlap of two atomic orbitals. The two electrons in the orbital attract both nuclei, binding them together in a σ bond. A π orbital (or π bond) lies predominantly in two lobes along either side of a σ bond. Overlap of two atomic p orbitals produces a π molecular orbital. To ensure maximum overlap, ethene must be a planar molecule. A single covalent bond, such as C–C or C–H, is made up of a σ orbital. Double bonds such as C=C consist of one σ bond and one π bond. This is shown in *figure 6.8*.

Compounds that contain π bonds, such as ethene, are called **unsaturated** compounds. The term 'unsaturated' indicates that the compound will combine by *addition* reactions with hydrogen or other chemicals, losing its multiple bonds. **Saturated** compounds contain *only single* carbon–carbon bonds. The terms saturated or unsaturated are often used in connection with oils and fats. The molecules in vegetable oils contain several double bonds – they are described as polyunsaturated. In hard margarine, hydrogen has been added to these double bonds so the margarine is now saturated. Several of the fatty acids that are essential to our diet are polyunsaturated and hence the fats in much modern margarine are only partially saturated.

The molecules of sight: cis–trans *isomerism*

The molecule that is responsible for initiating the signal to our brain, which allows us to see, is called retinal. This molecule is present in the rod and cone cells of the eye. One of its isomers is responsible for the absorption of light. Each double bond is locked into position,

 overlap of p atomic orbitals produces π molecular orbitals

● **Figure 6.8** The molecular orbitals in ethene. The green region shows the two lobes of the π orbital. Notice how they are exposed on either side of the molecule. The σ orbitals are not shown; they lie along the lines representing the covalent bonds.

preventing rotation. When this isomer absorbs light, one of the two electron-pairs in a double bond is split apart. This allows the retinal molecule to change its shape by rotating around the single bond left behind. After bond rotation, the two electrons that were split apart by the absorption of light come together, fixing the molecule in its new shape and preventing further rotation. This is shown in the reaction sequence in *figure 6.9*. The dramatic change of shape affects the shape of the protein to which the retinal is attached. This causes a signal to be sent via the optic nerve to the brain. The new *trans*-retinal isomer breaks away from the protein and is converted back to *cis*-retinal, ready for further light absorption.

The type of isomerism shown by the retinal molecule in this example is called *cis–trans* isomerism or geometric isomerism. It is frequently encountered in alkenes and arises because rotation about a double bond cannot occur (unless one of the bonds in the double bond is broken, as in retinal on absorption of light). In addition to a double bond, the molecule must have two identical groups on each of the two carbon atoms involved in the double bond. The other two groups must be different to this identical pair. But-2-ene is the simplest alkene to show *cis–trans* isomerism:

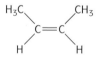

cis-but-2-ene

trans-but-2-ene

In the *cis* isomer, two methyl groups are on the same side of the double bond; in the *trans* isomer, they are on opposite sides. The breaking of one of the bonds in a double bond by light absorption is not a usual reaction for alkenes.

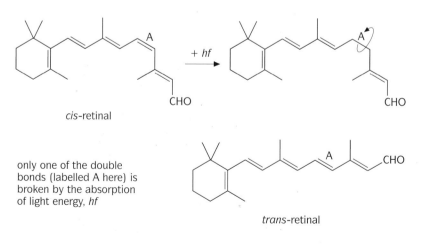

cis-retinal

+ *hf*

only one of the double bonds (labelled A here) is broken by the absorption of light energy, *hf*

trans-retinal

● *Figure 6.9* The change of shape of a retinal molecule by rotation about the single bond that results from absorption of light.

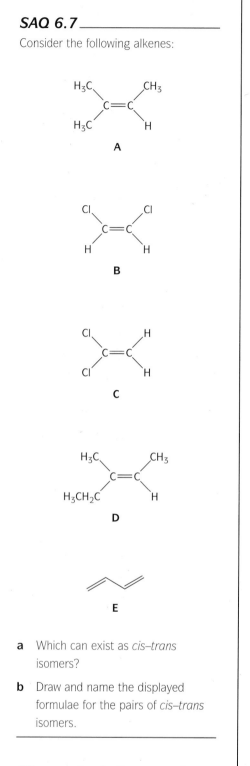

SAQ 6.7

Consider the following alkenes:

A

B

C

D

E

a Which can exist as *cis–trans* isomers?

b Draw and name the displayed formulae for the pairs of *cis–trans* isomers.

Characteristic reactions of alkenes

Apart from combustion, most alkene reactions involve breaking the π bond. This is weaker than the C–C σ bond and reacts with a variety of reagents.

Combustion

Like other hydrocarbons, alkenes will burn completely in an excess of oxygen to form carbon dioxide and water only.

SAQ 6.8

Write a balanced equation, including state symbols, for the complete combustion of propene.

When alkenes burn in air, combustion is less complete than that of the corresponding alkane. The flame from the alkene is more orange and more soot (carbon) is formed.

Oxidation of the double bond

Alkenes decolourise acidified potassium manganate(VII). The alkene is itself oxidised to a diol. Two alcohol functional groups (–OH) become attached to the carbon atoms on either side of the π bond. The potassium manganate(VII) acts as an oxidising agent, providing one of the oxygen atoms; the other oxygen and the hydrogen atoms come from a water molecule. In organic reactions, the oxygen from an oxidising agent is often represented by [O]. This enables a simpler equation to be written. For example,

$$CH_2{=}CH_2 + [O] + H_2O \longrightarrow CH_2OHCH_2OH$$

Molecular models of the organic compounds are:

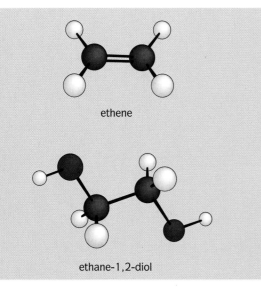

ethene

ethane-1,2-diol

The product from the oxidation of ethene in this way is ethane-1,2-diol. Industrially this reaction is

carried out using oxygen from the air and a silver catalyst.

SAQ 6.9

Draw the displayed formula for

a   propene;

b   the product obtained by oxidation of propene in the presence of a silver catalyst.

Addition reactions to the double bond

The characteristic reaction of an alkene involves a simple molecule (such as hydrogen, water or bromine) joining across the double bond to form a single product. Such reactions are called **addition reactions**. Addition reactions are the second important type of organic reactions that you will meet.

■ *Addition of hydrogen*:
This converts the unsaturated alkene to a saturated alkane. Hydrogen gas and a gaseous alkene are passed over a finely divided nickel catalyst. Margarine is manufactured from vegetable oil at a temperature of 420 K and a hydrogen pressure of 5×10^2 kPa.

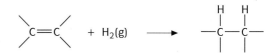

■ *Addition of water*:
This is a route to making alcohols. Industrially, steam and a gaseous alkene are passed over a solid catalyst. A temperature of 600 K and a pressure of 6 MPa are used in the presence of a phosphoric acid catalyst. Ethene and steam produce ethanol:

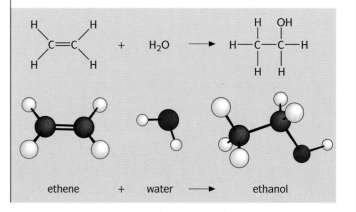

ethene   +   water $\longrightarrow$ ethanol

■ *Addition of bromine*:

When an alkene such as propene is bubbled through an alcoholic solution of bromine, the bromine solution is rapidly decolourised from its characteristic orange colour. The bromine joins to the propene to form 1,2-dibromopropane.

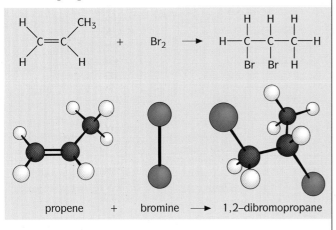

propene + bromine ⟶ 1,2–dibromopropane

Mechanism of the addition of bromine to ethene

Although bromine and ethene are non-polar reagents, the bromine molecule becomes polarised when close to a region of negative charge such as the ethene π bond. The π bond then breaks, with its electron-pair forming a new covalent bond to the bromine atom that carries a partial positive charge. At the same time the bromine molecule undergoes **heterolytic fission**. Heterolytic fission involves both electrons in the bond moving to the same atom. These changes produce a bromide ion and a positively charged carbon atom (called a **carbocation**) in the ethene molecule. A full-headed curly arrow is used to show the movement of two electrons (contrast with half-headed curly arrow for movement of one electron, page 104).

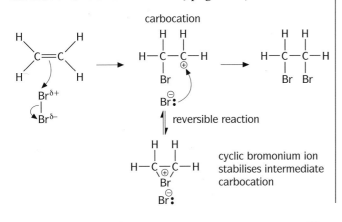

Carbocations are highly reactive and the bromide ion rapidly forms a second C–Br covalent bond to give 1,2-dibromoethane.

In this mechanism, the polarised bromine molecule has behaved as an **electrophile**. An electrophile is a reactant that is attracted to an electron-rich centre or atom where it accepts a pair of electrons to form a new covalent bond. The reaction is an example of one that proceeds by an **electrophilic addition** mechanism.

SAQ 6.10

a   If the reaction of bromine with ethene is carried out in ethanol containing some lithium chloride, a second, chlorine-containing, product is formed, as well as 1,2-dibromoethane. Suggest a structure for this second product.

b   Which of the following are likely to behave as electrophiles: $Cl_2(g)$, $Na^+(aq)$, $F^-(aq)$, $H_2(g)$, $SO_3(g)$, $ICl(g)$? Give an explanation in each case.

c   Draw a dot-and-cross diagram of the carbocation formed in an electrophilic addition to ethene. How many electrons are there on the positively charged carbon atom? Explain how this atom completes its outer electron shell when it combines with the bromide ion.

Simple tests for alkenes	
Test	*Observation if an alkene is present*
Shake alkene with bromine water	Orange bromine water is decolourised
Shake alkene with acidified aqueous potassium manganate(VII)	Purple potassium manganate(VII) is decolourised

Polymerisation of alkenes

During polymerisation, an alkene undergoes an addition reaction to itself. As one molecule joins to a second, a long molecular chain is built up. The reactions are initiated in various ways and the initiator may become incorporated at the start of the polymer chain. Ignoring the initiator, the empirical formula of an addition polymer is the same as the alkene it comes from. This type of reaction is called **addition polymerisation**. Many useful polymers are obtained via addition polymerisation of different alkenes.

Poly(ethene) was first produced accidentally by two scientists (Eric Fawcett and Reginald Gibson) in 1933. The reaction involves ethene adding to itself in a chain reaction. It is a very rapid reaction, chains of up to 10 000 ethene units being formed in one second. The product is a high-molecular-mass straight-chain alkane. It is a polymer and is a member of a large group of materials generally known as plastics. The alkene from which it is made is called the **monomer**.

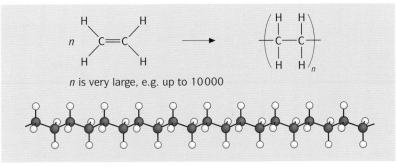

n is very large, e.g. up to 10 000

Other important poly(alkene)s include poly(chloroethene) and poly(phenylethene).

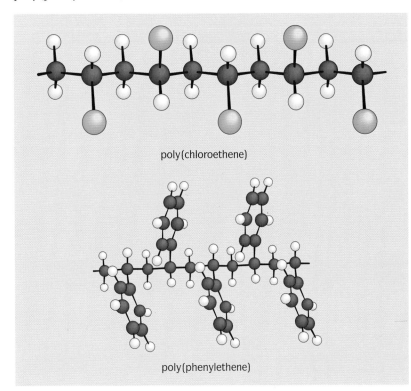

poly(chloroethene)

poly(phenylethene)

They are more commonly known as PVC and polystyrene respectively. Note how the systematic name is derived by putting the systematic name of the alkene in brackets, and prefixing this with 'poly'. The displayed formulae of chloroethene (traditionally vinyl chloride) and phenylethene (styrene) are as follows:

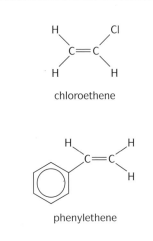

chloroethene

phenylethene

Note that when a benzene ring becomes a group attached to an alkene its name changes to phenyl (from 'phene', an old name for benzene). The phenyl group may also be written as C_6H_5-.

SAQ 6.11

Write balanced equations for the formation of poly(chloroethene) and poly(phenylethene) using displayed formulae.

We now have several methods for the addition polymerisation of alkenes. These methods provide the wide variety of poly(alkene)s for the many applications of these versatile materials. *Figure 6.10*

● *Figure 6.10* Some products made from poly(alkene)s.

● **Figure 6.11** A beach littered with poly(alkene) waste products, on the Pitcairn Islands in the south-eastern part of the Pacific Ocean.

shows some examples of these uses. The use of poly(alkene)s has created a major problem when we wish to dispose of them. *Figure 6.11* is a sight familiar to us all. As they are alkanes, they break down very slowly in the environment. They are resistant to most chemicals and to bacteria (they are non-biodegradable). It might seem desirable to collect waste poly(ethene), sort it and recycle it into new products (as in *figure 6.12*).

Some praiseworthy attempts at recycling are being made. However, the current costs of recycling in terms of the energy used in collecting and reprocessing the material is often greater than that used in making new material. One option is to burn the poly(ethene) to provide energy. The energy released on its combustion is about the same as the energy used in its production. It is potentially a good fuel as it is a hydrocarbon and would reduce the amount of oil or other fossil fuels burned. It

● **Figure 6.12** Recycling poly(alkene)s into a new product.

could be burnt with other combustible household waste. This would save considerable landfill costs and provide a substantial alternative energy source. Modern technology is such that the waste could be burnt cleanly and with less pollution than from traditional fossil-fuel power stations. The carbon dioxide produced would not add to the total emissions of this greenhouse gas but replace emissions from burning other fossil fuels. Other pollutant gases, such as hydrogen chloride from PVC, can be removed by the use of gas scrubbers. In a gas scrubber, acidic gases are dissolved and neutralised in a spray of alkali. New European Union legislation will require household waste incinerators to use gas scrubbers.

A second option, currently being developed by BP, is to subject the polymers to high-temperature pyrolysis. This enables the polymers to be broken down into smaller useful molecules. This is a process similar to the cracking of alkanes (see page 102).

Arenes

The simplest arene is benzene. It is not a compound that you will use in the laboratory as it is carcinogenic. However, it is a very important industrial chemical. One of its major uses, in unleaded petrol, has already been mentioned (page 103).

It has also been used to manufacture the insecticide Lindane. Use of chlorinated insecticides like Lindane has decreased considerably in view of the damage they have caused environmentally. Chlorinated insecticides build up in food chains and have been identified as a significant factor in the decline in populations of birds of prey. Lindane is an isomer of 1,2,3,4,5,6-hexachlorocyclohexane. This compound is formed by addition of three moles of chlorine to one mole of benzene in ultraviolet light:

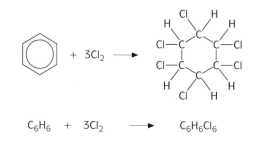

$$C_6H_6 + 3Cl_2 \longrightarrow C_6H_6Cl_6$$

Carbon compounds: Introduction to organic chemistry

SAQ 6.12

a Calculate the volume of chlorine gas required to convert 10 tonnes of benzene to 1,2,3,4,5,6-hexachlorocyclohexane at room temperature and pressure. (Under these conditions, one mole of a gas occupies $24\,dm^3$.)

b How many isomers can you draw for 1,2,3,4,5,6-hexachlorocyclohexane? You will find it easier to answer this question if you build a model. One of the isomers is:

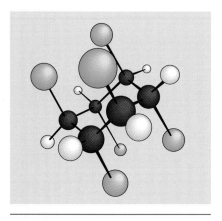

Bonding in benzene

Kekulé was first to suggest that benzene was a cyclic molecule with alternating single and double carbon–carbon bonds. Such a structure would have two different lengths for the carbon–carbon bonds. The single and double bonds may be placed in two alternative positions:

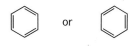

(It may help you to see these as alternative positions if you imagine that you are standing on the carbon atom at 12 o'clock: one structure will have the double bond on your left, the other has the double bond on the right.)

The Kekulé structure for benzene would be expected to show the typical addition reactions of an alkene. However, benzene undergoes addition reactions far less easily than a typical alkene. For example, an alkene such as cyclohexene will rapidly decolourise aqueous bromine in the dark. Bromine (or chlorine) must be dissolved in boiling benzene and exposed to ultraviolet light before addition occurs.

Also, the carbon–carbon bond lengths in benzene molecules are all identical, with lengths intermediate between those of single and double bonds:

	C–C	C=C	benzene C–C
bond length/nm	0.154	0.134	0.139

The current model of the bonding in benzene accounts for these observations. Each carbon atom contributes one electron to a π bond. However, the π bonds formed do not lie between pairs of carbon atoms as in an alkene. The π bonds spread over all six carbon atoms. The electrons now occupy three **delocalised** π orbitals. They are said to be delocalised as they are not localised between adjacent pairs of carbon atoms but spread over all six. (An alkene π bond is localised between a pair of carbon atoms.) The π molecular orbitals are formed by overlap of carbon p atomic orbitals. To achieve maximum overlap, the benzene molecule must be planar. One of the delocalised π molecular orbitals is shown below:

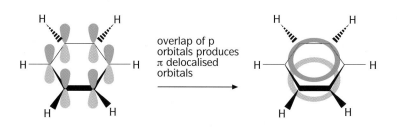

overlap of p orbitals produces π delocalised orbitals

This model produces six C–C bonds of the same length, as observed. The reluctance of benzene to undergo addition reactions is due to the additional energetic stability that the delocalised system gives it. A measure of this additional stability can be seen by considering the enthalpy changes for the hydrogenation of cyclohexene and benzene.

The addition of hydrogen to cyclohexene releases $120\,kJ\,mol^{-1}$:

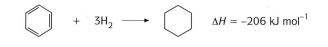

$\Delta H = -120\ kJ\ mol^{-1}$

The Kekulé structure for benzene with three localised double bonds should release $360\,kJ\,mol^{-1}$. However, only $206\,kJ\,mol^{-1}$ are released.

$$+ \quad 3H_2 \longrightarrow \qquad \Delta H = -206\ kJ\ mol^{-1}$$

Where has the 'extra' $154 \, kJ \, mol^{-1}$ gone? This is the amount of energy that is needed to disrupt the delocalised π orbitals in benzene. As it is equivalent to the additional energetic stability of benzene, it is sometimes known as the **delocalisation energy.**

SUMMARY

■ In general, organic compounds divide into aromatic compounds, which contain arene rings, and aliphatic compounds, which do not. Hydrocarbons may be classified as alkanes, alkenes or arenes. Each of these groups produces a series (called a homologous series) of compounds with increasing numbers of atoms.

■ Alkanes do not contain multiple bonds between pairs of carbon atoms and are described as saturated compounds. Alkenes and arenes, which do contain multiple bonds, are described as unsaturated compounds.

■ The geometry and structures of alkanes, alkenes and arenes (including the electron delocalisation model) may be described in terms of σ and π bonds.

■ There are many examples of different organic compounds with the same molecular formula in which the atoms are joined together in different arrangements. Such compounds are called isomers.

■ Chemists use a variety of types of formulae to represent organic molecules and to help distinguish between isomers. Such formulae include structural and displayed formulae. Structural isomers have the same molecular formula but have different structural formulae.

■ Many hydrocarbons exist as structural isomers. Geometric or *cis–trans* isomers have the same molecular formulae but have different displayed formulae. Alkenes may exist as geometric isomers.

■ Crude oil provides society with a wide range of hydrocarbons and is the source of many other compounds of major social and economic importance. It is the work of chemists (involved in research, development and production of these organic chemicals) that has helped society to achieve our current high standards of living.

■ Alkanes are non-polar molecules with strong bonds. They are thus relatively inert, their reactions having high activation energies. All hydrocarbons are potential fuels, the highly exothermic nature of their combustion providing the activation energy.

■ Free radicals are highly reactive chemical species that have one unpaired electron. They are produced in photochemical reactions involving ultraviolet light. Free radicals, such as a chlorine atom, will cause replacement of a hydrogen atom attached to a carbon atom. This type of reaction is called a substitution reaction.

■ Alkenes and arenes are more reactive than alkanes as the π bonds they contain are weaker than σ bonds. Arenes are less reactive than alkenes as the delocalisation of π electrons over the arene ring increases the strength of the bonding present.

■ Both alkenes and arenes undergo addition reactions in which molecules join together to produce a new molecule. Under suitable conditions, addition reactions occur with hydrogen, halogens and water.

■ Alkene molecules may also join to each other, producing a long chain molecule. This process is called addition polymerisation.

■ Many addition reactions involve reagents (called electrophiles) that are attracted by the π electron charge, with the subsequent formation of a covalent bond between the electrophile and carbon.

■ Most reactions do not occur as the single step shown by the balanced equation for the reaction. Instead, a sequence of steps is involved. This sequence is known as the reaction mechanism.

■ Substitution of hydrogen on alkanes by chlorine proceeds via a free-radical mechanism. Addition of chlorine to an alkene proceeds via an electrophilic addition mechanism.

Questions

1 The following compounds **A** to **E** can be obtained from crude oil:

compounds **A** and **B** are isomers of the alkane C_4H_{10};

compound **C**, C_8H_{18}, is an alkane;

compound **D**, C_6H_{12}, is a saturated hydrocarbon;

compound **E**, C_7H_8, is an arene.

a What is meant by the term **hydrocarbon**?

b Draw displayed formulae for possible structures of compounds **A** to **E**.

c The compound C_3H_6 reacts readily with bromine to produce $C_3H_6Br_2$. Draw displayed formulae for these two compounds.

d Addition polymerisation of C_3H_6 produces the polymer $(C_3H_6)_n$.

Draw a displayed formula for this polymer, indicating clearly the repeating unit.

2 a Discuss, with suitable examples and diagrams of carbon–carbon bonds, the structures of and geometry associated with:

(i) single bonds;

(ii) double bonds;

(iii) delocalised bonding electrons.

Your answer should describe, with suitable diagrams, the bonds in terms of σ and π orbitals, and discuss the effect of the bonds on the associated molecular shapes.

b Discuss the following reactions of ethene:

(i) combustion;

(ii) addition;

(iii) polymerisation.

Appendix: Periodic Table of the elements

Key:

```
  a
  X
Name
  b
```

a = relative atomic mass
X = symbol
b = proton number

Period / Group (s-Block, d-Block, p-Block)

Period	I	II	d-Block →										III	IV	V	VI	VII	O
1	1.0 H Hydrogen 1																	4.0 He Helium 2
2	6.9 Li Lithium 3	9.0 Be Beryllium 4											10.8 B Boron 5	12.0 C Carbon 6	14.0 N Nitrogen 7	16.0 O Oxygen 8	19.0 F Fluorine 9	20.2 Ne Neon 10
3	23.0 Na Sodium 11	24.3 Mg Magnesium 12											27.0 Al Aluminium 13	28.1 Si Silicon 14	31.0 P Phosphorus 15	32.1 S Sulphur 16	35.5 Cl Chlorine 17	39.9 Ar Argon 18
4	39.1 K Potassium 19	40.1 Ca Calcium 20	45.0 Sc Scandium 21	47.9 Ti Titanium 22	50.9 V Vanadium 23	52.0 Cr Chromium 24	54.9 Mn Manganese 25	55.9 Fe Iron 26	58.9 Co Cobalt 27	58.7 Ni Nickel 28	63.5 Cu Copper 29	65.4 Zn Zinc 30	69.7 Ga Gallium 31	72.6 Ge Germanium 32	74.9 As Arsenic 33	79.0 Se Selenium 34	79.9 Br Bromine 35	83.8 Kr Krypton 36
5	85.5 Rb Rubidium 37	87.6 Sr Strontium 38	88.9 Y Yttrium 39	91.2 Zr Zirconium 40	92.9 Nb Niobium 41	95.9 Mo Molybdenum 42	– Tc Technetium 43	101 Ru Ruthenium 44	103 Rh Rhodium 45	106 Pd Palladium 46	108 Ag Silver 47	112 Cd Cadmium 48	115 In Indium 49	119 Sn Tin 50	122 Sb Antimony 51	128 Te Tellurium 52	127 I Iodine 53	131 Xe Xenon 54
6	133 Cs Caesium 55	137 Ba Barium 56	La to Lu	178 Hf Hafnium 72	181 Ta Tantalum 73	184 W Tungsten 74	186 Re Rhenium 75	190 Os Osmium 76	192 Ir Iridium 77	195 Pt Platinum 78	197 Au Gold 79	201 Hg Mercury 80	204 Tl Thallium 81	207 Pb Lead 82	209 Bi Bismuth 83	– Po Polonium 84	– At Astatine 85	– Rn Radon 86
7	– Fr Francium 87	– Ra Radium 88	Ac to Lr	– Unq Unnilquadium 104	– Unp Unnilpentium 105	– Unh Unnilhexium 106	– Uns Unnilseptium 107	– Uno Unniloctium 108	– Une Unnilennium 109									

f-Block

139 La Lanthanum 57	140 Ce Cerium 58	141 Pr Praseodymium 59	144 Nd Neodymium 60	Pm Promethium 61	150 Sm Samarium 62	152 Eu Europium 63	157 Gd Gadolinium 64	159 Tb Terbium 65	163 Dy Dysprosium 66	165 Ho Holmium 67	167 Er Erbium 68	169 Tm Thulium 69	173 Yb Ytterbium 70	175 Lu Lutetium 71
Ac Actinium 89	Th Thorium 90	Pa Protactinium 91	U Uranium 92	Np Neptunium 93	Pu Plutonium 94	Am Americium 95	Cm Curium 96	Bk Berkelium 97	Cf Californium 98	Es Einsteinium 99	Fm Fermium 100	Md Mendelevium 101	No Nobelium 102	Lr Lawrencium 103

Answers to self-assessment questions

Chapter 1

1.1 **a** U-235 has 92 protons, 92 electrons and 143 neutrons.
U-238 has 92 protons, 92 electrons and 146 neutrons.

b K^+-40 has 19 protons, 18 electrons and 21 neutrons.
Cl^--37 has 17 protons, 18 electrons and 20 neutrons.

1.2 All the isotopes have the same number and arrangement of electrons and this controls their chemical properties.

1.3 **a**

Mg	(2,8,2)	S	(2,8,6)
Al	(2,8,3)	Cl	(2,8,7)
Si	(2,8,4)	Ar	(2,8,8)
P	(2,8,5)		

b They have the same number of electrons in their outer shells.

1.4 **a** Sodium has 11 electrons in all. There is one electron in its outer shell ($n=3$) and this is the easiest to remove. The second ionisation energy shows the energy required to remove an electron from the next inner (filled) shell ($n=2$).

The ninth electron to be removed is in shell $n=2$ and the tenth is in shell $n=1$, which is closest to the nucleus.

b The first electron is in the outer shell $n=3$.

The relatively low increases from the second to the ninth ionisation energies show that eight electrons are in the same shell $n=2$. The tenth and eleventh electrons are in the shell $n=1$.

1.5 Group II. The first and second ionisation energies are fairly close in value. There is a large increase between the second and third ionisation energies, which shows that the second and third electrons are in different shells. This indicates that there are two electrons in the outer shell.

1.6 See *figure*.

● **Answer for** SAQ 1.6

Chapter 2

2.1 Relative atomic mass of carbon
$$= \frac{98.89 \times 12 + 1.11 \times 13.003}{100} = 12.011$$

2.2 **a** $24.3 + 2 \times 35.5 = 95.3$

b $63.5 + 32.1 + 4 \times 16.0 = 159.6$

c $2 \times 23.0 + 12.0 + 3 \times 16.0 + 10(2 \times 1.0 + 16.0) = 286.0$

2.3 **a** $\dfrac{35.5}{35.5} = 1\,mol\;Cl$ atoms

b $\dfrac{71}{2 \times 35.5} = 1\,mol\;Cl_2$ molecules

2.4 **a** $6 \times 10^{23}\;Cl$ atoms

b $1\,mol\;Cl_2$ molecules $= 2\,mol\;Cl$ atoms
$= 2 \times 6 \times 10^{23} = 1.2 \times 10^{24}$

2.5 **a** $CO_2 = 12.0 + 2 \times 16.0 = 44.0\,g$
$\therefore$ mass $0.1\,mol\;CO_2 = 0.1 \times 44.0$
$= 4.40\,g$

b $CaCO_3 = 40.1 + 12.0 + 3 \times 16.0$
$= 100.1\,g$
$\therefore$ mass $10\,mol\;CaCO_3 = 10 \times 100.1$
$= 1001\,g$

2.6 a From equation, mole ratio $H_2 : Cl_2 = 1 : 1$

$\therefore$ mass ratio $= 2.0 : 71.0$ or $1 : 35.5$

  b $HCl = 1.0 + 35.5 = 36.5 = 1\,mol\ HCl$

$\therefore$ as $1\,mol\ H_2$ produces $2\,mol\ HCl$,

$0.5\,mol\ H_2$ produces $1\,mol\ HCl$.

$\therefore 2.0 \times 0.5$

$= 1.0\,g\ H_2$ produces $36.5\,g\ HCl$.

2.7 1000 tonnes Fe_2O_3 produce

$112 \times \dfrac{1000}{160}$ tonne $= 700$ tonnes Fe

$\therefore 1$ tonne Fe requires $\dfrac{1000}{700}$ tonne Fe_2O_3

$= 1.43$ tonne

$\therefore$ mass ore $= 1.43 \times \dfrac{100}{12} = 11.9$ tonne

2.8 a ^{90}Zr, ^{91}Zr, ^{92}Zr, ^{94}Zr, ^{96}Zr

  b $A_r(Zr)$

$= \dfrac{51.5 \times 90 + 11.2 \times 91 + 17.1 \times 92 + 17.4 \times 94 + 2.8 \times 96}{100}$

$= 91.3$

2.9 a 190

  b

Peak	m/e	Fragment ion
P	91	⟨benzene ring⟩—CH_2^+
Q	57	$CH_3CH_2CH_2CH_2^+$

2.10

m/e	Ion	Probability ratio	
84	$CH_2{}^{35}Cl_2{}^+$	$75 \times 75 = 5625$;	$5625 \div 625 = 9$
86	$CH_2{}^{35}Cl{}^{37}Cl{}^+$	$2 \times 75 \times 25 = 3750$;	$3750 \div 625 = 6$
88	$CH_2{}^{37}Cl_2{}^+$	$25 \times 25 = 625$;	$625 \div 625 = 1$

2.11 a N_2 2×14.0067

$= 28.0134$

  C_2H_4 $2 \times 12.0111 + 4 \times 1.0079$

$= 28.0538$

  CO $12.0111 + 15.9994$

$= 28.0105$

  b CO

2.12 a C_3H_7 b HO

2.13

	Cu	O
Amount/mol	$\dfrac{0.635}{63.5} = 0.0100$	$\dfrac{0.080}{16.0} = 0.00500$
Ratio/mol	2	1

$\therefore$ Empirical formula is Cu_2O.

2.14 a Mass C in $1.257\,g\ CO_2$

$= \dfrac{12.0}{44.0} \times 1.257 \quad = 0.343\,g$

  Mass H in $0.514\,g\ H_2O$

$= \dfrac{2 \times 1.0}{18.0} \times 0.514 \quad = 0.057\,g$

(Check: $0.343 + 0.057 = 0.400\,g =$ mass of hydrocarbon sample.)

	C	H
Amount/mol	$\dfrac{0.343}{12.0} = 0.0286$	$\dfrac{0.057}{1.0} = 0.057$
Ratio/mol	1	1.99

$\therefore$ Empirical formula is CH_2; $M_r(CH_2) = 14$.

  b As $84 = 6 \times 14$, molecular formula is C_6H_{12}.

2.15 a $MgBr_2$ d Na_2SO_4

  b HI e KNO_3

  c CaS f NO_2

2.16 a Potassium carbonate

  b Aluminium sulphide

  c Lithium nitrate

  d Calcium phosphate

  e Silicon dioxide

  f Nitrogen monoxide or nitrogen(II) oxide

2.17 a $2Al + Fe_2O_3 \rightarrow Al_2O_3 + 2Fe$

  b $2C_8H_{18} + 25O_2 \rightarrow 16CO_2 + 18H_2O$

  or $C_8H_{18} + \frac{25}{2}O_2 \rightarrow 8CO_2 + 9H_2O$

  c $2Pb(NO_3)_2 \rightarrow 2PbO + 4NO_2 + O_2$

2.18 a Amount nitric acid

$= \dfrac{25}{1000} \times 0.1 = 2.5 \times 10^{-3}\,mol$

  b Volume $= \dfrac{50}{1000} = 5 \times 10^{-2}\,dm^3$

$\therefore$ concentration $= \dfrac{0.125}{5 \times 10^{-2}}$

$= 2.5\,mol\,dm^{-3}$

2.19 a $CH_3COOH = 12.0 + 3 \times 1.0 + 12.0 + 2 \times 16.0 + 1.0 = 60.0$

$\therefore$ concentration $= 0.50 \times 60 = 30.0\,g\,dm^{-3}$

b $NaOH = 23.0 + 16.0 + 1.0 = 40.0$

$\therefore$ concentration $= \dfrac{4.00}{40.0} = 0.100\,mol\,dm^{-3}$

(N.B. Three significant figures in these answers.)

2.20 a Amount KOH

$= \dfrac{20}{1000} \times 0.100 = 2 \times 10^{-3}\,mol$

$KOH + HCl \rightarrow KCl + H_2O$

$\therefore$ amount KOH = amount HCl

$= 2 \times 10^{-3}\,mol$

Volume HCl $= \dfrac{25.0}{1000} = 2.5 \times 10^{-2}\,dm^3$

$\therefore$ concentration HCl

$= \dfrac{2 \times 10^{-3}}{2.5 \times 10^{-2}} = 0.08\,mol\,dm^{-3}$

b $36.5 \times 0.08 = 2.92\,g\,dm^{-3}$

2.21 Amount HNO_3

$= \dfrac{24}{1000} \times 0.050 = 1.20 \times 10^{-3}\,mol$

$\therefore$ stoichiometric mole ratio nitric acid : iron hydroxide is

$1.20 \times 10^{-3} : 4.00 \times 10^{-4}$ i.e. 3:1

Iron hydroxide contains three hydroxide ions to exactly neutralise three HNO_3 molecules. So equation is

$3HNO_3(aq) + Fe(OH)_3(s)$
$\rightarrow Fe(NO_3)_3(aq) + 3H_2O(l)$

2.22 a Amount He $= \dfrac{2.4}{24} = 0.10\,mol$

b 0.5 mol propane $= 0.5 \times 24 = 12\,dm^3$
1.5 mol butane $= 1.5 \times 24 = 36\,dm^3$
$\therefore$ total volume $= 48\,dm^3$

Chapter 3

3.1 At negative electrode: $Cu^{2+} + 2e^- \rightarrow Cu$;
At positive electrode: $2Br^- \rightarrow Br_2 + 2e^-$

3.2 a–d See *figure.*

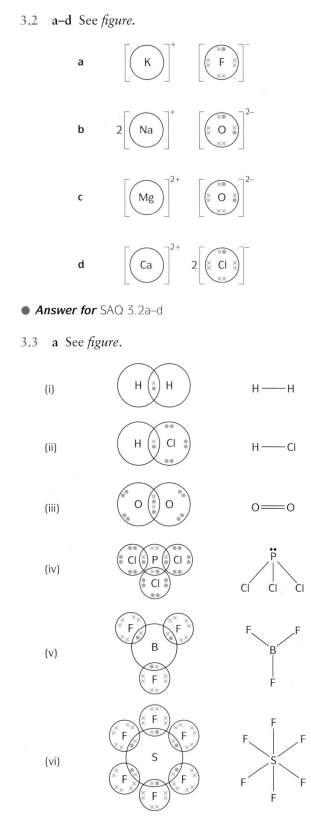

● *Answer for* SAQ 3.2a–d

3.3 a See *figure.*

● *Answer for* SAQ 3.3a

b BF_3: Outer shell of boron contains six electrons. SF_6: Outer shell of sulphur contains 12 electrons.

3.4 **a–c** See *figure*.

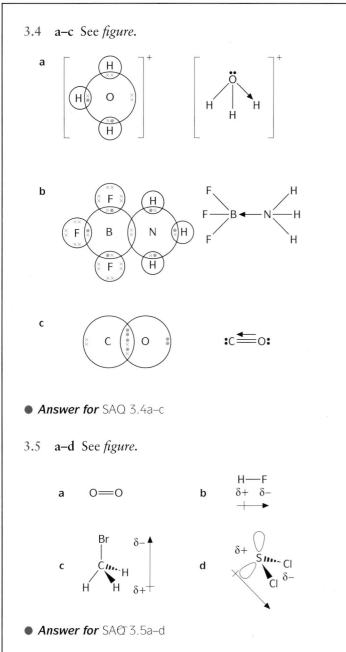

● *Answer for* SAQ 3.4a–c

3.5 **a–d** See *figure*.

a O=O **b** H—F
δ+ δ−

c **d**

● *Answer for* SAQ 3.5a–d

Thus, **a** is non-polar; and **b**, **c** and **d** are polar.

3.6 **a** Copper provides better heat transfer as it has a thermal conductivity that is five times higher than that of iron (stainless steel has a lower thermal conductivity than iron).

b Copper has more than three times the density of aluminium. The electrical conductivity of copper is 1.5 times that of aluminium. Aluminium cables will be lighter than copper whilst still being good conductors of electricity. The lighter cables enable less massive (and less unsightly) pylons to be used. As the tensile strength of aluminium is low, aluminium cables are reinforced with a steel core to increase their strength.

c Copper has the highest electrical and thermal conductivities. Its high thermal conductivity helps to keep equipment such as transformers cool.

3.7 As water molecules are free to rotate, the positive charge on the rod repels the positive end of a water molecule whilst attracting the negative end. The overall effect is thus an attraction. The effect will be the same if the charge on the rod is negative rather than positive.

3.8 See *figure*.

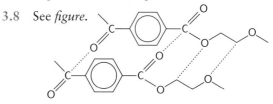

● *Answer for* SAQ 3.8

Dotted lines show the dipole–dipole forces.

Extrusion through spinnerets causes more molecules to line up closely, increasing the intermolecular forces (and hence the strength of the fibre) by the closer contact.

3.9 Underlying increase is due to increasing instantaneous dipole–induced dipole forces as the number of electrons and protons present in the molecules rise. The value for water based on this underlying trend would be about $18\,\text{kJ}\,\text{mol}^{-1}$.

The much higher value observed for water is due to the presence of much stronger intermolecular forces.

3.10 The O–H···O distance in ice is $0.159 + 0.096\,\text{nm}$ $= 0.255\,\text{nm}$. The effect of this is to produce a structure that occupies more space than that required when ice melts and many hydrogen bonds break. For a given mass, ice occupies a greater volume than water, so its density is less.

3.11 Washing-up liquid lowers the surface tension of water. This reduces the hydrogen bonding at the surface to the point where it is no longer sufficient to keep the needle afloat.

3.12 **a** Underlying increase is due to increasing instantaneous dipole–induced dipole forces as the number of electrons and protons present in the molecules rise.

b The much higher value observed for ammonia is due to the presence of hydrogen bonds, N–H···N.

3.13 See *figure*.

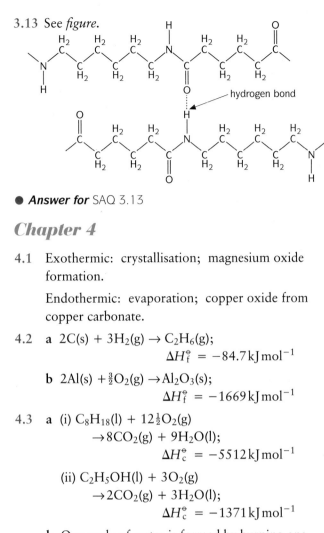

● **Answer for** SAQ 3.13

Chapter 4

4.1 Exothermic: crystallisation; magnesium oxide formation.

Endothermic: evaporation; copper oxide from copper carbonate.

4.2 **a** $2C(s) + 3H_2(g) \rightarrow C_2H_6(g)$;
$$\Delta H_f^{\ominus} = -84.7\,kJ\,mol^{-1}$$

b $2Al(s) + \frac{3}{2}O_2(g) \rightarrow Al_2O_3(s)$;
$$\Delta H_f^{\ominus} = -1669\,kJ\,mol^{-1}$$

4.3 **a** (i) $C_8H_{18}(l) + 12\frac{1}{2}O_2(g)$
$$\rightarrow 8CO_2(g) + 9H_2O(l);$$
$$\Delta H_c^{\ominus} = -5512\,kJ\,mol^{-1}$$

(ii) $C_2H_5OH(l) + 3O_2(g)$
$$\rightarrow 2CO_2(g) + 3H_2O(l);$$
$$\Delta H_c^{\ominus} = -1371\,kJ\,mol^{-1}$$

b One mole of water is formed by burning one mole of hydrogen.

4.4 $\Delta H_c^{\ominus}(H_2)$ is calculated directly from experimental measurements. $\Delta H_f^{\ominus}(H_2O)$ is found from bond energies, which are average values calculated from measurements in a number of different experiments.

4.5 The value in the data book was calculated from much more accurate experimental data. Some of the energy transferred from the burning propanol would not change the temperature but would be 'lost' in heating the apparatus and surroundings.

4.6 The reaction that produces the enthalpy change is the same in each case of reaction between these acids and alkalis. Only $H^+(aq)$ and $OH^-(aq)$ are involved:
$$H^+(aq) + OH^-(aq) \rightarrow H_2O(l)$$

4.7 A kilogram of hydrogen contains 500 moles of $H_2(g)$, whereas a kilogram of methane contains 62.5 moles of $CH_4(g)$.

4.8 **a** The volume of a liquid is much smaller than the volume of a gas of the same mass.

b A spherical shape gives the lowest surface area for the container of any given volume of liquid or gas. This saves material for making the container, and helps to keep the surface area of contents, affected by heating from the Sun, as small as possible.

4.9 $2NO_2(g) + H_2O(l) \rightarrow HNO_2(aq) + HNO_3(aq)$
         nitrous acid nitric acid

$SO_2(g) + H_2O(l) \rightarrow H_2SO_3(aq)$
        sulphurous acid

$SO_3(g) + H_2O(l) \rightarrow H_2SO_4(aq)$
        sulphuric acid

4.10 See *figure*.

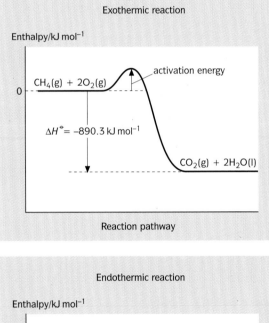

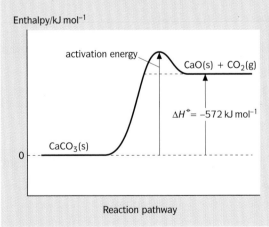

● **Answer for** SAQ 4.10

4.11 The order is
$$Ca(OH)_2 > Zn(OH)_2 > Fe(OH)_2 > Cu(OH)_2.$$

Chapter 5

5.1 The properties predicted for eka-silicon are close to those now known for germanium.

5.2 **a** Elements may have several isotopes – atoms with the same number of protons but different numbers of neutrons and hence different masses. The mass of an isotope of an element is the same as its nucleon number. This equals the number of protons plus the number of neutrons. The relative atomic mass of the element is the 'weighted average' of the nucleon numbers of its isotopes.

b Tellurium and iodine have several isotopes each. The weighted average A_r of tellurium is higher than the average for iodine. Thus, in a table based on relative atomic masses only, tellurium would have been placed higher than iodine.

5.3 **a** Electronic configurations are:

Na $1s^2 2s^2 2p^6 3s^1$
Mg $1s^2 2s^2 2p^6 3s^2$
Al $1s^2 2s^2 2p^6 3s^2 3p^1$

Mg has a higher nuclear charge than Na. This makes it more difficult to remove a 3s electron and thus Mg has a higher first ionisation energy. Al has a lower first ionisaton energy than Mg as the electron being removed is in a 3p orbital, a little further from the nuclear charge than the 3s orbital.

b Si $1s^2 2s^2 2p^6 3s^2 3p^2$
P $1s^2 2s^2 2p^6 3s^2 3p^3$
S $1s^2 2s^2 2p^6 3s^1 3p^4$

The general increase in ionisation energy is mainly due to the increasing nuclear charge effect upon the 3p electrons. The first ionisation energy of S is slightly lower than that of P for the same reason as the first ionisation energy of oxygen is lower than that of nitrogen (see text).

5.4 Francium is the most likely: it has only one electron in an s orbital, distant from the nucleus and well screened by several filled inner shells.

5.5 The noble gases exist only as individual atoms, not in molecules.

5.6 Both P_4 and S_8 are molecular structures with weak bonds between the molecules and these are fairly easily separated at relatively low temperatures. Their molecular masses, however, are much higher than for Cl_2 molecules. More energy is needed to move P_4 or S_8 molecules into the vapour phase than Cl_2 molecules. S_8 and P_4 do not boil until a higher temperature than the boiling point of Cl_2.

5.7 **a** Group I to Group III elements are all metals with metallic structure and bonding. The number of shell $n=3$ electrons, which are available to join the conduction band, increases from one to three per atom and this gives greater electrical conductivity.

b This is due to their metallic structures, with one or more electrons per atom joining a conduction band, which allows electrons to move throughout the whole structure. The p-block elements are molecular in structure with electrons kept in strong covalent bonds; their conductivity is much lower than the conductivity of metals.

5.8 C in CO_3^{2-} has an ox. no. of +4.
Al in Al_2Cl_6 has an ox. no. of +3.

5.9 Action of chlorine in water of the pool produces hydrochloric acid. This should be neutralised by alkaline materials to keep the pools safe for swimmers.

5.10 Oxidation:
$$6Fe^{2+}(aq) \rightarrow 6Fe^{3+}(aq) + 6e^-$$
Reduction:
$$Cr_2O_7^{2-}(aq) + 14H^+(aq) + 6e^-$$
$$\rightarrow 2Cr^{3+}(aq) + 7H_2O(l)$$
Full redox equation:
$$6Fe^{2+}(aq) + Cr_2O_7^{2-}(aq) + 14H^+(aq)$$
$$\rightarrow 6Fe^{3+}(aq) + 2Cr^{3+}(aq) + 7H_2O(l)$$

Chapter 6

6.1 **a** Heptane   **b** 3-methylhexane
c Cyclopentane   **d** 4,5-diethyloctane

6.2 See *figure*.

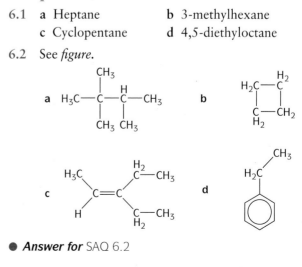

● **Answer for** SAQ 6.2

6.3 Some of the possibilities are:

$$CH_3CH_2CH_2CH_2CH_3$$
$$\rightarrow CH_3CH_2CH_3 + CH_2{=}CH_2$$

$$CH_3CH_2CH_2CH_2CH_3$$
$$\rightarrow CH_3CH_3 + CH_3CH{=}CH_2$$

$$CH_3CH_2CH_2CH_2CH_3$$
$$\rightarrow CH_4 + CH_3CH_2CH{=}CH_2$$

$$CH_3CH_2CH_2CH_2CH_3$$
$$\rightarrow CH_4 + CH_3CH{=}CHCH_3$$

$$CH_3CH_2CH_2CH_2CH_3$$
$$\rightarrow CH_4 + (CH_3)_2C{=}CH_2$$

$$CH_3CH_2CH_2CH_2CH_3$$
$$\rightarrow H_2 + CH_3CH_2CH_2CH{=}CH_2$$

$$CH_3CH_2CH_2CH_2CH_3$$
$$\rightarrow H_2 + CH_3CH_2CH{=}CHCH_3$$

$$CH_3CH_2CH_2CH_2CH_3$$
$$\rightarrow 2H_2 + CH_2{=}CHCH_2CH{=}CH_2$$

6.4 a (i) bonds broken

Bond	Bond energy	Number broken	Total energy/ kJ mol^{-1}
C–H	413	4	1652
O=O	498	2	996
energy absorbed			2648

(ii) bonds formed

Bond	Bond energy	Number formed	Total energy/ kJ mol^{-1}
C–O	805	2	1610
O–H	464	4	1856
energy released			3466

(iii) Percentage of energy released used to break bonds

$$= \frac{2648}{3466} \times 100 = 76.4\%$$

b The covalent bonds to be broken are very strong. More than three-quarters of the energy released is used to break them. The enthalpy change is

$$\Delta H = +2648 + (-3466) = -818\,\text{kJ mol}^{-1}$$

c Conditions are not standard, as H_2O is formed as a gas (not liquid) in this example.

Bond energies used are average values.

6.5 a $CH_3Cl + Cl_2 \rightarrow CH_2Cl_2 + HCl$
$CH_2Cl_2 + Cl_2 \rightarrow CHCl_3 + HCl$
$CHCl_3 + Cl_2 \rightarrow CCl_4 + HCl$

b CH_3CH_2Br bromoethane
CH_3CHBr_2 1,1-dibromoethane
CH_2BrCH_2Br 1,2-dibromoethane
CH_3CBr_3 1,1,1-tribromoethane
$CH_2BrCHBr_2$ 1,1,2-tribromoethane
CH_2BrCBr_3 1,1,1,2-tetrabromoethane
$CHBr_2CHBr_2$ 1,1,2,2-tetrabromoethane
$CHBr_2CBr_3$ pentabromoethane
CBr_3CBr_3 hexabromoethane
HBr hydrogen bromide

6.6 See *figure*.

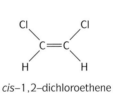

● *Answer for* SAQ 6.6

All angles approximately 120° and molecule is planar.

6.7 a B, D

b See *figure*.

cis–1,2–dichloroethene   *trans*–1,2–dichloroethene

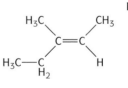 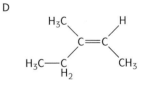

cis–3–methylpent–2–ene   *trans*–3–methylpent–2–ene

● *Answer for* SAQ 6.7

6.8 $CH_3CH{=}CH_2(g) + \frac{9}{2}O_2(g)$
$\rightarrow 3CO_2(g) + 3H_2O(l)$

6.9 a, b See *figure*.

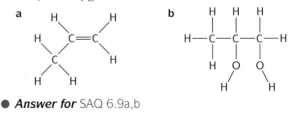

● *Answer for* SAQ 6.9a,b

6.10 a CH_2ClCH_2Br

b Cl_2 Electrophile, polarisable like Br_2.

   Na^+ No; does not usually form a covalent bond.

   F^- No; negative charge, hence repelled by electron-rich centre.

   H_2 No; not sufficiently polarisable.

   SO_3 Electrophile, as sulphur will accept more electrons to form a new covalent bond.

   ICl Electrophile, as polar; iodine is positive (electrophilic) end of molecule.

c See *figure*.

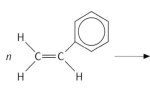

● **Answer for** SAQ 6.10c

   The carbocation accepts a pair of electrons from the bromide ion, Br^-, forming a new covalent bond.

6.11 See *figure*.

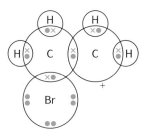

chloroethene   poly(chloroethene)

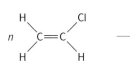

phenylethene   poly(phenylethene)

● **Answer for** SAQ 6.11

6.12 a See *figure*.

● **Answer for** SAQ 6.12

One mole of benzene reacts with three moles of chlorine.

$M_r(C_6H_6) = 78$.

10 tonnes of benzene

$$= 10 \times 10^6 \text{g or } \frac{1 \times 10^7}{78} = 1.3 \times 10^5 \text{mol}$$

1.3×10^5 mol benzene reacts with
$3 \times 1.3 \times 10^5$ mol chlorine

$$= 24 \times 3 \times 1.3 \times 10^5$$

$$= 9.4 \times 10^6 \text{dm}^3 \text{ chlorine}$$

b See *figure*. There are eight isomers of 1,2,3,4,5,6-hexachlorocyclohexane, including the one shown in the question. All eight are shown here.

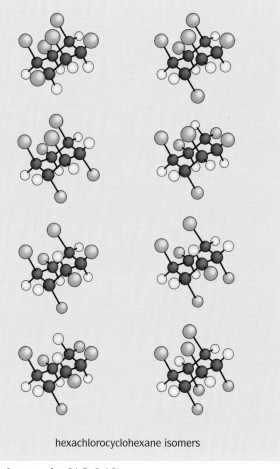

hexachlorocyclohexane isomers

● **Answer for** SAQ 6.12b

Index (Numbers in italics refer to figures.)